THE FAITH
OF
OUR FATHERS

AFFECTIONATELY DEDICATED

TO THE

Clergy and Laity

OF THE

ARCHDIOCESE AND PROVINCE OF BALTIMORE.

THE
FAITH OF OUR FATHERS

Being a Plain Exposition and Vindication of the Church Founded by Our Lord Jesus Christ

BY

JAMES CARDINAL GIBBONS

Archbishop of Baltimore

TAN BOOKS AND PUBLISHERS, INC.
Rockford, Illinois 61105

Originally published in 1876 by The John Murphy Company of Baltimore, Maryland, with new editions issued in 1879, 1895, 1904 and 1917. This printing is taken from the 110th printing, published by P. J. Kenedy & Sons, New York, New York.

Library of Congress Catalog No.: 80-51331

ISBN: 0-89555-158-6

Printed and bound in the United States of America

111th Printing

TAN BOOKS AND PUBLISHERS, INC.
P. O. Box 424
Rockford, Illinois 61105

1980

PREFACE TO THE ELEVENTH EDITION

The first edition of "The Faith of Our Fathers" was issued in December, 1876. From that time to the present fifty thousand copies of the work have been disposed of in the United States, Canada, Great Britain and Ireland, and in the British Colonies of Oceanica.

This gratifying result has surpassed the author's most sanguine expectations, and is a consoling evidence that the investigation of religious truths is not wholly neglected even in this iron age, so engrossed by material considerations.

Besides carefully revising the book, the author has profited by the kind suggestion of some friends, and inserted a chapter on the prerogatives and sanctity of the Blessed Virgin, which, it is hoped, will be not less acceptable to his readers than the other portions of the work.

He is also happy to announce that German editions have been published both in this country and in Germany.

He takes this occasion to return his hearty thanks to the editors of the Catholic periodicals, as well as of the secular press, for their favorable notices, which have no doubt contributed much to the large circulation of the book.

BALTIMORE,
Feast of St. Thomas Aquinas, 1879.

PREFACE TO THE FORTY-SEVENTH EDITION

It is very gratifying to the author to note the large increase in the sale of "The Faith of Our Fathers." Apart from personal considerations, it is pleasing to know that the popular interest in the Catholic Church and whatever pertains to her doctrines and discipline, is growing more widespread and earnest.

Since 1879, when the eleventh revised edition was given to the public, there have been thirty-five editions, and the number of copies sold reaches nearly a quarter of a million.

This desire to understand the teachings of the Church of our Fathers is not confined to our own country. It is manifest in other lands, as shown by the translations that have been made of this exposition of Catholic belief into French, German, Spanish, Italian, Norwegian and Swedish.

In the hope that they will add to the usefulness of the book, several passages upon doctrinal subjects have been inserted.

With these few remarks, the forty-seventh edition of "The Faith of Our Fathers" is presented to the sincere and earnest seeker after religious truth by

THE AUTHOR

Feast of St. Anselm, 1895.

PREFACE

The object of this little volume is to present in a plain and practical form an exposition and vindication of the principal tenets of the Catholic Church. It was thought sufficient to devote but a brief space to such Catholic doctrines and practices as are happily admitted by Protestants, while those that are controverted by them are more elaborately elucidated.

The work was compiled by the author during the uncertain hours which he could spare from the more active duties of the ministry. It substantially embodies the instructions and discourses delivered by him before mixed congregations in Virginia and North Carolina.

He has often felt that the salutary influence of such instructions, especially on the occasion of a mission in the rural districts, would be much augmented if they were supplemented by books or tracts circulated among the people, and which could be read and pondered at leisure.

As his chief aim has been to bring home the truths of the Catholic faith to our separated brethren, who generally accept the Scripture as the only source of authority in religious matters, he has endeavored to fortify his statements by abundant reference to the sacred text. He has thought proper, however, to add frequent quotations from the early Fathers, whose testimony, at least as witnesses of the faith of their times, must be accepted even by those who call in question their personal authority.

Though the writer has sought to be exact in all his assertions, an occasional inaccuracy may have inadvertently crept in. Any emendations which the venerated Prelates or Clergy may deign to propose will be gratefully attended to in a subsequent edition.

RICHMOND,
November 21st, 1876.

PREFACE TO EIGHTY-THIRD REVISED EDITION.

The new edition of "The Faith of Our Fathers" has been carefully revised, and enriched with several pages of important matter.

It is gratifying to note that since the first edition appeared, in 1876, up to the present time, fourteen hundred thousand copies have been published, and the circulation of the book is constantly increasing.

The work has also been translated into nearly all the languages of Europe.

BALTIMORE,
May 1st, 1917.

J. Card Gibbons

CONTENTS

INTRODUCTION

MY DEAR READER:—Perhaps this is the first time in your life that you have handled a book in which the doctrines of the Catholic Church are expounded by one of her own sons. You have, no doubt, heard and read many things regarding our Church; but has not your information come from teachers justly liable to suspicion? You asked for bread, and they gave you a stone. You asked for fish, and they reached you a serpent. Instead of the bread of truth, they extended to you the serpent of false-hood. Hence, without intending to be unjust, is not your mind biased against us because you listened to false witnesses? This, at least, is the case with thousands of my countrymen whom I have met in the brief course of my missionary career. The Cath-olic Church is persistently misrepresented by the most powerful vehicles of information.

She is assailed in romances of the stamp of María Monk, and in pictorial papers. It is true that the falsehood of those illustrated periodicals has been fully exposed. But the antidote often comes too late to counteract the poison. I have seen a picture represent-ing Columbus trying to demonstrate the practicability of his design to discover a new Continent before certain monks who are shaking their fists and gnashing their teeth at him. It matters not to the artist that Columbus could probably never have under-taken his voyage and discovery, as the explorer himself avows, were it not for the benevolent zeal of the monks, Antonio de Mar-chena and Juan Perez, and other ecclesiastics, as well as for the munificence of Queen Isabella and the Spanish Court.

The Church is misrepresented in so-called Histories like Foxe's Book of Martyrs. It is true that he has been successfully refuted by Lingard and Gairdner. But, how many have read the fictitious narratives of Foxe, who have never perused a page of Lingard or Gairdner? In a large portion of the press, and in pamphlets, and especially in the pulpit, which should be consecrated to truth and charity, she is the victim of the foulest slanders. Upon her fair and heavenly brow her enemies put a hideous mask, and in that guise they exhibit her to the insults and mockery of the public; just as Jesus, her Spouse, was treated when, clothed with a scarlet cloak and crowned with thorns, He was mocked by a thoughtless rabble.

They are afraid to tell the truth of her, for

> "Truth has such a face and such a mien,
> As to be loved needs only to be seen." [1]

It is not uncommon for a dialogue like the following to take place between a Protestant Minister and a convert to the Catholic Church:

MINISTER.—You cannot deny that the Roman Catholic Church teaches gross errors—the worship of images, for instance.

CONVERT.—I admit no such charge, for I have been taught no such doctrines.

MINISTER.—But the Priest who instructed you did not teach you all. He held back some points which he knew would be objectionable to you.

CONVERT.—He withheld nothing; for I am in possession of books treating fully of all Catholic doctrines.

MINISTER.—Deluded soul! Don't you know that in Europe they are taught differently?

CONVERT.—That cannot be, for, the Church teaches the same creed all over the world, and most of the doctrinal books which I read, were originally published in Europe.

Yet ministers who make these slanderous statements are surprised if we feel indignant, and accuse us of being too sensitive. We have been vilified so long, that they think we have no right to complain.

[1] Dryden. *Hind and Panther.*

We cannot exaggerate the offense of those who thus wilfully malign the Church. There is a commandment which says: "Thou shalt not bear false witness against thy neighbor."

If it is a sin to bear false testimony against one individual, how can we characterize the crime of those who calumniate three hundred millions of human beings, by attributing to them doctrines and practices which they repudiate and abhor. I do not wonder that the Church is hated by those who learn what she is from her enemies. It is natural for an honest man to loathe an institution whose history he believes to be marked by bloodshed, crime and fraud.

Had I been educated as they were, and surrounded by an atmosphere hostile to the Church, perhaps I should be unfortunate enough to be breathing vengeance against her today, instead of consecrating my life to her defence.

It is not of their hostility that I complain, but because the judgment they have formed of her is based upon the reckless assertions of her enemies, and not upon those of impartial witnesses.

Suppose that I wanted to obtain a correct estimate of the Southern people, would it be fair in me to select, as my only sources of information, certain Northern and Eastern periodicals which, during our Civil War, were bitterly opposed to the race and institutions of the South? Those papers have represented you as men who always appeal to the sword and pistol, instead of the law, to vindicate your private grievances. They heaped accusations against you which I will not here repeat. Instead of taking these publications as the basis of my information, it was my duty to come among you; to live with you; to read your life by studying your public and private character. This I have done, and I here cheerfully bear witness to your many excellent traits of mind and heart.

Now I ask you to give to the Catholic Church the same measure of fairness which you reasonably demand of me when judging of Southern character. Ask not her enemies what she is, for they are blinded by passion; ask not her ungrateful, renegade children, for you never heard a son speaking well of the mother whom he had abandoned and despised.

Study her history in the pages of truth. Examine her creed. Read her authorized catechisms and doctrinal books. You will find them everywhere on the shelves of booksellers, in the libraries of her clergy, on the tables of Catholic families.

There is no Freemasonry in the Catholic Church; she has no secrets to keep back. She has not one set of doctrines for Bishops and Priests, and another for the laity. She has not one creed for the initiated and another for outsiders. Everything in the Catholic Church is open and above board. She has the same doctrines for all—for the Pope and the peasant.

Should not I be better qualified to present to you the Church's creed than the unfriendly witnesses whom I have mentioned?

I have imbibed her doctrine with my mother's milk. I have made her history and theology the study of my life. What motive can I have in misleading you? Not temporal reward, since I seek not your money, but your soul, for which Jesus Christ died. I could not hope for an eternal reward by deceiving you, for I would thereby purchase for myself eternal condemnation by gaining proselytes at the expense of truth.

This, friendly reader, is my only motive. I feel in the depth of my heart that, in possessing Catholic faith, I hold a treasure compared with which all things earthly are but dross. Instead of wishing to bury this treasure in my breast, I long to share it with you, especially as I lose no part of my spiritual riches by communicating them to others.

It is to me a duty and a labor of love to speak the truth concerning my venerable Mother, so much maligned in our days. Were a tithe of the accusations which are brought against her true, I would not be attached to her ministry, nor even to her communion, for a single day. I know these charges to be false. The longer I know her, the more I admire and venerate her. Every day she develops before me new spiritual charms.

Ah! my dear friend, if you saw her as her children see her, she would no longer appear to you as typified by the woman of

Babylon. She would be revealed to you, "Bright as the sun, fair as the moon;" with the beauty of Heaven stamped upon her brow, glorious "as an army in battle array." You would love her, you would cling to her and embrace her. With her children, you would rise up in reverence "and call her blessed."

Consider what you lose and what you gain in embracing the Catholic religion.

Your loss is nothing in comparison with your gain. You do not surrender your manhood or your dignity or independence or reasoning powers. You give up none of those revealed truths which you may possess already. The only restraint imposed upon you is the restraint of the Gospel, and to this you will not reasonably object.

You gain everything that is worth having. You acquire a full and connected knowledge of God's revelation. You get possession of the whole truth as it is in Jesus. You no longer see it in fragments, but reflected before you in all its beauty, as in a polished mirror. While others are outside criticising the architecture of the temple, you are inside worshiping the divine Architect and saying devoutly with the Psalmist: "I have loved, O Lord, the beauty of Thy house and the place where Thy glory dwelleth." While others from without find in the stained-glass windows only blurred and confused figures without symmetry or attraction or meaning, you from within, are gazing with silent rapture on God's glorified saints, with their outlines clearly defined on the windows, and all illuminated with the sunlight of heaven. Your knowledge of the truth is not only complete and harmonious, but it becomes fixed and steady. You exchange opinion for certainty. You are no longer "tossed about by every wind of doctrine," but you are firmly grounded on the rock of truth. Then you enjoy that profound peace which springs from the conscious possession of the truth.

In coming to the Church, you are not entering a strange place, but you are returning to your Father's home. The house and furniture may look odd to you, but it is just the same as your forefather's left it three hundred years ago. In coming back to the Church, you worship where your fathers worshiped before you, you kneel before the altar at which they knelt, you receive the Sacraments which they received, and respect the authority of the clergy whom they venerated. You come back like the Prodigal Son to the home of your father and mother. The garment of joy is placed upon you, the banquet of love is set before you, and you receive the kiss of peace as a pledge of your filiation and adoption. One hearty embrace of your tender Mother will compensate you for all the sacrifices you may have made, and you will exclaim with the penitent Augustine: "Too late have I known thee, O Beauty, ever ancient and ever new, too late have I loved thee." Should the perusal of this book bring one soul to the knowledge of the Church, my labor will be amply rewarded.

Remember that nothing is so essential as the salvation of your immortal soul, "for what doth it profit a man, if he gain the whole world, and lose his own soul? Or what shall a man give in exchange for his soul?" [2] Let not, therefore, the fear of offending friends and relatives, the persecution of men, the loss of earthly possessions, nor any other temporal calamity, deter you from investigating and embracing the true religion. "For our present tribulation, which is momentary and light, worketh for us above measure exceedingly an eternal weight of glory." [3]

May God give you light to see the truth, and, having seen it, may He give you courage and strength to follow it!

[2] Matt. xvi. 26.   [3] II. Cor. iv. 17.

THE FAITH
OF
OUR FATHERS

CHAPTER I

THE BLESSED TRINITY, THE INCARNATION, ETC.

THE Catholic Church teaches that there is but one God, who is infinite in knowledge, in power, in goodness, and in every other perfection; who created all things by His omnipotence, and governs them by His Providence.

In this one God there are three distinct Persons,—the Father, the Son, and the Holy Ghost, who are perfectly equal to each other.

We believe that Jesus Christ, the Second Person of the Blessed Trinity, is perfect God and perfect Man. He is God, for He "is over all things, God blessed forever."[1] "He is God of the substance of the Father, begotten before time; and He is Man of the substance of His Mother, born in time."[2] Out of love for us, and in order to rescue us from the miseries entailed upon us by the disobedience of our first parents, the Divine Word descended from heaven, and became Man in the womb of the Virgin Mary, by the operation of the Holy Ghost. He was born on Christmas day, in a stable at Bethlehem.

After having led a life of obscurity for about thirty years, chiefly at Nazareth, He commenced His public career. He associated with Him a number of men who are named Apostles, whom He instructed in the doctrines of the religion which He established.

For three years He went about doing good, giving sight to the blind, hearing to the deaf, healing all kinds of diseases, raising the dead to life, and preaching throughout Judea the new Gospel of peace.[3]

---

[1] Rom. ix. 5.   [2] Athanasian Creed.   [3] Matt. xi.

On Good Friday He was crucified on Mount Calvary, and thus purchased for us redemption by His death. Hence Jesus exclusively bears the titles of *Savior* and *Redeemer,* because "there is no other name under heaven given to men whereby we must be saved." [4] "He was wounded for our iniquities; He was bruised for our sins, . . . and by His bruises we are healed." [5]

We are commanded by Jesus, suffering and dying for us, to imitate Him by the crucifixion of our flesh, and by acts of daily mortification. "If anyone," He says, "will come after Me, let him deny himself, and take up his cross daily and follow Me." [6]

Hence we abstain from the use of flesh meat on Friday—the day consecrated to our Savior's sufferings—not because the eating of flesh meat is sinful in itself, but as an act of salutary mortification. Loving children would be prompted by filial tenderness to commemorate the anniversary of their father's death rather by prayer and fasting than by feasting. Even so we abstain on Fridays from flesh meat that we may in a small measure testify our practical sympathy for our dear Lord by the mortification of our body, endeavoring, like St. Paul, "to bear about in our body the mortification of Jesus, that the life also of Jesus may be made manifest in our bodies." [7]

The Cross is held in the highest reverence by Catholics, because it was the instrument of our Savior's crucifixion. It surmounts our churches and adorns our sanctuaries. We venerate it as the emblem of our salvation. "Far be it from me," says the Apostle, "to glory save in the cross of our Lord Jesus Christ." [8] We do not, of course, attach any intrinsic virtue to the Cross; this would be sinful and idolatrous. Our veneration is referred to Him who died upon it.

It is also a very ancient and pious practice for the faithful to make on their person the sign of the Cross, saying at the same time: "In the name of the Father, and of the Son, and of the Holy Ghost." Tertullian, who lived in the second century of the Christian era, says: "In all our actions, when we come in or go

---

[4] Acts iv. 12.   [5] Isaiah liii. 5.   [6] Luke ix. 23.
[7] II. Cor. iv. 10.   [8] Gal. vi. 14.

out, when we dress, when we wash, at our meals, before retiring to sleep, . . . we form on our foreheads the sign of the cross. These practices are not commanded by a formal law of Scripture; but tradition teaches them, custom confirms them, faith observes them." [9] By the sign of the cross we make a profession of our faith in the Trinity and the Incarnation, and perform a most salutary act of religion.

We believe that on Easter Sunday Jesus Christ manifested His divine power by raising Himself to life, and that having spent forty days on earth, after His resurrection, instructing His disciples, He ascended to heaven from the Mount of Olives.

On the Feast of Pentecost, or Whitsunday, ten days after His Ascension, our Savior sent, as He had promised, His Holy Spirit to His disciples, while they were assembled together in prayer. The Holy Ghost purified their hearts from sin, and imparted to them a full knowledge of those doctrines of salvation which they were instructed to preach. On the same Feast of Pentecost the Apostles commenced their sublime mission, from which day, accordingly, we date the active life of the Catholic Church.

Our Redeemer gave the most ample authority to the Apostles to teach in His name; commanding them to "preach the Gospel to every creature," [10] and directing all, under the most severe penalties, to hear and obey them: "He that heareth you, heareth Me; and he that despiseth you, despiseth Me. And He that despiseth Me, despiseth Him that sent Me." [11]

And lest we should be mistaken in distinguishing between the true Church and false sects, which our Lord predicted would arise, He was pleased to stamp upon His Church certain shining marks, by which every sincere inquirer could easily recognize her as His only Spouse. The principal marks or characteristics of the true Church are, her Unity, Sanctity, Catholicity, and Apostolicity,[12] to which may be added the Infallibility of her teaching and the Perpetuity of her existence.

I shall treat successively of these marks.

[9] De Corona, C. iii.　　　　[10] Mark xvi. 15.
[11] Luke x. 16.　　　　[12] Symb. Constantinop.

CHAPTER II

THE UNITY OF THE CHURCH

BY unity is meant that the members of the true Church must be united in the belief of the same doctrines of revelation and in the acknowledgment of the authority of the same pastors. Heresy and schism are opposed to Christian unity. By heresy, a man rejects one or more articles of the Christian faith. By schism, he spurns the authority of his spiritual superiors. That our Savior requires this unity of faith and government in His members is evident from various passages of Holy Writ. In His admirable prayer immediately before His passion He says: "I pray for them also who through their word shall believe in Me; that they all may be one, as Thou, Father, in Me and I in Thee, that they also may be one in Us; that the world may believe that Thou hast sent Me," [1] because the unity of the Church is the most luminous evidence of the Divine mission of Christ. Jesus prayed that His followers may be united in the bond of a common faith, as He and His Father are united in essence, and certainly the prayer of Jesus is always heard.

St. Paul ranks schism and heresy with the crimes of murder and idolatry, and he declares that the authors of sects shall not possess the Kingdom of God.[2] He also addresses a letter to the Ephesians from his prison in Rome, and if the words of the Apostle should always command our homage, with how much reverence are they to be received when he writes in chains from the Imperial City! In this Epistle he insists upon unity of faith in the following

[1] John xvii. 20, 21.　　　　　[2] Gal. v. 20, 21.

emphatic language: "Be careful to keep the unity of the Spirit in the bond of peace; one body and one Spirit, as you are called in one hope of your calling; one Lord, one faith, one baptism, one God and Father of all, who is above all, and through all, and in us all." [3] As you all, he says, worship one God, and not many gods; as you acknowledge the same Divine Mediator of redemption, and not many mediators; as you are sanctified by the same Divine Spirit, and not by many spirits; as you all hope for the same heaven, and not different heavens, so must you all profess the same faith.

Unity of government is not less essential to the Church of Christ than unity of doctrine. Our Divine Saviour never speaks of His Churches, but of His *Church*. He does not say: "Upon this rock I will build My Churches," but "upon this rock I will build My Church," [4] from which words we must conclude that it never was His intention to establish or to sanction various conflicting denominations, but one corporate body, with all the members united under one visible Head; for as the Church is a visible body, it must have a visible head.

The Church is called a kingdom: "He shall reign over the house of Jacob forever, and of His kingdom there shall be no end." [5] Now in every well-regulated kingdom there is but *one king, one form of government, one uniform body of laws,* which all are obliged to observe. In like manner, in Christ's spiritual kingdom, there must be one Chief to whom all owe spiritual allegiance; one form of ecclesiastical government; one uniform body of laws which all Christians are bound to observe; for, "every kingdom divided against itself shall be made desolate." [6]

Our Savior calls His Church a sheepfold. "And there shall be one fold and one shepherd." [7] What more beautiful or fitting illustration of unity can we have than that which is suggested by a sheepfold? All the sheep of a flock cling together. If they are momentarily separated, they are impatient till reunited. They follow in the same path. They feed on the same pastures.

[3] Eph. iv. 3-6. [4] Matt. xvi. 18. [5] Luke i. 32, 33.
[6] Matt. xii. 25. [7] John x. 16.

They obey the same shepherd, and fly from the voice of strangers. So did our Lord intend that all the sheep of His fold should be nourished by the same sacraments and the same bread of life; that they should follow the same rule of faith as their guide to heaven; that they should listen to the voice of one Chief Pastor, and that they should carefully shun false teachers.

His Church is compared to a human body. "As in one body we have many members, but all the members have not the same office; so we, being many, are one body in Christ, and every one members one of another." [8] In one body there are many members, all inseparably connected with the head. The head commands and the foot instantly moves, the hand is raised and the lips open. Even so our Lord ordained that His Church, composed of many members, should be all united to one supreme visible Head, whom they are bound to obey.

The Church is compared to a vine. "I am the Vine; ye the branches; he that abideth in Me and I in him, the same beareth much fruit, for without Me ye can do nothing." [9] All the branches of a vine, though spreading far and wide, are necessarily connected with the main stem, and from its sap they are nourished. In like manner, our Saviour will have all the saplings of His Vineyard connected with the main stem, and all draw their nourishment from the parent stock.

The Church, in fine, is called in Scripture by the beautiful title of bride or spouse of Christ,[10] and the Christian law admits only of one wife.

In fact, our common sense alone, apart from revelation, is sufficient to convince us that God could not be the author of various opposing systems of religion. God is essentially one. He is Truth itself. How could the God of truth affirm, for instance, to one body of Christians that there are three persons in God, and to another there is only one person in God? How could He say to one individual that Jesus Christ is God, and to another that He is only man. How can He tell me that the punishments of the wicked are eternal, and tell another that they are not eternal? One

[8] Rom. xii. 4, 5.   [9] John xv. 5.   [10] Apoc. xxi. 9.

of these contradictory statements must be false. "God is not the God of dissension, but of peace." [11]

I see perfect harmony in the laws which govern the physical world that we inhabit. I see a marvelous unity in our planetary system. Each planet moves in its own sphere, and all are controlled by the central Sun.

Why should there not be also harmony and concord in that spiritual world, the Church of God, the grandest conception of His omnipotence, and the most bounteous manifestation of His goodness and love for mankind!

Hence, it is clear that Jesus Christ intended that His Church should have one common doctrine which all Christians are bound to believe, and one uniform government to which all should be loyally attached.

With all due respect for my dissenting brethren, truth compels me to say that this unity of doctrine and government is not to be found in the Protestant sects, taken collectively or separately. That the various Protestant denominations differ from one another not only in minor details, but in most essential principles of faith, is evident to every one conversant with the doctrines of the different Creeds. The multiplicity of sects in this country, with their mutual recriminations, is the scandal of Christianity, and the greatest obstacle to the conversion of the heathen. Not only does sect differ from sect, but each particular denomination is divided into two or more independent or conflicting branches.

In the State of North Carolina we have several Baptist denominations, each having its own distinctive appellation. There is also the Methodist Church North and the Methodist Church South. There was the Old and the New School Presbyterian Church. And even in the Episcopal Communion, which is the most conservative body outside the Catholic Church, there is the ritualistic, or high church, and the low church. Nay, if you question closely the individual members composing any one fraction of these denominations, you will not rarely find them giving a contradictory view of their tenets of religion.

[11] I. Cor. xiv. 33.

Protestants differ from one another not only in doctrine, but in the form of ecclesiastical government and discipline. The Church of England acknowledges the reigning Sovereign as its Spiritual Head. Some denominations recognize Deacons, Priests, and Bishops as an essential part of their hierarchy; while the great majority of Protestants reject such titles altogether.

Where, then, shall we find this essential unity of faith and government? I answer, confidently, nowhere save in the Catholic Church.

The number of Catholics in the world is computed at three hundred millions. They have all "one Lord, one faith, one baptism," one creed. They receive the same sacraments, they worship at the same altar, and pay spiritual allegiance to one common Head. Should a Catholic be so unfortunate as contumaciously to deny a single article of faith, or withdraw from the communion of his legitimate pastors, he ceases to be a member of the Church, and is cut off like a withered branch. The Church had rather sever her right hand than allow any member to corrode her vitals. It was thus she excommunicated Henry VIII. because he persisted in violating the sacred law of marriage, although she foresaw that the lustful monarch would involve a nation in his spiritual ruin. She anathematized, more recently, Dr. Döllinger, though the prestige of his name threatened to engender a schism in Germany. She says to her children: "You may espouse any political party you choose; with this I have no concern." But as soon as they trench on matters of faith she cries out: "Hitherto thou shalt come, and shalt go no further; and here thou shalt break thy swelling waves" [12] of discord. The temple of faith is the asylum of peace, concord and unity.

How sublime and consoling is the thought that whithersoever a Catholic goes over the broad world, whether he enters his Church in Pekin or in Melbourne, in London, or Dublin, or Paris, or Rome, or New York, or San Francisco, he is sure to hear the selfsame doctrine preached, to assist at the same sacrifice, and to partake of the same sacraments.

[12] Job xxxviii. 11.

This is not all. Her Creed is now identical with what it was in past ages. The same Gospel of peace that Jesus Christ preached on the Mount; the same doctrine that St. Peter preached at Antioch and Rome; St. Paul at Ephesus; St. John Chrysostom at Constantinople; St. Augustine in Hippo; St. Ambrose in Milan; St. Remigius in France; St. Boniface in Germany; St. Athanasius in Alexandria; the same doctrine that St. Patrick introduced into Ireland; that St. Augustine brought into England, and St. Pelagius into Scotland, and that Columbus brought to this American Continent, and this is the doctrine that is ever preached in the Catholic Church throughout the globe, from January till December—"Jesus Christ, yesterday, and today, and the same for ever." [13]

The same admirable unity that exists in matters of faith is also established in the government of the Church. All the members of the vast body of Catholic Christians are as intimately united to one visible Chief as the members of the human body are joined to the head. The faithful of each Parish are subject to their immediate Pastor. Each Pastor is subordinate to his Bishop, and each Bishop of Christendom acknowledges the jurisdiction of the Bishop of Rome, the successor of St. Peter, and Head of the Catholic Church.

But it may be asked, is not this unity of faith impaired by those doctrinal definitions which the Church has promulgated from time to time? We answer: No new dogma, unknown to the Apostles, not contained in the primitive Christian revelation, can be admitted. (John xiv. 26; xv. 15; xvi. 13.) For the Apostles received the whole deposit of God's word, according to the promise of our Lord: "When He shall come, the Spirit of truth, He shall teach you all truth." And so the Church proposes the doctrines of faith, such as came from the lips of Christ, and as the Holy Spirit taught them to the Apostles at the birth of the Christian law—doctrines which know neither variation nor decay.

Hence, whenever it has been defined that any point of doctrine pertained to the Catholic faith, it was always understood

[13] Heb. xiii. 8.

that this was equivalent to the declaration that the doctrine in
question had been revealed to the Apostles, and had come down
to us from them, either by Scripture or tradition. And as the acts
of all the Councils, and the history of every definition of faith
evidently show, it was never contended that a *new revelation*
had been made, but every inquiry was directed to this one point—
whether the doctrine in question was contained in the Sacred
Scriptures or in the Apostolic traditions.

A revealed truth frequently has a very extensive scope, and is
directed against error under its many changing forms. Nor is it
necessary that those who receive this revelation in the first
instance should be explicitly acquainted with its full import, or
cognizant of all its bearings. Truth never changes; it is the same
now, yesterday, and forever, *in itself;* but our relations towards
truth may change, for that which is hidden from us today may
become known to us tomorrow. "It often happens," says St.
Augustine, "that when it becomes necessary to defend certain
points of Catholic doctrine against the insidious attacks of heretics
they are more carefully studied, they become *more clearly understood,* they are *more earnestly inculcated;* and so the very
questions raised by heretics give occasion to a more thorough
knowledge of the subject in question." [14]

Let us illustrate this. In the Apostolic revelation and preaching
some truths might have been contained *implicitly, e. g.,* in the
doctrine that grace is necessary for every salutary work, it is
implicitly asserted that the assistance of grace is required for the
inception of every good and salutary work. This was denied by
the semi-Pelagians, and their error was condemned by an explicit
definition. And so in other matters, as the rising controversies or
new errors gave occasion for it, there were more *explicit* declarations of what was formerly *implicitly* believed. In the doctrine
of the supreme power of Peter, as the visible foundation of the
Church, we have the *implied* assertion of many rights and duties
which belong to the centre of unity. In the revelation of the

[14] De Civitate Dei, Lib. 16, Cap. ii., No. 1.

supereminent dignity and purity of the Blessed Virgin there is
implied her exemption from original sin, etc., etc.

So, too, in the beginning many truths might have been proposed somewhat *obscurely* or *less clearly;* they might have been
less urgently insisted upon, because there was no heresy, no
contrary teaching to render a more explicit declaration necessary.
Now, a doctrine which is *implicitly, less clearly, not so earnestly.*
proposed, may be overlooked, misunderstood, called in question;
consequently, it may happen that some articles are now universally believed in the Church, in regard to which doubts and controversies existed in former ages, even within the bosom of the
Church. "Those who err in belief do but serve to bring out more
clearly the soundness of those who believe rightly. For there are
many things which *lay hidden in the Scriptures,* and when heretics were cut off they vexed the Church of God with disputes;
then the hidden things were *brought to light,* and the will of
God was made known." (St. Augustine on the 54th Psalm, No.
22.)

This kind of *progress in faith* we can and do admit; but the
truth is not changed thereby. As Albertus Magnus says: "It would
be more correct to style this the progress of the believer in the
faith, than of the faith in the believer."

To show that this kind of progress is to be admitted only two
things are to be proved: 1: That some divinely revealed truths
should be contained in the Apostolic teaching *implicitly, less
clearly explained, less urgently pressed.* And this can be denied
only by those who hold that the Bible is the only rule of Faith,
that it is clear in every part, and could be readily understood by
all from the beginning. This point I shall consider farther on in
this work. 2. That the Church can, in process of time, as occasions
arise, *declare, explain, urge.* This is proved not only from the
Scriptures and the Fathers, but even from the conduct of Protestants themselves, who often boast of the care and assiduity with
which they "search the Scriptures," and study out their meaning,
even now that so many Commentaries on the sacred Text have

been published. And why? To obtain more light; to understand better what is revealed. It would appear from this that the only question which could arise on this point is, not about the possibility of arriving by degrees at a clearer understanding of the true sense of revelation, as circumstances may call for successive developments, but about the authority of the Church to propose and to determine that sense. So that, after all, we are always brought back to the only real point of division and dispute between those who are not Catholics and ourselves, namely, to the authority of the Church, of which I shall have more to say hereafter. I cannot conclude better than by quoting the words of St. Vincent of Lerins: "Let us take care that it be with us in matters of religion, which affect our souls, as it is with material bodies, which, as time goes on, pass through successive phases of growth and development and multiply their years, but yet remain always the same individual bodies as they were in the beginning. . . . It very properly follows from the nature of things that, with a perfect agreement and consistency between the beginnings and the final results, when we reap the harvest of dogmatic truth which has sprung from the seeds of doctrine sown in the spring-time of the Church's existence, we should find no substantial difference between the grain which was first planted and that which we now gather. For though the germs of the early faith have in some respects been evolved in the course of time, and still receive nourishment and culture, yet nothing in them that is substantial can ever suffer change. The Church of Christ is a faithful and ever watchful guardian of the dogmas which have been committed to her charge. In this sacred deposit she changes nothing, she takes nothing from it, she adds nothing to it."

CHAPTER III

THE HOLINESS OF THE CHURCH

HOLINESS is also a mark of the true Church; for in the Creed we say, "I believe in the *holy* Catholic Church."

Every society is founded for a special object. One society is formed with the view of cultivating social intercourse among its members; a second is organized to advance their temporal interests; and a third for the purpose of promoting literary pursuits. The Catholic Church is a society founded by our Lord Jesus Christ for the sanctification of its members; hence, St. Peter calls the Christians of his time "a chosen generation, a royal priesthood, *a holy nation,* a purchased people." [1]

The example of our Divine Founder, Jesus Christ, the sublime moral lessons He has taught us, the Sacraments He has instituted —all tend to our sanctification. They all concentre themselves in our soul, like so many heavenly rays, to enlighten and inflame it with the fire of devotion.

When the Church speaks to us of the attributes of our Lord, of His justice and mercy and sanctity and truth, her object is not merely to extol the Divine perfections, but also to exhort us to imitate them, and to be like Him, just and merciful, holy and truthful. Behold the sublime Model that is placed before us! It is not man, nor angel, nor archangel, but Jesus Christ, the Son of God, "who is the brightness of His glory, and the figure of His substance." [2] The Church places His image over our altars, admonishing us to "look and do according to the pattern shown

---

[1] I. Pet. ii. 9.   [2] Heb. i. 3.

13

on the Mount." [3] And from that height He seems to say to us: "Be ye holy, for I the Lord your God am holy." [4] "Be ye perfect, even as your heavenly Father is perfect." [5] "Be ye followers of God as most dear children." [6]

We are invited to lead holy lives, not only because our Divine Founder, Jesus Christ, was holy, but also because we bear His sweet and venerable name. We are called *Christians.* That is a name we would not exchange for all the high-sounding titles of Prince or Emperor. We are justly proud of this appellation of *Christian;* but we are reminded that it has annexed to it a corresponding obligation. It is not an idle name, but one full of solemn significance; for a Christian, as the very name implies, is a follower or disciple of Christ—one who walks in the footsteps of his Master by observing His precepts; who reproduces in his own life the character and virtues of his Divine Model. In a word, a Christian is another Christ. It would, therefore, be a contradiction in terms, if a Christian had nothing in common with his Lord except the name. The disciple should imitate his Master, the soldier should imitate his Commander, and the members should be like the Head.

The Church constantly allures her children to holiness by placing before their minds the Incarnation, life and death of our Savior. What appeals more forcibly to a life of piety than the contemplation of Jesus born in a stable, living an humble life in Nazareth, dying on a cross, that His blood might purify us? If He sent forth Apostles to preach the Gospel to the whole world; if in His name temples are built in every nation, and missionaries are sent to the extremities of the globe, all this is done that we may be Saints. "God," says St. Paul, "gave some Apostles, and some Prophets, and others Evangelists, and others Pastors and Doctors, for the perfecting of the Saints, for the work of the ministry, for the building up of the body of Christ, until we all meet unto the unity of faith and of the knowledge of the Son of God unto a perfect man." [7]

[3] Exod. xxv. 40.   [4] Lev. xix. 2.   [5] Matt. v. 48.
[6] Eph. v. 1.   [7] Eph. iv. 11, 13.

The moral law which the Catholic Church inculcates on her children is the highest and holiest standard of perfection ever presented to any people, and furnishes the strongest incentives to virtue.

The same Divine precepts delivered through Moses to the Jews, on Mount Sinai, the same salutary warnings which the Prophets uttered throughout Judea, the same sublime and consoling lessons of morality which Jesus gave on the Mount—these are the lessons which the Church teaches from January till December. The Catholic preacher does not amuse his audience with speculative topics or political harangues, or any other subjects of a transitory nature. He preaches only "Christ, and Him crucified."

This code of Divine precepts is enforced with as much zeal by the Church as was the Decalogue of old by Moses, when he said: "These words, which I command thee this day, shall be in thy heart; and thou shalt tell them to thy children; and thou shalt meditate upon them, sitting in thy house, and walking on thy journey, sleeping and rising." [8]

The first lesson taught to children in our Sunday-schools is their duty to know, love and serve God, and thus to be Saints; for if they know, love and serve God aright they shall be Saints indeed. Their tender minds are instructed in this great truth that though they had the riches of Dives, and the glory and pleasures of Solomon, and yet fail to be righteous, they have missed their vocation, and are "wretched, and miserable, and poor, and blind, and naked." [9] "For, what doth it profit a man, if he gain the whole world and lose his own soul?" [10] On the contrary though they are as poor as Lazarus, and as miserable as Job in the days of his adversity, they are assured that their condition is a happy one in the sight of God, if they live up to the maxims of the Gospel.

The Church quickens the zeal of her children for holiness of life by impressing on their minds the rigor of God's judgments, who "will bring to light the hidden things of darkness, and make

[8] Deut. vi. 6, 7.   [9] Apoc. iii. 7.   [10] Matt. xvi. 26.

manifest the counsels of the hearts," by reminding them of the terrors of Hell and of the sweet joys of Heaven.

Not only are Catholics instructed in church on Sundays but they are exhorted to peruse the Word of God, and manuals of devotion, at home. The saints whose lives are there recorded serve like bright stars to guide them over the stormy ocean of life to the shores of eternity; while the history of those who have fallen from grace stands like a beacon light, warning them to shun the rocks against which a Solomon and a Judas made shipwreck of their souls.

Our books of piety are adapted to every want of the human soul, and are a fruitful source of sanctification. Who can read without spiritual profit such works as the almost inspired *Following of Christ* by Thomas à Kempis; the *Christian Perfection* of Rodriguez; the *Spiritual Combat* of Scupoli; the writings of St. Francis de Sales, and a countless host of other ascetical authors?

You will search in vain outside the Catholic Church for writers comparable in unction and healthy piety to such as I have mentioned. Compare, for instance, *Kempis* with *Bunyan's Pilgrim's Progress,* or *Butler's Lives of the Saints* with *Foxe's Book of Martyrs.* You lay down *Butler* with a sweet and tranquil devotion, and with a profound admiration for the Christian heroes whose lives he records; while you put aside *Foxe* with a troubled mind and a sense of vindictive bitterness. I do not speak of the *Book of Common Prayer,* because the best part of it is a translation from our Missal. Protestants also publish *Kempis,* though sometimes in a mutilated form; every passage in the original being carefully omitted which alludes to Catholic doctrines and practices.

A distinguished Episcopal clergyman of Baltimore once avowed to me that his favorite books of devotion were our standard works of piety. In saying this, he paid a merited and graceful tribute to the superiority of Catholic spiritual literature.

The Church gives us not only the most pressing motives, but also the most potent means for our sanctification. These means are furnished by prayer and the Sacraments. She exhorts us to frequent communion with God by prayer and meditation, and so imperative is this obligation in our eyes that we would justly hold ourselves guilty of grave dereliction of duty if we neglected for a considerable time the practice of morning and evening prayer.

The most abundant source of graces is also found in the seven Sacraments of the Church. Our soul is bathed in the Precious Blood of Jesus Christ at the font of Baptism, from which we come forth "new creatures." We are then and there incorporated with Christ, becoming "bone of His bone and flesh of His flesh;" "for as many of you," says the Apostle, "as have been baptized in Christ have put on Christ." [11] And as the Holy Ghost is inseparable from Christ, our bodies are made the temples of the Spirit of God and our souls His Sanctuary. "Christ loved the Church and delivered Himself up for it, that He might sanctify it, cleansing it by the laver of water, in the word of life; that He might present it to Himself a glorious Church, not having spot or wrinkle, or any such thing, but that it should be holy and without blemish." [12]

In Confirmation we receive new graces and new strength to battle against the temptations of life.

In the Eucharist we are fed with the living Bread which cometh down from Heaven.

In Penance are washed away the stains we have contracted after Baptism.

Are we called to the Sacred Ministry, or to the married state, we find in the Sacraments of Orders and Matrimony ample graces corresponding with the condition of life which we have embraced.

And our last illness is consoled by Extreme Unction, wherein we receive the Divine succor necessary to fortify and purify us before departing from this world.

In a word, the Church, like a watchful mother, accompanies us

[11] Gal. iii. 27.
[12] Eph. v. 25-27.

from the cradle to the grave, supplying us at each step with the medicine of life and immortality.

As the Church offers to her children the strongest motives and the most powerful means for attaining to sanctity of life, so does she reap among them the most abundant fruits of holiness. In every age and country she is the fruitful mother of saints. Our Ecclesiastical calendar is not confined to the names of the twelve Apostles. It is emblazoned with the lists of heroic Martyrs who "were stoned, and cut asunder, and put to death by the sword;"[13] of innumerable Confessors and Hermits who left all things and followed Christ; of spotless virgins who preserved their chastity for the Kingdom of Heaven's sake. Every day in the year is consecrated in our Martyrology to a large number of Saints.

And in our own times, in every quarter of the globe and in every department of life, the Church continues to raise up Saints worthy of the primitive days of Christianity.

If we seek for *Apostles,* we find them conspicuously among the Bishops of Germany, who are now displaying in prison and in exile a serene heroism worthy of Peter and Paul.

Every year records the tortures of Catholic missioners who die *Martyrs* to the Faith in China, Corea, and other Pagan countries.

Among her *confessors* are numbered those devoted priests who, abandoning home and family ties, annually go forth to preach the Gospel in foreign lands. Their worldly possessions are often confined to a few books of devotion and their modest apparel.

And who is a stranger to her consecrated *virgins,* those sisters of various Orders who in every large city of Christendom are daily reclaiming degraded women from a life of shame, and bringing them back to the sweet influences of religion; who snatch the abandoned offspring of sin from temporal and spiritual death, and make them pious and useful members of society, becoming more than mothers to them; who rescue children from ignorance, and instill into their minds the knowledge and love of God.

We can point to numberless saints also among the laity. I dare

[13] Heb. xi. 37.

assert that in almost every congregation in the Catholic world, men and women are to be found who exhibit a fervent piety and a zeal for religion which render them worthy of being named after the *Annas, the Aquilas* and the *Priscillas* of the New Testament. They attract not indeed the admiration of the public, because true piety is unostentatious and seeks a "life hidden with Christ in God." [14]

It must not be imagined that, in proclaiming the sanctity of the Church, I am attempting to prove that all Catholics are holy. I am sorry to confess that corruption of morals is too often found among professing Catholics. We cannot close our eyes to the painful fact that too many of them, far from living up to the teachings of their Church, are sources of melancholy scandal. "It must be that scandals come, but woe to him by whom the scandal cometh." I also admit that the sin of Catholics is more heinous in the sight of God than that of their separated brethren, because they abuse more grace.

But it should be borne in mind that neither God nor His Church forces any man's conscience. To all He says by the mouth of His Prophet: "Behold I set before you the way of life and the way of death." (Jer. xxi. 8.) The choice rests with yourselves.

It is easy to explain why so many disedifying members are always found clinging to the robes of the Church, their spiritual Mother, and why she never shakes them off nor disowns them as her children. The Church is animated by the spirit of her Founder, Jesus Christ. He "came into this world to save sinners." [15] He "came not to call the just but sinners to repentance." He was the Friend of Publicans and Sinners that He might make them the friends of God. And they clung to Him, knowing His compassion for them.

The Church, walking in the footsteps of her Divine Spouse, never repudiates sinners nor cuts them off from her fold, no matter how grievous or notorious may be their moral delinquencies; not because she connives at their sin, but because she wishes to reclaim them. She bids them never to despair, and tries, at least,

[14] Coloss. iii. 3.   [15] I. Tim. i. 15.

to weaken their passions, if she cannot altogether reform their lives.

Mindful also of the words of our Lord: "The poor have the Gospel preached to them," [16] the Church has a tender compassion for the victims of poverty, which has its train of peculiar temptations and infirmities. Hence, the poor and the sinners cling to the Church, as they clung to our Lord during His mortal life.

We know, on the other hand, that sinners who are guilty of gross crimes which shock public decency are virtually excommunicated from Protestant Communions. And as for the poor, the public press often complains that little or no provision is made for them in Protestant Churches. A gentleman informed me that he never saw a poor person enter an Episcopal Church which was contiguous to his residence.

These excluded sinners and victims of penury either abandon Christianity altogether, or find refuge in the bosom of their true Mother, the Catholic Church, who, like her Divine Spouse, claims the afflicted as her most cherished inheritance. The parables descriptive of this Church which our Lord employed also clearly teach us that the good and bad shall be joined together in the Church as long as her earthly mission lasts. The kingdom of God is like a field in which the cockle is allowed to grow up with the good seed until the harvest-time; [17] it is like a net which encloses good fish and bad until the hour of separation comes.[18] So, too, the Church is that great house[19] in which there are not only vessels of gold and silver, but also of wood and clay.

The Fathers repeat the teaching of Scripture. St. Jerome says: "The ark of Noah was a type of the Church. As every kind of animal was in that, so in this there are men of every race and character. As in that were the leopard and the kids, the wolf and the lambs, so in this there are to be found the just and the sinful—that is, vessels of gold and silver along with those of wood and clay." [20]

---

[16] Matt. xi. 5.   [17] Matt. xiii, 24-37.   [18] Ibid. xiii. 47.
[19] II. Tim. ii. 20.   [20] Dial. contra Lucif.

St. Gregory the Great writes: "Because in it (the Church) the good are mingled with the bad, the reprobate with the elect, it is rightly declared to be similar to the wise and the foolish virgins." [21]

Listen to St. Augustine: "Let the mind recall the threshing-floor containing straw and wheat; the nets in which are inclosed good and bad fish; the ark of Noah in which were clean and unclean animals, and you will see that the Church from now until the judgment day *contains not only sheep and oxen*—that is, saintly laymen and holy ministers—*but also the beasts of the field.* . . . For the beasts of the field are men who take delight in carnal pleasures, *the field being that broad way which leads to perdition."* [22]

The occasional scandals existing among members of the Church do not invalidate or impair her claim to the title of sanctity. The spots on the sun do not mar his brightness. Neither do the moral stains of some members sully the brilliancy of her "who cometh forth as the morning star, fair as the moon, bright as the sun." [23] The cockle that grows amidst the wheat does not destroy the beauty of the ripened harvest. The sanctity of Jesus was not sullied by the presence of Judas in the Apostolic College. Neither can the moral corruption of a few disciples tarnish the holiness of the Church. St. Paul calls the Church of Corinth a congregation of Saints,[24] though he reproves some scandalous members among them.[25]

It cannot be denied that corruption of morals prevailed in the sixteenth century to such an extent as to call for a sweeping reformation, and that laxity of discipline invaded even the sanctuary.

But how was this reformation of morals to be effected? Was it to be accomplished by a force operating inside the Church, or outside? I answer that the proper way of carrying out this reformation was by battling against iniquity within the Church; for there was not a single weapon which men could use in wag-

---

[21] Hom. 12, in Evang. [22] In Ps. viii., n. 13. [23] Cant. vi. 9.
[24] I. Cor. i. [25] I. Cor. v.

ing war with vice outside the Church, which they could not wield with more effective power when fighting under the authority of the Church. The true weapons of an Apostle, at all times, have been personal virtue, prayer, preaching, and the Sacraments. Every genuine reformer had those weapons at his disposal within the Church.

She possesses, at all times, not only the principle of undying vitality, but, besides, all the elements of reformation, and all the means of sanctification. With the weapons I have named she purified morals in the first century, and with the same weapons she went to work with a right good will, and effected a moral reformation in the sixteenth century. She was the only effectual spiritual reformer of that age.

What was the Council of Trent but a great reforming tribunal? Most of its decrees are directed to the reformation of abuses among the clergy and the laity, and the salutary fruits of its legislation are reaped even to this day.

St. Charles Borromeo, the nephew of a reigning Pope, was the greatest reformer of his time. His whole Episcopal career was spent in elevating the morals of his clergy and people. Bartholomew, Archbishop of Braga, in Portugal, preached an incessant crusade against iniquity in high and low places. St. Ignatius of Loyola and St. Alphonsus, with their companions, were conspicuous and successful reformers throughout Europe. St. Philip Neri was called the modern Apostle of Rome because of his happy efforts in dethroning vice in that city. All these Catholic Apostles preach by example as well as by word.

How do Luther and Calvin, and Zuinglius and Knox, and Henry VIII. compare with these genuine and saintly reformers, both as to their moral character and the fruit of their labors? The private lives of these pseudo-reformers were stained by cruelty, rapine, and licentiousness; and as the result of their propagandism, history records civil wars, and bloodshed, and bitter religious strife, and the dismemberment of Christianity into a thousand sects.

Instead of co-operating with the lawful authorities in extinguishing the flames which the passions of men had enkindled in the city of God, these faithless citizens fly from the citadel which they had vowed to defend; then joining the enemy, they hasten back to fan the conflagration, and to increase the commotion. And they overturn the very altars before which they previously sacrificed as consecrated priests.[26] They sanctioned rebellion by undermining the principle of authority.

What a noble opportunity they lost of earning for themselves immortal honors from God and man! If, instead of raising the standard of revolt, they had waged war upon their own passions, and fought with the Catholic reformers against impiety, they would be hailed as true soldiers of the cross. They would be welcomed by the Pope, the Bishops and clergy, and by all good men. They might be honored today on our altars, and might have a niche in our temples, side by side with those of Charles Borromeo and Ignatius Loyola; and instead of a divided army of Christians, we should behold today a united Christendom, spreading itself irresistibly from nation to nation, and bringing all kingdoms to the knowledge of Jesus Christ.

[26] Luther, Zuinglius, and Knox had been ordained priests. Calvin had studied for the priesthood, but did not receive Orders.

CHAPTER IV

CATHOLICITY

THAT Catholicity is a prominent note of the Church is evident from the Apostles' Creed, which says: "I believe in the Holy *Catholic* Church." The word *Catholic,* or Universal, signifies that the true Church is not circumscribed in its extent, like human empires, nor confined to one race of people, like the Jewish Church, but that she is diffused over every nation of the globe, and counts her children among all tribes and peoples and tongues of the earth.

This glorious Church is foreshadowed by the Psalmist, when he sings: "All the ends of the earth shall be converted to the Lord, and all the kindreds of the Gentiles shall adore in His sight; for the kingdom is the Lord's, and He shall have dominion over the nations." [1] The Prophet Malachy saw in the distant future this world-wide Church, when he wrote: "From the rising of the sun, to the going down, My name is great among the Gentiles; and in *every place* there is sacrifice, and there is offered to My name a clean oblation; for My name is great among the Gentiles, saith the Lord of Hosts." [2]

When our Savior gave commission to his Apostles He assigned to them the whole world as the theatre of their labors, and the entire human race, without regard to language, color, or nationality, as the audience to whom they were to preach. Unlike the religion of the Jewish people, which was national, or that of the

[1] Ps. xxi. 28, 29. [2] Mal. i. 11.

Mohammedans, which is local, the Catholic religion was to be cosmopolitan, embracing all nations and all countries. This is evident from the following passages: "Go ye, therefore, and teach *all nations.*" [3] "Go ye into the *whole world,* and preach the Gospel to every creature." [4] "Ye shall be witnesses unto Me in Jerusalem, and in all Judea, and Samaria, and even *to the uttermost part of the earth.*" [5]

These prophecies declaring that the Church was to be worldwide and to embrace even the Gentile nations may not strike us today as specially remarkable, accustomed as we are now to meet with Christian civilization everywhere, and to see the nations of the world bound so closely together by social and commercial relations. But we must remember that when they were uttered the true God was known and adored only in an obscure, almost isolated, corner of the earth, while triumphant idolatry was the otherwise universal religion of the world.

The prophecies were fulfilled. The Apostles scattered themselves over the surface of the earth, preaching the Gospel of Christ. "Their sound," says St. Paul, "went over all the earth and their words unto the ends of the whole world." [6] Within thirty years after our Savior's Crucifixion the Apostle of the Gentiles was able to say to the Romans: "I give thanks to my God through Jesus Christ because your faith is spoken of in the entire world" [7]—spoken of assuredly by those who were in sympathy and communion with the faith of the Romans.

St. Justin, Martyr, was able to say, about one hundred years after Christ, that there was no race of men, whether Barbarians or Greeks, or any other people of what name soever, among whom the name of Jesus Christ was not invoked.

St. Irenaeus, writing at the end of the second century, tells us that the religion so marvelously propagated throughout the whole world was not a vague, ever-changing form of Christianity, but that "this faith and doctrine and tradition preached throughout the globe is as uniform as if the Church consisted of

---

[3] Matt. xxviii. 19.   [4] Mark xvi. 15.   [5] Acts i. 8.
[6] Rom. x 18.   [7] Rom. i. 8.

one family, possessing one soul, one heart, and as if she had but one mouth. For, though the languages of the world are dissimilar, her doctrine is the same. The churches founded in Germany, in the Celtic nations, in the East in Egypt, in Lybia, and in the centres of civilization, do not differ from each other; but as the sun gives the same light throughout the world, so does the light of faith shine everywhere the same and enlighten all men who wish to come to the knowledge of the truth." [8]

"We are but of yesterday," says Tertullian, "and already have we filled your cities, towns, islands, your council halls and camps, . . . the palace, senate, forum; we have left you only the temples." [9]

Clement of Alexandria, at the end of the second century, writes: "The word of our Master did not remain in Judea, as philosophy remained in Greece, but has been poured out over the whole world, persuading Greeks and Barbarians alike, race by race, village by village, every city, whole houses and hearers one by one—nay, not a few of the philosophers themselves."

And Origen, in the early part of the next century, observes: "In all Greece, and in all barbarous races within our world, there are tens of thousands who have left their national law and customary gods for the law of Moses and the Word of Jesus Christ, though to adhere to that law is to incur the hatred of idolaters and the risk of death besides to have embraced that Word; and considering how, in so few years, in spite of the attack made on us, even to the loss of life or property, and with no great store of teachers, the preaching of that Word has found its way into every part of the world, so that Greek and Barbarian, wise and unwise, adhere to the religion of Jesus, doubtless it is a work greater than any work of man."

This Catholicity, or universality, is not to be found in any, or in all, of the combined communions separated from the Roman Catholic Church.

The Schismatic churches of the East have no claim to this title

[8] Adv. Hær., i. 1.   [9] Apologet. c. 37.

because they are confined within the Turkish and Russian dominions, and number not more than sixty million souls.

The Protestant churches, even taken collectively, (as separate communions they are a mere handful) are too insignificant in point of numbers, and too circumscribed in their territorial extent, to have any pretensions to the title of Catholic. All the Protestant denominations are estimated at sixty-five million, or less than one-fifth of those who bear the Christian name. They repudiate, moreover, and protest against the name of Catholic, though they continue to say in the Apostles' Creed "I believe in the Holy Catholic Church."

That the Roman Catholic Church alone deserves the name of *Catholic* is so evident that it is ridiculous to deny it. Ours is the only Church which adopts this name as her official title. We have possession, which is nine-tenths of the law. We have exclusively borne this glorious appellation in troubled times, when the assumption of this venerable title exposed us to insult, persecution and death; and to attempt to deprive us of it at this late hour, would be as fruitless as the efforts of the French Revolutionists who sought to uproot all traces of the old civilization by assigning new names to the days and seasons of the year.

Passion and prejudice and bad manners may affix to us the epithets of *Romish* and *Papist* and *Ultramontane,* but the calm, dispassionate mind, of whatever faith, all the world over, knows us only by the name of *Catholic*. There is a power in this name and an enthusiasm aroused by it akin to the patriotism awakened by the flag of one's country.

So great is the charm attached to the name of Catholic that a portion of the Episcopal body sometimes usurps the title of *Catholic,* though in their official books they are named *Protestant Episcopalians*. If they think that they have any just claim to the name of *Catholic,* why not come out openly and write it on the title-pages of their Bibles and Prayer-Books? Afraid of going so far, they gratify their vanity by privately calling themselves Catholic. But the delusion is so transparent that the attempt must provoke a smile even among themselves.

Should a stranger ask them to direct him to the Catholic Church they would instinctively point out to him the Roman Catholic Church.

The sectarians of the fourth and fifth centuries, as St. Augustine tells us, used to attempt the same pious fraud, but signally failed:

"We must hold fast to the Christian religion and to the communion of that Church which is Catholic, and which is called Catholic not only by those who belong to her, but also by all her enemies. Whether they will it or not, the very heretics themselves and followers of schism, when they converse, not with their own but with outsiders, call that only Catholic which is really Catholic. For they cannot be understood unless they distinguish her by that name, by which she is known throughout the whole earth." [10]

We possess not only the name, but also the reality. A single illustration will suffice to exhibit in a strong light the widespread dominion of the Catholic Church and her just claims to the title of *Catholic*. Take the Ecumenical Council of the Vatican, opened in 1869 and presided over by Pope Pius IX. Of the thousand Bishops and upwards now comprising the hierarchy of the Catholic Church, nearly eight hundred attended the opening session, the rest being unavoidably absent. All parts of the habitable globe were represented at the Council.

The Bishops assembled from Great Britain, Ireland, France, Germany, Switzerland and from almost every nation and principality in Europe. They met from Canada, the United States, Mexico and South America, and from the islands of the Atlantic and the Pacific. They were gathered together from different parts of Africa and Oceanica. They went from the banks of the Tigris and Euphrates, the cradle of the human race, and from the banks of the Jordan, the cradle of Christianity. They traveled to Rome from Mossul, built near ancient Nineveh, and from Bagdad, founded on the ruins of Babylon. They flocked from Damascus and Mount Libanus and from the Holy Land, sanctified by the footprints of our blessed Redeemer.

[10] St. Aug. de Ver. Rel., c. 7. n. 12.

Those Bishops belonged to every form of government, from the republic to the most absolute monarchy.[11] Their faces were marked by almost every shade and color that distinguished the human family. They spoke every civilized language under the sun. Kneeling together in the same great Council-Hall, truly could those Prelates exclaim, in the language of the Apocalypse: "Thou hast redeemed us, O Lord, to God in Thy blood, out of every tribe, and tongue, and people, and nation.[12]

What the Catholic Church lost by the religious revolution of the sixteenth century in the old world she has more than regained by the immense accessions to her ranks in the East and West Indies, in North and South America.

Never, in her long history, was she numerically so strong as she is at the present moment, when her children amount to about three hundred millions, or double the number of those who bear the name of Christians outside of her communion.

In her alone is literally fulfilled the magnificent prophecy of Malachy; for in every clime, and in every nation under the sun, are erected thousands of Catholic altars upon which the "clean oblation"[13] is daily offered up to the Most High.

It is said, with truth, that the sun never sets on British dominions. It may also be affirmed, with equal assurance, that wherever the British drumbeat sounds, aye, and wherever the English language is spoken, there you will find the English-speaking Catholic Missionary planting the cross—the symbol of salvation—side by side with the banner of St. George.

Quite recently a number of European emigrants arrived in Richmond. They were strangers to our country, to our customs and to our language. Every object that met their eye sadly reminded them that they were far from their own sunny Italy. But when they saw the cross surmounting our Cathedral they hastened to it with a joyful step. I saw and heard a group of them

---

[11] Does not this fact conclusively demonstrate the truth that the Catholic Church can subsist under every form of government? And is it not an eloquent refutation of the oft-repeated calumny that a republic is not a favorable soil for her development?

[12] Apoc. v. 9.   [13] Mal. i. 11.

giving earnest expression to their deep emotions. Entering this sacred temple, they felt that they had found an oasis in the desert. Once more they were at home. They found one familiar spot in a strange land. They stood in the church of their fathers, in the home of their childhood; and they seemed to say in their hearts, as a tear trickled down their sun-burnt cheeks, "How lovely are thy tabernacles, O Lord of Hosts! My soul longeth and fainteth for the courts of the Lord. My heart and my flesh have rejoiced in the living God." [14] They saw around them the paintings of familiar Saints whom they had been accustomed to reverence from their youth. They saw the baptismal font and the confessionals. They beheld the altar and the altar-rails where they received their Maker. They observed the Priest at the altar in his sacred vestments. They saw a multitude of worshipers kneeling around them, and they felt in their heart of hearts that they were once more among brothers and sisters, with whom they had "one Lord, one faith, one baptism, one God and Father of all."

Everywhere a Catholic is at home. Secret societies, of whatever name, form but a weak and counterfeit bond of union compared with the genuine fellowship created by Catholic faith, hope and charity.

The Roman Catholic Church, then, exclusively merits the title of Catholic, because her children abound in every part of the globe and comprise the vast majority of the Christian family.

God forbid that I should write these lines, or that my Catholic readers should peruse them in a boasting and vaunting spirit. God estimates men not by their numbers, but by their intrinsic worth. It is no credit to us to belong to the body of the Church Catholic if we are not united to the soul of the Church by a life of faith, hope and charity. It will avail us nothing to be citizens of that Kingdom of Christ which encircles the globe, unless the Kingdom of God is within us by the reign of the Holy Spirit in our hearts.

One righteous soul that reflects the beauty and perfections of

[14] Ps. lxxxiii.

the Lord, is more precious in His sight than the mass of humanity that has no spiritual life, and is dead to the inspirations of grace.

The Patriarch Abraham was dearer to Jehovah than all the inhabitants of the corrupt city of Sodom.

Elias was of greater worth before the Almighty than the four hundred prophets of Baal who ate at the table of Jezabel.

The Apostles with the little band of disciples that were assembled in Jerusalem after our Lord's ascension, were more esteemed by Him than the great Roman Empire, which was seated in darkness and the shadow of death.

While we rejoice, then, in the inestimable blessing of being incorporated in the visible body of the Catholic Church, whose spiritual treasures are inexhaustible, let us rejoice still more that we have not received that blessing in vain.

CHAPTER V

APOSTOLICITY

THE true Church must be Apostolical. Hence in the Creed framed in the first Ecumenical Council of Nicæa, in the year 325, we find these words: "I believe in the One, Holy, Catholic and *Apostolic* Church."

This attribute or note of the Church implies that the true Church must always teach the identical doctrines once delivered by the Apostles, and that her ministers must derive their powers from the Apostles by an uninterrupted succession.

Consequently, no church can claim to be the true one whose doctrines differ from those of the Apostles, or whose ministers are unable to trace, by an unbroken chain, their authority to an Apostolic source; just as our Minister to England can exercise no authority in that country unless he is duly commissioned by our Government and represents its views.

The Church, says St. Paul, is "built upon the foundation of the Apostles," [1] so that the doctrine which it propagates must be based on Apostolic teachings. Hence St. Paul says to the Galatians: "Though an angel from heaven preach a Gospel to you besides that which we have preached to you, let him be anathema." [2] The same Apostle gives this admonition to Timothy: "The things which thou hast heard from me before many witnesses the *same* commend to faithful men who shall be fit to teach others also." [3] Timothy must transmit to his disciples only such doctrines as he heard from the lips of his Master.

---

[1] Eph. ii. 20.   [2] Gal. i. 8.   [3] II. Tim. ii 2.

Not only is it required that ministers of the Gospel should conform their teaching to the doctrine of the Apostles, but also that these ministers should be ordained and commissioned by the Apostles or their legitimate successors. "Neither doth any man," says the Apostle, "take the honor to himself, but he that is called by God, as Aaron was." [4] This text evidently condemns all self-constituted preachers and reformers; for, "how shall they preach, unless they be sent?" [5] *Sent,* of course, by legitimate authority, and not directed by their own caprice. Hence, we find that those who succeeded the Apostles were ordained and commissioned by them to preach, and that no others were permitted to exercise this function. Thus we are told that Paul and Barnabas "had ordained for them priests in every church." [6] And the Apostle says to Titus: "For this cause I left thee in Crete, ... that thou shouldst ordain Priests in every city, as I also appointed thee." [7] Even St. Paul himself, though miraculously called and instructed by God, had hands imposed on him,[8] lest others should be tempted by his example to preach without Apostolic warrant.

To discover, therefore, the Church of Christ among the various conflicting claimants we have to inquire, first, which church teaches whole and entire those doctrines that were taught by the Apostles; second, what ministers can trace back, in an unbroken line, their missionary powers to the Apostles.

The Catholic Church *alone* teaches doctrines which are *in all respects* identical with those of the first teachers of the Gospel. The following parallel lines exhibit some examples of the departure of the Protestant bodies from the primitive teachings of Christianity, and the faithful adhesion of the Catholic Church to them.

[4] Heb. v. 4.   [5] Rom. x. 15.   [6] Acts xiv. 22.
[7] Tit. i. 5.   [8] Acts xiii. 2, 3.

Apostolic Church	Catholic Church	Protestant Churches
1. Our Savior gives pre-eminence to Peter over the other Apostles: "I will give to thee the keys of the kingdom of heaven." [9] "Confirm thy brethren." [10] "Feed My lambs; feed My sheep." [11]	The Catholic Church gives the primacy of honor and jurisdiction to Peter and to his successors.	All other Christian communions practically deny Peter's supremacy over the other Apostles.
2. The Apostolic Church claimed to be infallible in her teachings. Hence the Apostles spoke with unerring authority, and their words were received not as human opinions, but as Divine truths. "When you have received from us the word of God, you received it not as the word of men, but (as it is indeed) the word of God." [12] "It hath seemed good to the Holy Ghost and to us," say the assembled Apostles, "to lay no further burden upon you than these necessary things." [13] "Though an angel from heaven preach a gospel to you besides that which we have preached to you, let him be anathema." [14]	The Catholic Church alone, of all the Christian communions, claims to exercise the prerogative of infallibility in her teaching. Her ministers always speak from the pulpit as having authority, and the faithful receive with implicit confidence what the Church teaches, without once questioning her veracity.	All the Protestant churches repudiate the claim of infallibility. They deny that such a gift is possessed by any teachers of religion. The ministers pronounce no authoritative doctrines, but advance opinions as embodying their private interpretation of the Scripture. And their hearers are never required to believe them, but are expected to draw their own conclusions from the Bible.
3. Our Savior enjoins and prescribes rules for fasting: "When thou fastest, anoint thy head and wash thy face, that thou appear not to men	The Church prescribes fasting to the faithful at stated seasons, particularly during Lent. A Catholic Priest is always fasting when he	Protestants have no law prescribing fasts, though some may fast from private devotion. They even try to cast ridicule on fasting as a

[9] Matt. xvi. 18.
[12] Thess. ii. 13.

[10] Luke xxii. 32.
[13] Acts xv. 28.

[11] John xxi. 15.
[14] Gal. i. 8.

Apostolic Church	Catholic Church	Protestant Churches
to fast . . . and thy Father, who seeth in secret, will repay thee."[15] The Apostles fasted before engaging in sacred functions: "They ministered to the Lord, and fasted."[16] "And when they ordained Priests in every city, they prayed with fasting."[17]	officiates at the altar. He breaks his fast only after he says Mass. When Bishops ordain Priests they are always fasting, as well as the candidates for ordination.	work of supererogation, detracting from the merits of Christ. Neither candidates for ordination, nor the ministers who ordain them, ever fast on such occasions.
4. "Let women," says the Apostle, "keep silence in the churches. For, it is not permitted them to speak . . . It is a shame for a woman to speak in the church."[18]	The Catholic Church never permits women to preach in the house of God.	Women, especially in this country, publicly preach in Methodist and other churches with the sanction of the church elders.
5. St. Peter and St. John confirmed the newly baptized in Samaria: "They laid hands on them and they received the Holy Ghost."[19]	Every Catholic Bishop, as a successor of the Apostles, likewise imposes hands on baptized persons in the Sacrament of Confirmation, by which they receive the Holy Ghost.	No denomination performs the ceremony of imposing hands in this country except Episcopalians, and even they do not recognize Confirmation as a Sacrament.
6. Our Savior and His Apostles taught that the Eucharist contains the Body and Blood of Christ: "Take ye, and eat; this is My Body. . . . Drink ye all of this, for this is my Blood."[20] "The chalice of benediction which we bless, is it not the communion of the Blood of Christ;	The Catholic Church teaches, with our Lord and His Apostles, that the Eucharist contains really and indeed the Body and Blood of Jesus Christ under the appearance of bread and wine.	The Protestant churches (except, perhaps, a few Ritualists) condemn the doctrine of the Real Presence as idolatrous, and say that, in partaking of the communion, we receive only a memorial of Christ.

[15] Matt. vi. 17.
[18] I. Cor. xiv. 34, 35.

[16] Acts xiii. 2.
[19] Acts viii. 17.

[17] Acts xiv. 22.
[20] Matt. xxvi. 26-28.

Apostolic Church	Catholic Church	Protestant Churches
and the bread which we break, is it not the participation of the Body of the Lord?"[21]		
7. The Apostles were empowered by our Savior to forgive sins:— "Whose sins ye shall forgive, they are forgiven."[22] "God," says St. Paul, "hath given to us the ministry of reconciliation."[23]	The Bishops and Priests of the Catholic Church, as the inheritors of Apostolic prerogatives, profess to exercise the ministry of reconciliation, and to forgive sins in the name of Christ.	Protestants affirm, on the contrary, that God delegates to no man the power of pardoning sin.
8. Regarding the sick, St. James gives this instruction: "Is any man sick among you, let him bring in the priests of the Church, and let them pray over him, anointing him with oil in the name of the Lord."[24]	One of the most ordinary duties of a Catholic Priest is to anoint the sick in the Sacrament of Extreme Unction. If a man is sick among us he is careful to call in the Priest of the Church, that he may anoint him with oil in the name of the Lord.	No such ceremony as that of anointing the sick is practised by any Protestant denomination, notwithstanding the Apostle's injunction.
9. Of marriage our Savior says: "Whoever shall put away his wife and marry another committeth adultery against her. And if the wife shall put away her husband and be married to another she committeth adultery."[25] And again St. Paul says: "To them that are	Literally following the Apostle's injunction, the Catholic Church forbids the husband and wife to separate from one another; or, if they separate, neither of them can marry again during the life of the other.	The Protestant churches, as is well known, have so far relaxed this rigorous law of the Gospel as to allow divorced persons to remarry. And divorce *a vinculo* is granted on various and even trifling pretenses.

[21] I. Cor. x. 16. [22] John xx. 28. [23] II. Cor. v. 18.
[24] James v. 14. [25] Mark x. 11, 12.

Apostolic Church	Catholic Church	Protestant Churches
married . . . the Lord commandeth that the wife depart not from her husband, and if she depart that she remain unmarried . . . And let not the husband put away his wife."[26]		
10. Our Lord recommends not only by word, but by His example, to souls aiming at perfection, the state of perpetual virginity. St. Paul also exhorts the Corinthians by counsel and his own example to the same angelic virtue: "He that giveth his virgin in marriage," he says, "doeth well. And he that giveth her not doeth better."[27]	Like the Apostle and his Master, the Catholic clergy bind themselves to a life of perpetual chastity. The inmates of our convents of men and women voluntarily consecrate their virginity to God.	All the ministers of other denominations, with very rare exceptions, marry. And far from inculcating the Apostolic counsel of celibacy to any of their flock, they more than insinuate that the virtue of perpetual chastity, though recommended by St. Paul, is impracticable.

We now leave the reader to judge for himself which Church enforces the doctrines of the Apostles in all their pristine vigor.

To show that the Catholic Church is the only lineal descendant of the Apostles it is sufficient to demonstrate that she alone can trace her pedigree, generation after generation, to the Apostles, while the origin of all other Christian communities can be referred to a comparatively modern date.

The most influential Christian sects existing in this country at the present time are the Lutherans, Episcopalians, Methodists, Presbyterians and Baptists. The other Protestant denominations are comparatively insignificant in point of numbers, and are for the most part offshoots from the Christian communities just named.

Martin Luther, a Saxon monk, was the founder of the church

---

[26] I. Cor. vii, 10, 11.   [27] I. Cor. vii.

which bears his name. He was born at Eisleben, in Saxony, in 1483, and died in 1546.

The Anglican or Episcopal Church owes its origin to Henry VIII. of England. The immediate cause of his renunciation of the Roman Church was the refusal of Pope Clement VII. to grant him a divorce from his lawful wife, Catharine of Aragon, that he might be free to be joined in wedlock to Anne Boleyn. In order to legalize his divorce from his virtuous queen the licentious monarch divorced himself and his kingdom from the spiritual supremacy of the Pope.

"There is a close relationship," says D'Aubigné, "between these two divorces," meaning Henry's divorce from his wife and England's divorce from the Church. Yes, there is the relationship of cause and effect.

Bishop Short, an Anglican historian, candidly admits that "the existence of the Church of England as a distinct body, and her final separation from Rome, may *be dated* from the period of the divorce." [28]

The Book of Homilies, in the language of fulsome praise, calls Henry "the true and faithful minister," and gives him the credit for having abolished in England the Papal supremacy and established the new order of things.[29]

John Wesley is the acknowledged founder of the Methodist Church. Methodism dates from the year 1729, and its cradle was the Oxford University in England. John and Charles Wesley were students at Oxford. They gathered around them a number of young men who devoted themselves to the frequent reading of the Holy Scriptures and to prayer. Their methodical and exact mode of life obtained for them the name of *Methodists*. The Methodist Church in this country is the offspring of a colony sent hither from England.

As it would be tedious to give even a succinct history of each sect, I shall content myself with presenting a tabular statement

[28] History of the Church of England, by Thomas V. Short, Bishop of St. Asaph's, p. 44.
[29] Book of Homilies.

Name	Place of Origin	Founder	Year	Authority Quoted
Anabaptists	Germany	Nicolas Stork	1521	Vincent L. Milner, "Religious Denominations."
Baptists	Rhode Island	Roger Williams	1639	"The Book of Religions," by John Hayward.
Free-Will Baptists	New Hampshire	Benj. Randall	1780	Ibid.
Free Communion Baptists	New York	Benijah Corp	Close of 18th century	Rev. A. D. Williams in "History of All Denominations."
Seventh-Day Baptists	United States	General Conference	1833	W. B. Gillett, Ibid.
Campbellites, or Christians	Virginia	Alex. Campbell	1813	"Book of Religions."
Methodist Episcopal	England	John Wesley	1739	Rev. Nathan Bangs in "History of All Denominations."
Reformed Methodist	Vermont	Branch of the Meth. Episcopal Church	1814	Ibid.
Methodist Society	New York	Do.	1820	Rev. W. M. Stilwell, Ibid.
Methodist Protestant	Baltimore	Do.	1830	James R. Williams, Ibid.
True Wesleyan Methodist	New York	Delegates from Methodist denominations	1843	J. Timberman, Ibid.
Presbyterian (Old School)	Scotland	General Assembly	1560	John M. Krebs, Ibid.
Presbyterian (New School)	Philadelphia	General Assembly	1840	Joel Parker, D.D., Ibid.
Episcopalian	England	Henry VIII	1534	Macaulay and other English historians.
Lutheran	Germany	Martin Luther	1524	S. S. Schmucker in "History of All Denominations."
Unita'n Congregationalists	Germany	Celarius	About 1540	Alvan Lamson, Ibid.
Congregationalists	England	Robert Browne	1583	E. W. Andrews, Ibid.
Quakers	England	George Fox	1647	English Historians.
Do.	America	William Penn	1681	American Historians.
Catholic Church	Jerusalem	Jesus Christ	33	New Testament.

exhibiting the name and founder of each denomination, the place and date of its origin, and the names of the authors from whom I quote. My authorities in every instance are Protestants.

From this brief historical tableau we find that all the Christian *sects* now existing in the United States had their origin since the year 1500. Consequently, the oldest body of Christians among us, outside the Catholic Church, is not yet four centuries old. They all, therefore, come fifteen centuries too late to have any pretensions to be called the Apostolic Church.

But I may be told: "Though our public history as Protestants dates from the Reformation, we can trace our origin back to the Apostles." This I say is impossible. First of all, the very name you bear betrays your recent birth; for who ever heard of a Baptist or an Episcopal, or any other Protestant church, prior to the Reformation? Nor can you say: "We existed in every age as an invisible church." Your concealment, indeed, was so complete that no man can tell, to this day, where you lay hid for sixteen centuries. But even if you did exist you could not claim to be the Church of Christ; for our Lord predicted that His Church should ever be as a city placed upon the mountain top, that all might see it, and that its ministers should preach the truths of salvation from the watch-towers thereof, that all might hear them.

It is equally in vain to tell me that you were allied in faith to the various Christian sects that went out from the Catholic Church from age to age; for these sects proclaimed doctrines diametrically opposed to one another, and the true Church must be one in faith. And besides, the less relationship you claim with many of these seceders the better for you, as they all advocated errors against Christian truth, and some of them disseminated principles at variance with *decency* and morality.

The Catholic Church, on the contrary, can easily vindicate the title of Apostolic, because she derives her origin from the Apostles. Every Priest and Bishop can trace his genealogy to the first disciples of Christ with as much facility as the most remote branch of a vine can be traced to the main stem.

All the Catholic Clergy in the United States, for instance, were ordained only by Bishops who are in active communion with the See of Rome. These Bishops themselves received their commissions from the Bishop of Rome. The present Bishop of Rome, Pius IX., is the successor of Gregory XVI., who succeeded Pius VIII., who was the successor of Leo XII. And thus we go back from century to century till we come to Peter, the first Bishop of Rome, Prince of the Apostles and Vicar of Christ. Like the Evangelist Luke, who traces the genealogy of our Savior back to Adam and to God, we can trace the pedigree of Pius IX. to Peter and to Christ. There is not a link wanting in the chain which binds the humblest Priest in the land to the Prince of the Apostles. And although on a few occasions there happened to be two or even three claimants for the chair of Peter, these counter-claims could no more affect the validity of the legitimate Pope than the struggle of two contestants for the Presidency could invalidate the title of the recognized Chief Magistrate.

It was by pursuing this line of argument that the early Fathers demonstrated the Apostolicity of the Catholic Church, and refuted the pretensions of contemporary sectaries. St. Irenæus, Tertullian and St. Augustine give catalogues of the Bishops of Rome who flourished up to their respective times, with whom it was their happiness to be in communion, and then they challenged their opponents to trace their lineage to the Apostolic See. "Let them," says Tertullian, in the second century, "produce the origin of their church. Let them exhibit the succession of their Bishops, so that the first of them may appear to have been ordained by an *Apostle, or by an apostolic man who was in communion with the Apostles.*" [30]

And if the Fathers of the fifth century considered it a powerful argument in their favor that they could refer to an uninterrupted line of fifty Bishops who occupied the See of Rome, how much stronger is the argument to us who can now exhibit five times that number of Roman Pontiffs who have sat in the chair of Peter! I would affectionately repeat to my separated brethren

[30] Lib. de Præscrip., c. 32.

what Augustine said to the Donatists of his time: "Come to us, brethren, if you wish to be engrafted in the vine. We are afflicted in beholding you lying cut off from it. Count over the Bishops from the very See of St. Peter, and mark, in this list of Fathers, how one succeeded the other. This is the rock against which the proud gates of hell do not prevail." [31]

[31] Psal. contra part Donati.

CHAPTER VI

PERPETUITY OF THE CHURCH

PERPETUITY, or duration till the end of time, is one of the most striking marks of the Church. By perpetuity is not meant merely that Christianity in one form or another was always to exist, but that the Church was to remain forever in its *integrity,* clothed with *all* those attributes which God gave it in the beginning. For, if the Church lost any of her essential characteristics, such as her unity and sanctity, which our Lord imparted to her at the commencement of her existence, she could not be said to be perpetual because she would not be the same Institution.

The unceasing duration of the Church of Christ is frequently foretold in Sacred Scripture. The Angel Gabriel announces to Mary that Christ "shall reign over the house of Jacob *forever,* and of his kingdom *there shall be no end.*" [1] Our Savior said to Peter: "Thou art Peter, and upon this rock I will build My Church, and the gates of hell shall not prevail against it." [2] Our Blessed Lord clearly intimates here that the Church is destined to be assailed always, but to be overcome, never.

In the last words recorded of our Redeemer in the Gospel of St. Matthew the same prediction is strongly repeated, and the reason of the Church's indefectibility is fully expressed: "Go ye, teach all nations, ... and behold I am with you *all days,* even *to the consummation* of the world." [3] This sentence contains three important declarations: First—The presence of Christ with His Church—"Behold, I am with you." Second—His constant

[1] Luke i. 32, 33.   [2] Matt. xvi. 18.   [3] Matt. xxviii. 19, 20.

presence, without an interval of one day's absence—"I am with you all days." Third—His perpetual presence to the end of the world, and consequently the perpetual duration of the Church— "Even to the consummation of the world."

Hence it follows that the true Church must have existed from the beginning; it must have had not one day's interval of suspended animation, or separation from Christ, and must live to the end of time.

None of the Christian Communions outside the Catholic Church can have any reasonable claim to *Perpetuity,* since, as we have seen in the preceding chapter, they are all [4] of recent origin.

The indestructibility of the Catholic Church is truly marvelous and well calculated to excite the admiration of every reflecting mind, when we consider the number and variety, and the formidable power of the enemies with whom she had to contend from her very birth to the present time; this fact alone stamps divinity on her brow.

The Church has been constantly engaged in a double warfare, one foreign, the other domestic—in foreign war against Paganism and infidelity; in civil strife against heresy and schism fomented by her own rebellious children.

From the day of Pentecost till the victory of Constantine the Great over Maxentius, embracing a period of about two hundred and eighty years, the Church underwent a series of ten persecutions unparalleled for atrocity in the annals of history. Every torture that malice could invent was resorted to, that every vestige of Christianity might be eradicated. *"Christianos ad leones," the Christians to the lions,* was the popular war-cry.

They were clothed in the skins of wild beasts, and thus exposed to be devoured by dogs. They were covered with pitch and set on fire to serve as lamp-posts to the streets of Rome. To justify such atrocities, and to smother all sentiments of compassion, these persecutors accused their innocent victims of the most appalling crimes.

For three centuries the Christians were obliged to worship God

[4] Except some Oriental sects dating back to the fifth and ninth centuries.

in the secrecy of their chambers, or in the Roman catacombs, which are still preserved to attest the undying fortitude of the martyrs and the enormity of their sufferings.

And yet Pagan Rome, before whose standard the mightiest nations quailed, was unable to crush the infant Church or arrest her progress. In a short time we find this colossal Empire going to pieces, and the Head of the Catholic Church dispensing laws to Christendom in the very city from which the imperial Cæsars had promulgated their edicts against Christianity!

During the fifth and sixth centuries the Goths and Vandals, the Huns, Visigoths, Lombards and other immense tribes of Barbarians came down like a torrent from the North, invading the fairest portions of Southern Europe. They dismembered the Roman Empire and swept away nearly every trace of the old Roman civilization. They plundered cities, leveled churches and left ruin and desolation after them. Yet, though conquering for awhile, they were conquered in turn by submitting to the sweet yoke of the Gospel. And thus, as even the infidel Gibbon observes, "The progress of Christianity has been marked by two glorious and decisive victories over the learned and luxurious citizens of the Roman Empire and over the warlike Barbarians of Scythia and Germany, who subverted the empire and embraced the religion of the Romans." [5]

Mohammedanism took its rise in the seventh century in Arabia, and made rapid conquests in Asia. In the fifteenth century Constantinople was captured by the followers of the false prophet, who even threatened to subject all Europe to their sway. For nine centuries Mohammedanism continued to be a standing menace to christendom, till the final issue came when it was to be decided once for all whether Christianity and civilization on the one hand, or Mohammedanism and infidelity on the other, should rule the destinies of Europe and the world.

At the earnest solicitation of the Pope, the kingdom of Spain and the republic of Venice formed an offensive league against the Turks, who were signally defeated in the battle of Lepanto,

[5] Decline and Fall of the Roman Empire, ch. xxxvii, p. 450.

in 1571. And if the Cross, instead of the Crescent, surmounts the cities of Europe today, it is indebted for this priceless blessing to the vigilance of the Roman Pontiffs.

Another adversary more formidable and dangerous than those I have mentioned threatened the overthrow of the Church in the fourth and fifth centuries. I speak of the great heresy of Arius, which was followed by those of Nestorius and Eutyches.

The Arian schism, soon after its rise, spread rapidly through Europe, Northern Africa and portions of Asia. It received the support of immense multitudes, and flourished for awhile under the fostering care of several successive emperors. Catholic Bishops were banished from their sees, and their places were filled by Arian intruders. The Church which survived the sword of Paganism seemed for awhile to yield to the poison of Arianism. But after a short career of prosperity this gigantic sect became weakened by intestine divisions, and was finally swept away by other errors which came following in its footsteps.

You are already familiar with the great religious revolution of the sixteenth century, which spread like a tornado over Northern Europe and threatened, if that were possible, to engulf the bark of Peter. More than half of Germany followed the new Gospel of Martin Luther. Switzerland submitted to the doctrines of Zuinglius. The faith was lost in Sweden through the influence of its king, Gustavus Vasa. Denmark conformed to the new creed through the intrigues of King Christian II. Catholicity was also crushed out in Norway, England and Scotland. Calvinism in the sixteenth century and Voltaireism in the eighteenth had gained such a foothold in France that the faith of that glorious Catholic nation twice trembled in the balance. Ireland alone, of all the nations of Northern Europe, remained faithful to the ancient Church.

Let us now calmly survey the field after the din and smoke of battle have passed away. Let us examine the condition of the old Church after having passed through those deadly conflicts. We see her numerically stronger today than at any previous period of her history. The losses she sustained in the old world are more than compensated by her acquisitions in the new. She has already recovered a good portion of the ground wrested from her in the sixteenth century. She numbers now about three hundred million adherents. She exists today not an effete institution, but in all the integrity and fulness of life, with her organism unimpaired, more united, more compact and more vigorous than ever she was before.

The so-called Reformation of the sixteenth century bears many points of resemblance to the great Arian heresy. Both schisms originated with Priests impatient of the yoke of the Gospel, fond of novelty and ambitious for notoriety. Both were nursed and sustained by the reigning Powers, and were augmented by large accessions of proselytes. Both spread for awhile with the irresistible force of a violent hurricane, till its fury was spent. Both subsequently became subdivided into various bodies. The extinction of Protestantism would complete the parallel.

In this connection a remark of De Maistre is worth quoting: "If Protestantism bears always the same name, though its belief has been perpetually shifting, it is because its name is purely negative and means only the denial of Catholicity, so that the less it believes, and the more it protests, the more consistently Protestant it will be. Since, then, its name becomes continually truer, it must subsist until it perishes, just as an ulcer disappears with the last atom of the flesh which it has been eating away." [6]

But similar causes will produce similar results. As both revolutions were the offspring of rebellion; as both have been marked by the same vigorous youth, the same precocious manhood, the same premature decay and dismemberment of parts; so we are not rash in predicting that the dissolution which long since visited the former is destined, sooner or later, to overtake the latter. But the Catholic Church, because she is the work of God, is always "renewing her strength, like the eagle's." [7] You ask for a miracle, as the Jews asked our Saviour for a sign. You ask the Church to prove her divine mission by a miraculous agency. Is not her very survival the greatest of prodigies? If

[6] Du Pape, I, 2, c. 5.   [7] Psalm cii. 5.

you beheld some fair bride with all the weakness of humanity upon her, cast into a prison and starved and trampled upon, hacked and tortured, her blood sprinkled upon her dungeon walls, and if you saw her again emerging from her prison, in all the bloom and freshness of youth, and surviving for years and centuries beyond the span of human life, continuing to be the joyful mother of children, would you not call that scene a miracle?

And is not this a picture of our Mother the Church? Has she not passed through all these vicissitudes? Has she not tasted the bitterness of prison in every age? Has not her blood been shed in every clime?

And yet in her latter days, she is as fair as ever, and the nursing mother of children. Are not civil governments and institutions mortal as well as men? Why should the Republic of the Church be an exception to the law of decay and death? If this is not a miracle, I know not what a miracle is.

If Augustin, that profound Christian philosopher, could employ this argument in the fifth century, with how much more force may it be used today, fifteen hundred years after his time!

But far be it from us to ascribe to any human cause this marvelous survival of the Church.

Her indestructibility is not due, as some suppose, to her wonderful organization, or to the far-reaching policy of her Pontiffs, or to the learning and wisdom of her teachers. If she has survived, it is not because of human wisdom, but often in spite of human folly. Her permanence is due not to the arm of the flesh, but to the finger of God. "Not to us, O Lord, not to us, but to Thy name give glory."

I would now ask this question of all that are hostile to the Catholic Church and that are plotting her destruction: How can you hope to overturn an institution which for more than nineteen centuries has successfully resisted all the combined assaults of the world, of men, and of the powers of darkness? What means will you employ to encompass her ruin?

I. Is it the power of Kings, and Emperors, and Prime Ministers? They have tried in vain to crush her, from the days of the Roman Cæsars to those of the former Chancellor of Germany.

Many persons labor under the erroneous impression that the crowned heads of Europe have been the unvarying supporters of the Church, and that if their protection were withdrawn she would soon collapse. So far from the Church being sheltered behind earthly thrones, her worst enemies have been, with some honorable exceptions, so-called Christian Princes who were nominal children of the Church. They chafed under her salutary discipline; they wished to be rid of her yoke, because she alone, in time of oppression, had the power and the courage to stand by the rights of the people, and place her breast as a wall of brass against the encroachments of their rulers. With calm confidence we can say with the Psalmist: "Why have the Gentiles raged, and the people devised vain things? The kings of the earth stood up, and the princes met together, against the Lord, and against his Christ. Let us break their bonds asunder, and let us cast away their yoke from us.

"He that dwelleth in heaven shall laugh at them and the Lord shall deride them." [8]

II. Can the immense resources and organized power of rival religious bodies succeed in absorbing her and in bringing her to naught? I am not disposed to undervalue this power. Against any human force it would be irresistible. But if the colossal strength, and incomparable machinery of the Roman Empire could not prevent the establishment of the Church; if Arianism, Nestorianism, Eutychianism could not check her development, how can modern organizations stop her progress now, when in the fulness of her strength?

It is easier to preserve what is created, than to create anew.

III. But we have been told: "Take from the Pope his Temporal power and the Church is doomed to destruction. This is the secret of her strength; strip her of this, and, like Samson shorn of his hair, she will betray all the weakness of a poor mortal.

[8] Psalm ii. 1-4.

Then this brilliant luminary will wax pale and she will sink below the horizon, never more to rise again."

For more than seven centuries after the establishment of the Church the Popes had no sovereign territorial jurisdiction. How could she have outlived that period, if the temporal power were essential to her perpetuity? And even since 1870 the Pope has been deprived of his temporalities. This loss, however, does not bring a wrinkle on the fair brow of the Church, nor does it retard one inch her onward march.

IV. Is she unable to cope with modern inventions and the mechanical progress of the nineteenth century? We are often told so; but far from hiding our head, like the ostrich in the sand, at the approach of these inventions we hail them as messengers of God, and will use them as Providential instruments for the further propagation of the faith.

If we succeeded so well before, when we had no ships but frail canoes, no compass but our eyes; when we had no roads but eternal snows, virgin forests and trackless deserts; when we had no guide save faith, and hope, and God—if even then we succeeded so well in carrying the Gospel to the confines of the earth, how much more can we do now by the aid of telegraph, steamships and railroads?

Yes, O men of genius, we bless your inventions; we bless you, ye modern discoveries; and we will impress you into the service of the Church and say: "Fire and heat bless the Lord. Lightnings and clouds bless the Lord; all ye works of the Lord bless the Lord; praise and exalt him above all forever." [9]

The utility of modern inventions to the Church has lately been manifested in a conspicuous manner. The Pope called a council of all the Bishops of the world. Without the aid of steam it would have been almost impossible for them to assemble; by its aid they were able to meet from the uttermost bounds of the earth.

V. But may not the light of the Church grow pale and be extinguished before the intellectual blaze of the nineteenth cen-

[9] Daniel, iii.

tury? Has she not much to fear from literature, the arts and sciences? She has always been the Patroness of literature, and the fostering Mother of the arts and sciences. She founded and endowed nearly all the great universities of Europe.

Not to mention those of the continent, a bare catalogue of which would cover a large space, I may allude to the Universities of Oxford and Cambridge, the two most famous seats of learning in England, which were established under Catholic auspices centuries before the Reformation.

The Church also founded three of the four universities now existing in Scotland, viz: St. Andrew's in 1411, Glasgow in 1450 and Aberdeen in 1494.

Without her we should be deprived today of the priceless treasures of ancient literature; for, in preserving the languages of Greece and Rome from destruction, she rescued classical writers of those countries from oblivion. Hallam justly observes that, were it not for the diligent labors of the monks in the Middle Ages, our knowledge of the history of ancient Greece and Rome would be as vague today as our information regarding the Pyramids of Egypt.

And as for works of art, there are more valuable monuments of art contained in the single museum of the Vatican than are to be found in all our country. Artists are obliged to go to Rome to consult their best models. Our churches are not only temples of worship, but depositories of sacred art. For our intellectual progress we are in no small measure indebted to the much-abused Middle Ages. Tyndall has the candor to observe that "The nineteenth century strikes its roots into the centuries gone by and draws nutriment from them." [10]

VI. Is it liberty that will destroy tne Church? The Church breathes freely and expands with giant growth, where true liberty is found. She is always cramped in her operations wherever despotism casts its dark shadow. Nowhere does she enjoy more independence than here; nowhere is she more vigorous and more prosperous.

[10] Tyndall, Study of Physics.

Children of the Church, fear nothing, happen what will to her. Christ is with her and therefore she cannot sink. Cæsar, in crossing the Adriatic, said to the troubled oarsman: "Quid times? Cæsarem vehis." What Cæsar said in presumption Jesus says with truth: What fearest thou? Christ is in the ship. Are we not positive that the sun will rise tomorrow and next day, and so on to the end of the world? Why? Because God so ordained when He established it in the heavens; and because it has never failed to run its course from the beginning. Has not Christ promised that the Church should always enlighten the world? Has He not, so far, fulfilled His promise concerning His Church? Has she not gone steadily on her course amid storm and sunshine? The fulfilment of the past is the best security for the future.

Amid the continual changes in human institutions she is the one Institution that never changes. Amid the universal ruins of earthly monuments she is the one monument that stands proudly pre-eminent. Not a stone in this building falls to the ground. Amid the general destruction of kingdoms her kingdom is never destroyed. Ever ancient and ever new, time writes no wrinkles on her Divine brow.

The Church has seen the birth of every government of Europe, and it is not at all improbable that she shall also witness the death of them all and chant their requiem. She was more than fourteen hundred years old when Columbus discovered our continent, and the foundation of our Republic is but as yesterday to her.

She calmly looked on while the Goths and the Visigoths, the Huns and the Saxons swept like a torrent over Europe, subverting dynasties. She has seen monarchies changed into republics, and republics consolidated into empires—all this has she witnessed, while her own Divine Constitution has remained unaltered. Of Her we can truly say in the words of the Psalmist: "They shall perish, but thou remainest; and all of them shall grow old as a garment. And as a vesture Thou shalt change them, and they shall be changed. But thou art always the self-same, and thy years shalt not fail. The children of thy servants shall continue, and their seed shall be directed forever." [11] God forbid that we should ascribe to any human cause this marvelous survival of the Church. Her indestructibility is not due, as some suppose, to her wonderful organization, or to the far-reaching policy of her Pontiffs, or to the learning and wisdom of her teachers. If she has survived, it is not because of human wisdom, but often in spite of human folly. Her permanence is due not to the arm of the flesh, but to the finger of God.

In the brightest days of the Republic of Pagan Rome the Roman said with pride: "I am a Roman citizen." This was his noblest title. He was proud of the Republic, because it was venerable in years, powerful in the number of its citizens, and distinguished for the wisdom of its statesmen. What a subject of greater glory to be a citizen of the Republic of the Church which has lasted for nineteen centuries, and will continue till time shall be no more; which counts her millions of children in every clime; which numbers her heroes and her martyrs by the thousand; which associates you with the Apostles and Saints. "You are no more strangers and foreigners, but you are fellow-citizens with the Saints and the domestics of God, built upon the foundation of the Prophets and Apostles, Jesus Christ Himself being the chief cornerstone." [12] Though separated from earthly relatives and parents, you need never be separated from her. She is ever with us to comfort us. She says to us what her Divine Spouse said to His Apostles: "Behold, I am with you all days, even to the consummation of the world." [13]

[11] Psalm ci. 27-29.   [12] Eph. ii. 19, 20.   [13] Matt. xxviii. 20.

CHAPTER VII

INFALLIBLE AUTHORITY OF THE CHURCH

THE Church has authority from God to teach regarding faith and morals, and in her teaching she is preserved from error by the special guidance of the Holy Ghost.

The prerogative of infallibility is clearly deduced from the attributes of the Church already mentioned. The Church is One, Holy, Catholic, and Apostolic. Preaching the same creed everywhere and at all times; teaching holiness and truth, she is, of course, essentially unerring in her doctrine; for what is one, holy or unchangeable must be infallibly true.

That the Church was infallible in the Apostolic age is denied by no Christian. We never question the truth of the Apostles' declarations; [1] they were, in fact, the only authority in the Church for the first century. The New Testament was not completed till the close of the first century. There is no just ground for denying to the Apostolic teachers of the nineteenth century in which we live a prerogative clearly possessed by those of the first, especially as the Divine Word nowhere intimates that this unerring guidance was to die with the Apostles. On the contrary, as the Apostles transmitted to their successors their power to preach, to baptize, to ordain, to confirm, etc., they must also have handed down to them the no less essential gift of infallibility.

God loves us as much as He loved the primitive Christians; Christ died for us as well as for them and we have as much need of unerring teachers as they had.

[1] See Gal. iv. 14; 1 Thess. ii. 13.

54

It will not suffice to tell me: "We have an infallible Scripture as a substitute for an infallible apostolate of the first century," for an infallible book is of no use to me without an infallible interpreter, as the history of Protestantism too clearly demonstrates.

But besides these presumptive arguments, we have positive evidence from Scripture that the Church cannot err in her teachings. Our Blessed Lord, in constituting St. Peter Prince of His Apostles, says to him: "Thou art Peter, and upon this rock I will build My Church, and the gates of hell shall not prevail against it." [2] Christ makes here a solemn prediction that no error shall ever invade His Church, and if she fell into error the gates of hell have certainly prevailed against her.

The Reformers of the sixteenth century affirm that the Church did fall into error; that the gates of hell did prevail against her; that from the sixth to the sixteenth century she was a sink of iniquity. The Book of Homilies of the Church of England says that the Church "lay buried in damnable idolatry for eight hundred years or more." The personal veracity of our Savior and of the Reformers is here at issue, for our Lord makes a statement which they contradict. Who is to be believed, Jesus or the Reformers?

If the prediction of our Savior about the preservation of His Church from error be false, then Jesus Christ is not God, since God cannot lie. He is not even a prophet, since He predicted falsehood. Nay, He is an impostor, and all Christianity is a miserable failure and a huge deception, since it rests on a false Prophet.

But if Jesus predicted the truth when He declared that the gates of hell should not prevail against His Church—and who dare deny it?—then the Church never has and never could have fallen from the truth; then the Catholic Church is infallible, for she alone claims that prerogative, and she is the only Church that is acknowledged to have existed from the beginning. Truly is Jesus that wise Architect mentioned in the Gospel, "who built his house upon a rock; and the rain fell, and the floods came, and the

[2] Matt. xvi. 18.

winds blew, and they beat upon that house, and it fell not, for it was founded upon a rock." [3]

Jesus sends forth the Apostles with plenipotentiary powers to preach the Gospel. "As the Father," He says, "hath sent Me, I also send you." [4] "Going therefore, teach all nations, teaching them to observe all things whatsoever I have commanded you." [5] "Preach the Gospel to every creature." [6] "Ye shall be witnesses unto Me in Jerusalem, and in all Judea, and Samaria, and even to the uttermost part of the earth." [7]

This commission evidently applies not to the Apostles only, but also to their successors, to the end of time, since it was utterly impossible for the Apostles personally to preach to the whole world.

Not only does our Lord empower His Apostles to preach the Gospel, but He commands, and under the most severe penalties, those to whom they preach to listen and obey. "Whosoever will not receive you, nor hear your words, going forth from that house or city, shake the dust from your feet. Amen, I say to you, it shall be more tolerable for the land of Sodom and Gomorrha in the day of judgment than for that city." [8] "If he will not hear the Church, let him be to thee as the heathen and the publican." [9] "He that believeth shall be saved; he that believeth not shall be condemned." [10] "He that heareth you heareth Me; he that despiseth you despiseth Me; and he that despiseth Me despiseth Him that sent Me." [11]

From these passages we see, on the one hand, that the Apostles and their successors have received full powers to announce the Gospel; and on the other, that their hearers are obliged to listen with docility and to obey not merely by an external compliance, but also by an internal assent of the intellect. If, therefore, the Catholic Church could preach error, would not God Himself be responsible for the error? And could not the faithful soul say to God with all reverence and truth: Thou hast commanded me, O

---

[3] Matt. vii. 24, et seq.   [4] John xx. 21.   [5] Matt. xxviii. 19, 20.
[6] Mark xvi. 15.   [7] Acts i. 8.   [8] Matt. x. 14, 15.
[9] Matt. xviii. 17.   [10] Mark xvi. 16.   [11] Luke x. 16.

Lord, to hear Thy Church; if I am deceived by obeying her, Thou art the cause of my error?

But we may rest assured that an all-wise Providence who commands His Church to speak in His name will so guide her in the path of truth that she shall never lead into error those that follow her teachings.

But as this privilege of Infallibility was a very extraordinary favor, our Savior confers it on the rulers of His Church in language which removes all doubt from the sincere inquirer, and under circumstances which add to the majesty of His word. Shortly before His death Jesus consoles His disciples by this promise: "I will ask the Father, and He shall give you another Paraclete, *that He may abide with you forever.* . . . But when He, the Spirit of truth, shall come, *He will teach you all truth.*" [12]

The following text of the same import forms the concluding words recorded of our Savior in St. Matthew's Gospel: "All power is given to Me in heaven and on earth. Go ye, therefore, and teach all nations, . . . teaching them to observe all things whatsoever I have commanded you. And behold I am with you all days, even to the consummation of the world." [13]

He begins by asserting His own Divine authority and mission. "All power is given," etc. That power He then delegates to His Apostles and to their successors: "Go ye, therefore, and teach all nations," etc. He does not instruct them to scatter Bibles broadcast over the earth, but to teach by word of mouth. "And behold!" Our Savior never arrests the attention of His hearers by using the interjection, *behold,* unless when He has something unusually solemn and extraordinary to communicate. An important announcement is sure to follow this word. "Behold, I am with you." These words, *"I am with you,"* are frequently addressed in Sacred Scripture by the Almighty to His Prophets and Patriarchs, and they always imply a special presence and a particular supervision of the Deity.[14] They convey the same meaning in the present instance. Christ says equivalently I who "am the way, the

---

[12] John xiv. 16; xvi. 13.   [13] Matt. xxviii. 18-20.
[14] Ex. iii. 12; Jer. xv. 20, etc.

truth and the life," will protect you from error and will guide you in your speech. I will be with you, not merely during *your* natural lives, not for a century only, but all days, at all times, without intermission, even to the end of the world.

These words of Jesus Christ establish two important facts: First—A promise to guard His Church from error. Second—A promise that His presence with the Church will be continuous, without any interval of absence, to the consummation of the world.

And this is also the sentiment of the Apostle of the Gentiles writing to the Ephesians: God "gave some indeed Apostles, and some Prophets, and some Evangelists, and others, some Pastors and Teachers, for the perfecting of the Saints, for the work of the ministry, for the building up of the body of Christ, until we all meet in the unity of faith, . . . that we may no more be children, tossed to and fro, and carried about with every wind of doctrine, by the wickedness of men, in craft, by which they lie in wait to deceive." [15]

Notwithstanding these plain declarations of Scripture, some persons think it an unwarrantable assumption for the Church to claim infallibility. But mark the consequences that follow from denying it.

If your church is not infallible it is liable to err, for there is no medium between infallibility and liability to error. If your church and her ministers are fallible in their doctrinal teachings, as they admit, they may be preaching falsehood to you, instead of truth. If so, you are in doubt whether you are listening to truth or falsehood. If you are in doubt you can have no faith, for faith excludes doubt, and in that state you displease God, for "without faith it is impossible to please God." [16] Faith and infallibility must go hand in hand. The one cannot exist without the other. There can be no faith in the hearer unless there is unerring authority in the speaker—an authority founded upon such certain knowledge as precludes the possibility of falling into error

[15] Eph. iv. 11-14.
[16] Heb. xi. 6.

on his part, and including such unquestioned veracity as to prevent his deceiving him who accepts his word.

You admit infallible certainty in the physical sciences; why should you deny it in the science of salvation? The astronomer can predict with accuracy a hundred years beforehand an eclipse of the sun or moon. He can tell what point in the heavens a planet will reach on a given day. The mariner, guided by his compass, knows, amid the raging storm and the darkness of the night, that he is steering his course directly to the city of his destination; and is not an infallible guide as necessary to conduct you to the city of God in heaven? Is it not, moreover, a blessing and a consolation that, amid the ever-changing views of men, amid the conflict of human opinion and the tumultuous waves of human passion, there is one voice heard above the din and uproar, crying in clear, unerring tones: "Thus saith the Lord?"

It is very strange that the Catholic Church must apologize to the world for simply declaring that she speaks the truth, the whole truth, and nothing but the truth.

The Roman Pantheon was dedicated to all the gods of the Empire, and their name was legion. Formidable also in numbers are the Founders of the religious sects existing in our country. A Pantheon as vast as Westminster Abbey would hardly be spacious enough to contain life-sized statues for their accommodation.

If you were to confront those figures, and to ask them, one by one, to give an account of the faith they had professed, and if they were endowed with the gift of speech, you would find that no two of them were in entire accord, but that they all differed among themselves on some fundamental principle of revelation.

Would you not be acting very unwisely and be hazarding your soul's salvation in submitting to the teachings of so many discordant and conflicting oracles.

Children of the Catholic Church, give thanks to God that you are members of that Communion, which proclaims year after year the one same and unalterable message of truth, peace and love, and that you are preserved from all errors in faith, and from all

illusion in the practice of virtue. You are happily strangers to
those interior conflicts, to those perplexing doubts and to that
frightful uncertainty which distracts the souls of those whose
private judgment is their only guide, who are "ever learning and
never attaining to the knowledge of the truth." [17] You are not,
like others, drifting helplessly over the ocean of uncertainty and
"carried about by every wind of doctrine." You are not as "blind
men led by blind guides." You are not like those who are in the
midst of a spiritual desert intersected by various by-paths, not
knowing which to pursue; but you are on that high road spoken
of by the prophet Isaiah, which is so "straight a way that fools
shall not err therein." [18] You are a part of that universal Communion which has no "High Church" and "Low Church;" no
"New School" and "Old School," for you all belong to that
School which is "ever ancient and ever new." You enjoy that
profound peace and tranquillity which springs from the conscious
possession of the whole truth. Well may you exclaim: "Behold
how good and how pleasant it is for brethren to dwell together
in unity." [19]

Give thanks, moreover, to God that you belong to a Church
which has also a keen sense to detect and expose those moral
shams, those pious frauds, those socialistic schemes which are so
often undertaken in this country ostensibly in the name of religion and morality, but which, in reality, are subversive of morality and order, which are the offspring of fanaticism, and serve
as a mask to hide the most debasing passions. Neither Mormons
nor Millerites, nor the advocates of free love or of women's rights,
so called, find any recruits in the Catholic Church. She will
never suffer her children to be ensnared by these impostures, how
specious soever they may be.

From what has been said in the preceding pages, it follows
that the Catholic Church cannot be reformed. I do not mean, of
course, that the Pastors of the Church are personally impeccable
or not subject to sin. Every teacher in the Church, from the Pope
down to the humblest Priest, is liable at any moment, like any

[17] Tim. iii. 7.   [18] Isaiah xxxv. 8.   [19] Ps. cxxxii.

of the faithful, to fall from grace and to stand in need of moral reformation. We all carry "this treasure (of innocence) in earthen vessels."

My meaning is that the Church is not susceptible of being reformed in her doctrines. The Church is the work of an Incarnate God. Like all God's works, it is perfect. It is, therefore, incapable of reform. Is it not the height of presumption for men to attempt to improve upon the work of God? Is it not ridiculous for the Luthers, the Calvins, the Knoxes and the Henries and a thousand lesser lights to be offering their amendments to the Constitution of the Church, as if it were a human Institution?

Our Lord Himself has never ceased to rule personally over His Church. It is time enough for little men to take charge of the Ship when the great Captain abandons the helm.

A Protestant gentleman of very liberal education remarked to me, before the opening of the late Ecumenical Council: "I am assured, sir, by a friend, in confidence, that, at a secret Conclave of Bishops recently held in Rome it was resolved that the Dogma of the Immaculate Conception would be reconsidered and abolished at the approaching General Council; in fact, that the definition was a mistake, and that the blunder of 1854 would be repaired in 1869." I told him, of course, that no such question could be entertained in the Council; that the doctrinal decrees of the Church were irrevocable, and that the dogma of the Immaculate Conception was defined once and forever.

If only one instance could be given in which the Church ceased to teach a doctrine of faith which had been previously held, that single instance would be the death blow of her claim to infallibility. But it is a marvelous fact worthy of record that in the whole history of the Church, from the nineteenth century to the first, no solitary example can be adduced to show that any Pope or General Council ever revoked a decree of faith or morals enacted by any preceding Pontiff or Council. Her record in the past ought to be a sufficient warrant that she will tolerate no doctrinal variations in the future.

If, as we have seen, the Church has authority from God to

teach, and if she teaches nothing but the truth, is it not the duty of all Christians to hear her voice and obey her commands? She is the organ of the Holy Ghost. She is the Representative of Jesus Christ, who has said to her: "He that heareth you heareth Me; he that despiseth you despiseth Me." She is the Mistress of truth. It is the property of the human mind to embrace truth wherever it finds it. It would, therefore, be not only an act of irreverence, but of sheer folly, to disobey the voice of this ever-truthful Mother.

If a citizen is bound to obey the laws of his country, though these laws may not in all respects be conformable to strict justice; if a child is bound by natural and divine law to obey his mother, though she may sometimes err in her judgments, how much more strictly are not we obliged to be docile to the teachings of the Catholic Church, our Mother, whose admonitions are always just, whose precepts are immutable!

"For twenty years," observed a recently converted Minister of the Protestant Church, "I fought and struggled against the Church with all the energy of my will. But when I became a Catholic all my doubts ended, my inquiries ceased. I became as a little child, and rushed like a lisping babe into the arms of my mother." By Baptism Christians become children of the Church, no matter who pours upon them the regenerating waters. If she is our Mother, where is our love and obedience? When the infant seeks nourishment at its mother's breast it does not analyze its food. When it receives instructions from its mother's lips it never doubts, but instinctively believes. When the mother stretches forth her hand the child follows unhesitatingly. The Christian should have for his spiritual Mother all the simplicity, all the credulity, I might say, of a child, guided by the instincts of faith. "Unless ye become," says our Lord, "as little children, ye shall not enter into the Kingdom of Heaven." [20] "As new-born babes, desire the rational milk without guile; that thereby you may grow unto salvation." [21] In her nourishment there is no poison; in her doctrines there is no guile.

[20] Matt. xviii. 3.   [21] Pet. ii. 2.

CHAPTER VIII

THE CHURCH AND THE BIBLE

THE Church, as we have just seen, is the only Divinely constituted teacher of Revelation.

Now, the Scripture is the great depository of the Word of God. Therefore, the Church is the divinely appointed Custodian and Interpreter of the Bible. For, her office of infallible Guide were superfluous if each individual could interpret the Bible for himself.

That God never intended the Bible to be the Christian's rule of faith, independently of the living authority of the Church, will be the subject of this chapter.

No nation ever had a greater veneration for the Bible than the Jewish people. The Holy Scripture was their pride and their glory. It was their national song in time of peace; it was their meditation and solace in time of tribulation and exile. And yet the Jews never dreamed of settling their religious controversies by a private appeal to the Word of God.

Whenever any religious dispute arose among the people it was decided by the High Priest and the Sanhedrim, which was a council consisting of seventy-two civil and ecclesiastical judges. The sentence of the High Priest and of his associate judges was to be obeyed under penalty of death. "If thou perceive," says the Book of Deuteronomy, "that there be among you a hard and doubtful matter in judgment, . . . thou shalt come to the Priests of the Levitical race and to the judge, . . . and they shall show thee the truth of the judgment. . . . And thou shalt follow their sentence; neither shalt thou decline to the right hand, nor to the left. . . . But he that will . . . refuse to obey the commandment of the Priest, . . . that man shall die, and thou shalt take away the evil from Israel." [1]

From this clear sentence you perceive that God does not refer the Jews for the settlement of their controversies to the letter of the law, but to the living authority of the ecclesiastical tribunal which He had expressly established for that purpose.

Hence, the Priests were required to be intimately acquainted with the Sacred Scripture, because they were the depositaries of God's law, and were its expounders to the people. "The lips of the Priest shall keep knowledge, and they (the people) shall seek the law at his mouth, because he is the angel (or messenger) of the Lord of hosts." [2]

And, in fact, very few of the children of Israel, except the Priests, were in possession of the Divine Books. The holy manuscript was rare and precious. And what provision did God make that all the people might have an opportunity of hearing the Scriptures? Did He command the sacred volume to be multiplied? No; but He ordered the *Priests* and the *Levites* to be distributed through the different tribes, that they might always be at hand to instruct the people in the knowledge of the law. The Jews were even forbidden to read certain portions of the Scripture till they had reached the age of thirty years.

Does our Savior reverse this state of things when He comes on earth? Does He tell the Jews to be their own guides in the study of the Scriptures? By no means; but He commands them to obey their constituted teachers, no matter how disedifying might be their private lives. "Then said Jesus to the multitudes and to His disciples: The Scribes and Pharisees sit upon the chair of Moses. All things therefore whatsoever they shall say to you, observe and do." [3]

It is true our Lord said on one occasion: "Search the Scriptures, for you *think* in them to have life everlasting, and the same are they that give testimony to Me." [4] This passage is triumphantly

---

[1] Deut. xvii. 8, et seq.   [2] Mal. ii. 7.
[3] Matt. xxiii. 2, 3.   [4] John v. 39.

quoted as an argument in favor of private interpretation. But it proves nothing of the kind. Many learned commentators, ancient and modern, express the verb in the indicative mood: "Ye search the Scriptures." At all events, our Savior speaks here only of the Old Testament because the New Testament was not yet written. He addresses not the multitude, but the Pharisees, who were the teachers of the law, and reproaches them for not admitting His Divinity. "You have," He says, "the Scriptures in your hands; why then do you not recognize Me as the Messiah, since they give testimony that I am the Son of God?" He refers them to the Scriptures for a proof of His Divinity, not as to a source from which they were to derive all knowledge in regard to the truths of revelation.

Besides, He did not rest the proof of His Divinity upon the *sole* testimony of Scripture. For He showed it:

First—By the testimony of John the Baptist (v. 33), who had said, "Behold the Lamb of God; behold Him who taketh away the sins of the world." See also John i. 34.

Second—By the miracles which He wrought (v. 36).

Third—By the testimony of the Father (v. 37), when He said: "This is my beloved Son, in whom I am well pleased; hear ye Him." Matt. iii. 16; Luke ix. 35.

Fourth—By the Scriptures of the Old Testament; as if He were to say, "If you are unwilling to receive these three proofs, though they are most cogent, at least you cannot reject the testimony of the Scriptures, of which you boast so much."

Finally, in this very passage our Lord is explaining the sense of Holy Writ; therefore, its true meaning is not left to the private interpretation of every chance reader. It is, therefore, a grave perversion of the sacred text to adduce these words in vindication of private interpretation of the Scriptures.

But when our Redeemer abolished the Old Law and established His Church, did He intend that His Gospel should be disseminated by the circulation of the Bible, or by the living voice of His disciples? This is a vital question. I answer most emphatically, that it was by preaching alone that He intended to convert the nations, and by preaching alone they were converted. No nation has ever yet been converted by the agency of Bible Associations.

Jesus Himself never wrote a line of Scripture. He never once commanded His Apostles to write a word,* or even to circulate the Scriptures already existing. When He sends them on their Apostolic errand, He says: "Go *teach* all nations." [5] *"Preach* the Gospel to every creature." [6] "He that heareth you heareth Me." [7] And we find that Apostles acting in strict accordance with these instructions.

Of the twelve Apostles, the seventy-two disciples, and early followers of our Lord only eight have left us any of their sacred writings. And the Gospels and Epistles were addressed to particular persons or particular churches. They were written on the occasion of some emergency, just as Bishops issue Pastoral letters to correct abuses which may spring up in the Church, or to lay down some rules of conduct for the faithful. The Apostles are never reported to have circulated a single volume of the Holy Scripture, but "they going forth, *preached* everywhere, the Lord co-operating with them." [8]

Thus we see that in the Old and the New Dispensation the people were to be guided by a living authority, and not by their private interpretation of the Scriptures.

Indeed, until the religious revolution of the sixteenth century, it was a thing unheard of from the beginning of the world, that people should be governed by the dead letter of the law either in civil or ecclesiastical affairs. How are your civil affairs regulated in this State, for instance? Certainly not in accordance with your personal interpretation of the laws of Virginia, but in accordance with decisions which are rendered by the constituted judges of the State.

Now what the civil code is to the citizen, the Scripture is to

*NOTE: Except when He directed St. John to write the Apocalypse, i. 11.
[5] Matt. xxviii. 19.   [6] Mark xvi. 15.
[7] Luke x. 16.   [8] Mark xvi. 20.

the Christian. The Word of God, as well as the civil law, must have an interpreter, by whose decision we are obliged to abide.

We often hear the shibboleth: "The Bible, and the Bible only, must be your guide." Why, then, do you go to the useless expense of building fine churches and Sabbath-schools? What is the use of your preaching sermons and catechizing the young, if the Bible at home is a sufficient guide for your people? The fact is, you reverend gentlemen contradict in practice what you so vehemently advance in theory. Do not tell me that the Bible is all-sufficient; or, if you believe it is self-sufficient, cease your instructions. Stand not between the people and the Scriptures.

I will address myself now in a friendly spirit to a non-Catholic, and will proceed to show him that he cannot consistently accept the silent Book of Scripture as his sufficient guide.

A copy of the sacred volume is handed to you by your minister, who says: "Take this book; you will find it all-sufficient for your salvation." But here a serious difficulty awaits you at the very threshold of your investigations. What assurance have you that the book he hands you is the *inspired* Word of God; for every part of the Bible is far from possessing intrinsic evidences of inspiration? It may, for ought you know, contain more than the Word of God, or it may not contain all the Word of God. We must not suppose that the Bible was always, as it is now, a compact book, bound in a neat form. It was for several centuries in scattered fragments, spread over different parts of Christendom. Meanwhile, many spurious books, under the name of Scripture, were circulated among the faithful. There was, for instance, the spurious Gospel of St. Peter; there was also the Gospel of St. James and of St. Matthias.

The Catholic Church, in the plenitude of her authority, in the third Council of Carthage, (A. D. 397,) separated the chaff from the wheat, and declared what Books were Canonical, and what were apocryphal. Even to this day the Christian sects do not agree among themselves as to what books are to be accepted as genuine. Some Christians of continental Europe do not recognize the

Gospels of St. Mark and St. Luke because these Evangelists were not among the Apostles. Luther used to call the Epistle of St. James a letter of straw.

But even when you are assured that the Bible contains the Word of God, and nothing but the Word of God, how do you know that the translation is faithful? The Books of Scripture were originally written in Hebrew and Greek, and you have only the translation. Before you are certain that the translation is faithful you must study the Hebrew and Greek languages, and then compare the translation with the original. How few are capable of this gigantic undertaking!

Indeed, when you accept the Bible as the Word of God, you are obliged to receive it on the authority of the Catholic Church, who was the sole Guardian of the Scriptures for fifteen hundred years.

But after having ascertained to your satisfaction that the translation is faithful, still the Scriptures can never serve as a complete Rule of Faith and a complete guide to heaven independently of an authorized, living interpreter.

A competent guide, such as our Lord intended for us, must have three characteristics. It must be within the reach of everyone; it must be clear and intelligible; it must be able to satisfy us on all questions relating to faith and morals.

First—A complete guide of salvation must be within the reach of every inquirer after truth; for, God "wishes all men to be saved, and to come to the knowledge of the truth;"[9] and therefore He must have placed within the reach of everyone the means of arriving at the truth. Now, it is clear that the Scriptures could not at any period have been accessible to everyone.

They could not have been accessible *to the primitive Christians,* because they were not all written for a long time after the establishment of Christianity. The Christian religion was founded in the year 33. St. Matthew's Gospel, the first part of the New Testament ever written, did not appear till eight years after. The Church was established about twenty years when St. Luke

[9] I. Tim., ii. 4.

wrote his Gospel. And St. John's Gospel did not come to light till toward the end of the first century. For many years after the Gospels and Epistles were written the knowledge of them was confined to the churches to which they were addressed. It was not till the close of the fourth century that the Church framed her Canon of Scripture and declared the Bible, as we now possess it, to be the genuine Word of God. And this was the golden age of Christianity! The most perfect Christians lived and died and went to heaven before the most important parts of the Scriptures were written. And what would have become of them if the Bible alone had been their guide?

The art of printing was not invented till the fifteenth century (1440). How utterly impossible it was to supply everyone with a copy of the Scriptures *from the fourth to the fifteenth century!* During that long period Bibles had to be copied with the pen. There were but a few hundred of them in the Christian world, and these were in the hands of the clergy and the learned. "According to the Protestant system, the art of printing would have been much more necessary to the Apostles than the gift of tongues. It was well for Luther that he did not come into the world until a century after the immortal invention of Guttenberg. A hundred years earlier his idea of directing two hundred and fifty million men to read the Bible would have been received with shouts of laughter, and would inevitably have caused his removal from the pulpit of Wittenberg to a hospital for the insane." [10]

And even *at the present day,* with all the aid of steam printing presses, with all the Bible Associations extending through this country and England, and supported at enormous expense, it taxes all their energies to supply every missionary country with Bibles printed in the languages of the tribes and peoples for whom they are intended.

But even if the Bible were at all times accessible to everyone, how many millions exist in every age and country, not excepting our own age of boasted enlightenment, who are not accessible to

[10] Martinet, Religion in Society, Vol. II., c. 10.

the Bible because they are incapable of reading the Word of God! Hence, the doctrine of private interpretation would render many men's salvation not only difficult, but impossible.

Second—A competent religious guide must be clear and intelligible to all, so that everyone may fully understand the true meaning of the instructions it contains. Is the Bible a book intelligible to all? Far from it; it is full of obscurities and difficulties not only for the illiterate, but even for the learned. St. Peter himself informs us that in the Epistles of St. Paul there are "certain things hard to be understood, which the unlearned and the unstable wrest, as they do also the other Scriptures, to their own destruction." [11] And consequently he tells us elsewhere "that no prophecy of Scripture is made by private interpretation." [12]

We read in the Acts of the Apostles that a certain man was riding in his chariot, reading the Book of Isaiah, and being asked by St. Philip whether he understood the meaning of the prophecy he replied: "How can I understand unless some man show me?" [13] admitting, by these modest words, that he did not pretend of himself to interpret the Scriptures.

The Fathers of the Church, though many of them spent their whole lives in the study of the Scriptures, are unanimous in pronouncing the Bible a book full of knotty difficulties. And yet we find in our days pedants, with a mere smattering of Biblical knowledge, who see no obscurity at all in the Word of God, and who presume to expound it from Genesis to Revelation. "Fools rush in where angels fear to tread."

Does not the conduct of the Reformers conclusively show the utter folly of interpreting the Scriptures by private judgment? As soon as they rejected the oracle of the Church, and set up their own private judgment as the highest standard of authority, they could hardly agree among themselves on the meaning of a single important text. The Bible became in their hands a complete Babel. The sons of Noe attempted in their pride to ascend to heaven by building the tower of Babel, and their scheme ended in the confusion and multiplication of tongues. The children of

[11] II. Pet., iii. 16.   [12] Ibid., i. 20.   [13] Acts, viii. 31.

the Reformation endeavored in their conceit to lead men to heaven by the private interpretation of the Bible, and their efforts led to the confusion and the multiplication of religions. Let me give you one example out of a thousand. These words of the Gospel, "This is My Body," were understood only in one sense before the Reformation. The new lights of the sixteenth century gave no fewer than eighty different meanings to these four simple words, and since their time the number of interpretations has increased to over a hundred.

No one will deny that in our days there exists a vast multitude of sects, which are daily multiplying. No one will deny[14] that this multiplying of creeds is a crying scandal, and a great stumbling-block in the way of the conversion of heathen nations. No one can deny that these divisions in the Christian family are traceable to the assumption of the right of private judgment. Every new-fledged divine, with a superficial education, imagines that he has received a call from heaven to inaugurate a new religion, and he is ambitious of handing down his fame to posterity by stamping his name on a new sect. And every one of these champions of modern creeds appeals to the unchanging Bible in support of his ever-changing doctrines.

Thus, one body of Christians will prove from the Bible that there is but one Person in God, while the rest will prove from the same source that a Trinity of Persons is a clear article of Divine Revelation. One will prove from the Holy Book that Jesus Christ is not God. Others will appeal to the same text to attest His Divinity. One denomination will assert on the authority of Scripture that infant baptism is not necessary for salvation, while others will hold that it is. Some Christians, with Bible in hand, will teach that there are no sacraments. Others will say that there are only two. Some will declare that the inspired Word does not preach the eternity of punishments. Others will say that the Bible distinctly vindicates that dogma. Do not clergymen appear every day in the pulpit, and on the authority of the Book of

---

[14] Except, perhaps, Rev. H. W. Beecher, who thinks that God is glorified by the variety of sects.

Revelation point out to us with painful accuracy the year and the day on which this world is to come to an end? And when their prophecy fails of execution they coolly put off our destruction to another time.

Very recently several hundred Mormon women presented a petition to the government at Washington protesting against any interference with their abominable polygamy and they insist that their cherished system is sustained by the Word of God.

Such is the legitimate fruit of private interpretation! Our civil government is run not by private judgment, but by the constituted authorities. No one in his senses would allow our laws to be interpreted, and war to be declared by sensational journals, or by any private individuals. Why not apply the same principle to the interpretation of the Bible and the government of the Church?

Would it not be extremely hazardous to make a long voyage in a ship in which the officers and crew are fiercely contending among themselves about the manner of explaining the compass and of steering their course? How much more dangerous is it to trust to contending captains in the journey to heaven! Nothing short of an infallible authority should satisfy you when it is a question of steering your course to eternity. On this vital point there should be no conflict of opinion among those that guide you. There should be no conjecture. But there must be always someone at the helm whose voice gives assurance amid the fiercest storms that *all is well.*

Third—A rule of faith, or a competent guide to heaven, must be able to instruct in all the truths necessary for salvation. Now the Scriptures alone do not contain all the truths which a Christian is bound to believe, nor do they explicitly enjoin all the duties which he is obliged to practice. Not to mention other examples, is not every Christian obliged to sanctify Sunday and to abstain on that day from unnecessary servile work? Is not the observance of this law among the most prominent of our sacred duties? But you may read the Bible from Genesis to Revelation, and you will not find a single line authorizing the sanctification of Sunday. The Scriptures enforce the religious observance of Saturday, a day which we never sanctify.

The Catholic Church correctly teaches that our Lord and His Apostles inculcated certain important duties of religion which are not recorded by the inspired writers.[15] For instance, most Christians pray to the Holy Ghost, a practice which is nowhere found in the Bible.

We must, therefore, conclude that the Scriptures *alone* cannot be a sufficient guide and rule of faith because they cannot, at any time, be within the reach of every inquirer; because they are not of themselves clear and intelligible even in matters of the highest importance, and because they do not contain all the truths necessary for salvation.

God forbid that any of my readers should be tempted to conclude from what I have said that the Catholic Church is opposed to the reading of the Scriptures, or that she is the enemy of the Bible. The Catholic Church the enemy of the Bible! Good God! What monstrous ingratitude! What base calumny is contained in that assertion! As well might you accuse the Virgin Mother of trying to crush the Infant Savior at her breast as to accuse the Church, our Mother, of attempting to crush out of existence the Word of God. As well might you charge the patriotic statesman with attempting to destroy the constitution of his country, while he strove to protect it from being mutilated by unprincipled demagogues.

For fifteen centuries the Church was the sole guardian and depository of the Bible, and if she really feared that sacred Book, who was to prevent her, during that long period, from tearing it in shreds and scattering it to the winds? She could have thrown it into the sea, as the unnatural mother would have thrown away her offspring, and who would have been the wiser?

What has become of those millions of once famous books written in past ages? They have nearly all perished. But amid

[15] See John xxi. 25; II. Thess. ii. 14.

this wreck of ancient literature, the Bible stands almost a solitary monument like the Pyramids of Egypt amid the surrounding wastes. That venerable Volume has survived the wars and revolutions and the barbaric invasions of fifteen centuries. Who rescued it from destruction? The Catholic Church. Without her fostering care the New Testament would probably be as little known today as "the Book of the days of the kings of Israel." [16]

Little do we imagine, in our age of steam printing, how much labor it cost the Church to preserve and perpetuate the Sacred Scriptures. Learned monks, who are now abused in their graves by thoughtless men, were constantly employed in copying with the pen the Holy Bible. When one monk died at his post another took his place, watching like a faithful sentinel over the treasure of God's Word.

Let me give you a few plain facts to show the pains which the Church has taken to perpetuate the Scriptures.

The Canon of the Bible, as we have seen, was framed in the fourth century. In that same century Pope Damascus commanded a new and complete translation of the Scriptures to be made into the Latin language, which was then the living tongue not only of Rome and Italy, but of the civilized world.

If the Popes were afraid that the Bible should see the light, this was a singular way of manifesting their fear.

The task of preparing a new edition of the Scriptures was assigned to St. Jerome, the most learned Hebrew scholar of his time. This new translation was disseminated throughout Christendom, and on that account was called the *Vulgate,* or popular edition.

In the sixth and seventh centuries the modern languages of Europe began to spring up like so many shoots from the parent Latin stock. The Scriptures, also, soon found their way into these languages. The Venerable Bede, who lived in England in the eighth century, and whose name is profoundly reverenced in that country, translated the Sacred Scriptures into Saxon, which

[16] III. Kings xiv. 19.

was then the language of England. He died while dictating the last verses of St. John's Gospel.

Thomas Arundel, Archbishop of Canterbury, in a funeral discourse on Queen Anne, consort of Richard II., pronounced in 1394, praises her for her diligence in reading the four Gospels. The Head of the Church of England could not condemn in others what he commended in the queen.

Sir Thomas More affirms that, before the days of Wycliffe, there was an English version of the Scriptures, "by good and godly people with devotion and soberness well and reverently read." [17]

If partial restrictions began to be placed on the circulation of the Bible in England in the fifteenth century, these restrictions were occasioned by the conduct of Wycliffe and his followers, who not only issued a new translation, on which they engrafted their novelties of doctrine, but also sought to explain the sacred text in a sense foreign to the received interpretation of tradition.

While laboring to diffuse the Word of God it is the duty, as well as the right of the Church, as the guardian of faith, to see that the faithful are not misled by unsound editions.

Printing was invented in the fifteenth century, and almost a hundred years later came the Reformation. It is often triumphantly said, and I suppose there are some who, even at the present day, are ignorant enough to believe the assertion, that the first edition of the Bible ever published after the invention of printing was the edition of Martin Luther. The fact is, that before Luther put his pen to paper, no fewer than fifty-six editions of the Scriptures had appeared on the continent of Europe, not to speak of those printed in Great Britain. Of those editions, twenty-one were published in German, one in Spanish, four in French, twenty-one in Italian, five in Flemish and four in Bohemian.

Coming down to our own times, if you open an English Catholic Bible you will find in the preface a letter of Pope Pius VI., in

[17] Dialog. 3, 14.

which he strongly recommends the pious reading of the Holy Scriptures. A Pope's letter is the most weighty authority in the Church. You will also find in Haydock's Bible the letters of the Bishops of the United States, in which they express the hope that this splendid edition would have a wide circulation among their flocks.

These facts ought, I think, to convince every candid mind that the Church, far from being opposed to the reading of the Scriptures, does all she can to encourage their perusal.

A gentleman of North Carolina lately informed me that the first time he entered a Catholic bookstore he was surprised at witnessing on the shelves an imposing array of Bibles for sale. Up to that moment he had believed the unfounded charge that Catholics were forbidden to read the Scriptures. He has since embraced the Catholic faith.

And perhaps I may be permitted here to record my personal experiences during a long course of study. I speak of myself, not because my case is exceptional, but, on the contrary, because my example will serve to illustrate the system pursued toward ecclesiastical students in all colleges throughout the Catholic world in reference to the Holy Scriptures.

In our course of Humanities we listened every day to the reading of the Bible. When we were advanced to the higher branches of Philosophy and Theology the study of the Sacred Scriptures formed an important part of our education. We read, besides, every day a chapter of the New Testament, not standing or sitting, but on our knees, and then reverently kissed the inspired page. We listened at our meals each day to selections from the Bible, and we always carried about with us a copy of the New Testament.

So familiar, indeed, were the students with the sacred Volume that many of them, on listening to a few verses, could tell from what portion of the Scriptures you were reading. The only dread we were taught to have of the Scriptures was that of reading them without fear and reverence.

And after his ordination every Priest is obliged in conscience to devote upwards of an hour each day to the perusal of the Word of God. I am not aware that clergymen of other denominations are bound by the same duty.

What is good for the clergy must be good, also, for the laity. Be assured that if you become a Catholic you will never be forbidden to read the Bible. It is our earnest wish that every word of the Gospel may be imprinted on your memory and on your heart.

CHAPTER IX

THE PRIMACY OF PETER

THE Catholic Church teaches also, that our Lord conferred on St. Peter the first place of honor and jurisdiction in the government of His whole Church, and that the same spiritual supremacy has always resided in the Popes, or Bishops of Rome, as being the successors of St. Peter. Consequently, to be true followers of Christ all Christians, both among the clergy and the laity, must be in communion with the See of Rome, where Peter rules in the person of his successor.

Before coming to any direct proofs on this subject I may state that, in the Old Law, the High Priest appointed by Almighty God filled an office analogous to that of Pope in the New Law. In the Jewish Church there were Priests and Levites ordained to minister at the altar; and there was, also, a supreme ecclesiastical tribunal, with the High Priest at its head. All matters of religious controversy were referred to this tribunal and in the last resort to the High Priest, whose decision was enforced under pain of death. "If there be a hard matter in judgment between blood and blood, cause and cause, leprosy and leprosy, . . . thou shalt come to the Priests of the Levitical race and to the judge, . . . and they shall show thee true judgment. And thou shalt do whatever they say who preside in the place which the Lord shall choose, and thou shalt follow their sentence. And thou shalt not decline to the right hand, or to the left. . . . But he that . . . will refuse to obey the commandment of the Priest, who ministereth at the time, . . . that man shall die, and thou shalt take away the evil from Israel." [1]

From this passage it is evident that in the Hebrew Church the High Priest had the highest jurisdiction in religious matters. By this means unity of faith and worship was preserved among the people of God.

Now the Jewish synagogue, as St. Paul testifies, was the type and figure of the Christian Church; for "all these things happened to them (the Jews) in figure." [2] We must, therefore, find in the Church of Christ a spiritual judge, exercising the same supreme authority as the High Priest wielded in the Old Law. For if a supreme Pontiff was necessary, in the Mosaic dispensation, to maintain purity and uniformity of worship, the same dignitary is equally necessary now to preserve unity of faith.

Every well-regulated civil government has an acknowledged head. The President is the head of the United States Government. Queen Victoria is the ruler of Great Britain. The Sultan sways the Turkish Empire. If these nations had no authorized leader to govern them they would be reduced to the condition of a mere mob, and anarchy, confusion and civil war would inevitably follow, as recently happened to France after the fall of Napoleon III.

Even in every well-ordered family, domestic peace requires that someone preside.

Now, the Church of Christ is a visible society—that is, a society composed of human beings. She has, it is true, a spiritual end in view; but having to deal with men, she must have a government as well as every other organized society. This government, at least in its essential elements, our Lord must have established for His Church. For was He not as wise as human legislators? And shall we suppose that, of all lawgivers, the Wisdom Incarnate alone left His Kingdom on earth to be governed without a head?

But someone will tell me: "We do not deny that the Church has a head. God himself is its Ruler." This is evading the real

[1] Deut. xvii.
[2] I. Cor. x. 11.

question. Is not God the Ruler of all governments? "By Me," He says, "kings reign, and lawgivers decree just things." [3] He is the recognized Head of our Republic, and of every Christian family in the land; but, nevertheless, there is always presiding over the country a visible chief, who represents God on earth.

In like manner the Church, besides an invisible Head in heaven, must have a visible head on earth. The body and members of the Church are visible; why not also the Head? The Church without a supreme Ruler would be like an army without a general, a navy without an admiral, a sheepfold without a shepherd, or like a human body without a head.

The Christian communities separated from the Catholic Church deny that Peter received any authority over the other Apostles, and hence they reject the supremacy of the Pope.

The absence from the Protestant communions of a Divinely appointed, visible Head is to them an endless source of weakness and dissension. It is an insuperable barrier against any hope of a permanent reunion among themselves, because they are left without a common rallying centre or basis of union and are placed in an unhappy state of schism.

The existence, on the contrary, of a supreme judge of controversy in the Catholic Church is the secret of her admirable unity. This is the keystone that binds together and strengthens the imperishable arch of faith.

From the very fact, then, of the existence of a supreme Head in the Jewish Church; from the fact that a Head is always necessary for civil government, for families and corporations; from the fact, especially, that a visible Head is essential to the maintenance of unity in the Church, while the absence of a Head necessarily leads to anarchy, we are forced to conclude, even though positive evidence were wanting, that, in the establishment of His Church, it must have entered into the mind of the Divine Lawgiver to place over it a primate invested with superior judicial powers.

But have we any positive proof that Christ did appoint a su-

[3] Prov. viii. 15.

preme Ruler over His Church? To those, indeed, who read the Scriptures with the single eye of pure intention the most abundant evidence of this fact is furnished. To my mind the New Testament establishes no doctrine, unless it satisfies every candid reader that our Lord gave plenipotentiary powers to Peter to govern the whole Church. In this chapter I shall speak of the Promise, the Institution, and the exercise of Peter's Primacy, as recorded in the New Testament. The next chapter shall be devoted to its perpetuity in the Popes.

Promise of the Primacy. Our Saviour, on a certain occasion, asked His disciples, saying: "Whom do men say that the Son of Man is? And they said: Some say that Thou art John the Baptist; and others, Elias; and others, Jeremiah, or one of the Prophets. Jesus saith to them: But whom do ye say that I am?" Peter, as usual, is the leader and spokesman. "Simon Peter answering, said: Thou art Christ, the Son of the living God. And Jesus answering said to him: Blessed art thou, Simon Bar-Jona: because flesh and blood hath not revealed it to thee, but My Father who is in heaven. And I say to thee: that thou art Peter, and upon this rock I will build My Church, and the gates of hell shall not prevail against it. And I will give to thee the keys of the Kingdom of Heaven: and whatsoever thou shalt bind on earth shall be bound also in heaven; and whatsoever thou shalt loose on earth shall be loosed also in heaven." [4] Here we find Peter confessing the Divinity of Christ, and in reward for that confession he is honored with the promise of the Primacy.

Our Savior, by the words "thou art Peter," clearly alludes to the new name which He Himself had conferred upon Simon, when He received him into the number of His followers (John i. 42); and He now reveals the reason for the change of name, which was to insinuate the honor He was to confer on him, by appointing him President of the Christian Republic; just as God, in the Old Law, changed Abram's name to Abraham, when He chose him to be the father of a mighty nation.

The word *Peter,* in the Syro-Chaldaic tongue, which our

[4] Matt. xvi. 13-19.

Savior spoke, means *a rock*. The sentence runs thus in that language: *"Thou art a rock, and on this rock I will build My Church."* Indeed, all respectable Protestant commentators have now abandoned, and even ridicule, the absurdity of applying the word *rock* to anyone but to Peter; as the sentence can bear no other construction, unless our Lord's good grammar and common sense are called in question.

Jesus, our Lord, founded but one Church, which He was pleased to build on Peter. Therefore, any church that does not recognize Peter as its foundation stone is not the Church of Christ, and therefore cannot stand, for it is not the work of God. This is plain. Would to God that all would see it aright and with eyes free from prejudice.

He continues: "And I will give to thee the keys of the Kingdom of Heaven," etc. In ancient times, and particularly among the Hebrew people, keys were an emblem of jurisdiction. To affirm that a man had received the keys of a city was equivalent to the assertion that he had been appointed its governor. In the Book of Revelation our Savior says that He has "the keys of death and of hell," [5] which means that He is endowed with power over death and hell. In fact, even to this day does not the presentation of keys convey among ourselves the idea of authority? If the proprietor of a house, on leaving it for the summer, says to any friend: "Here are the keys of my house," would not this simple declaration, without a word of explanation, convey the idea, "I give you full control of my house; you may admit or exclude whom you please; you represent me in my absence?" Let us now apply this interpretation to our Redeemer's words. When He says to Peter: "I will give to thee the keys," etc., He evidently means: I will give the supreme authority over My Church, which is the citadel of faith, My earthly Jerusalem. Thou and thy successors shall be My visible representatives to the end of time. And be it remembered that to Peter alone, and to no other Apostle, were these solemn words addressed.

Fulfillment of the Promise. The promise which our Redeemer

[5] Rev. i. 18.

made of creating Peter the supreme Ruler of His Church is fulfilled in the following passage: "Jesus saith to Simon Peter: Simon, son of John, lovest thou Me more than these? He saith to Him: Yea, Lord, Thou knowest that I love Thee. He saith to him: Feed My lambs. He saith to him again: Simon, son of John, lovest thou Me? He saith to Him: Yea, Lord, Thou knowest that I love Thee. He saith to him: Feed My lambs. He saith to him the third time: Simon, son of John, lovest thou Me? Peter was grieved because He had said to him the third time: Lovest thou Me? And he said to Him: Lord, Thou knowest all things. Thou knowest that I love Thee. He said to him: Feed My sheep." [6]

These words were addressed by our Lord to Peter after His resurrection. The whole sheepfold of Christ is confided to him, without any exception or limitation. Peter has jurisdiction not only over the lambs—the weak and tender portion of the flock— by which are understood the faithful; but also over the sheep, *i. e.,* the Pastors themselves, who hold the same relations to their congregations that the sheep hold to the lambs, because they bring forth unto Jesus Christ, and nourish the spiritual lambs of the fold. To other Pastors a certain portion of the flock is assigned; to Peter the entire fold; for, never did Jesus say to any other Apostle or Bishop what He said to Peter: Feed My whole flock.

Candid reader, do you not profess to be a member of Christ's flock? Yes, you answer. Do you take your spiritual food from Peter and his successor, and do you hear the voice of Peter, or have you wandered into the fold of strangers who spurn Peter's voice? Ponder well this momentous question. For if Peter is authorized to feed the lambs of Christ's flock, the lambs should hear Peter's voice.

Exercise of the Primacy. In the Acts of the Apostles, which contain almost the only Scripture narrative that exists of the Apostles subsequent to our Lord's ascension, St. Peter appears before us, like Saul among the tribes, standing head and

[6] John xxi. 15-17.

shoulders over his brethren by the prominent part he takes in every ministerial duty.

The first twelve chapters of the Acts are devoted to Peter and to some of the other Apostles, the remaining chapters being chiefly occupied with the labors of the Apostles of the Gentiles. In that brief historical fragment, as well as in the Gospels, the name of Peter is everywhere pre-eminent.

Peter's name always stands first in the list of the Apostles, while Judas Iscariot is invariably mentioned last.[7] Peter is even called by St. Matthew *the first Apostle*. Now Peter was first neither in age nor in priority of election, his elder brother Andrew having been chosen before him. The meaning, therefore, of the expression must be that Peter was first not only in rank and honor, but also in authority.

Peter is the first Apostle who performed a miracle.[8] He is the first to address the Jews in Jerusalem while his Apostolic brethren stand respectfully around him, upon which occasion he converts three thousand souls.[9]

Peter is the first to make converts from the Gentile world in the persons of Cornelius and his friends.[10]

When there is question of electing a successor to Judas Peter *alone speaks*. He points out to the Apostles and disciples the duty of choosing another to succeed the traitor. The Apostles silently acquiesce in the instructions of their leader.[11]

In the Apostolic Council of Jerusalem Peter is the first whose sentiments are recorded. Before his discourse "there was much disputing." But when he had ceased to speak "all the multitude held their peace." [12]

St. James and the other Apostles concur in the sentiments of Peter without a single dissenting voice.

St. James is cast into prison by Herod and afterward beheaded. He was one of the three most favored Apostles. He was the cousin of our Lord and brother of St. John. He was most dear to

[7] Matt. x. 2; Mark iii. 16; Luke vi. 14; Acts i. 14.
[8] Acts iii.　　　　　[9] Acts ii.　　　　　[10] Acts x.
[11] Acts i.　　　　　[12] Acts xv.

the faithful. Yet no extraordinary efforts are made by the faithful to rescue him from death.

Peter is imprisoned about the same time. The whole Church is aroused. Prayers for his deliverance ascend to heaven, not only from Jerusalem but also from every Christian family in the land.[13]

The army of the Lord can afford to lose a chieftain in the person of James, but it cannot yet spare the commander-in-chief. The enemies of the Church had hoped that the destruction of the chief shepherd would involve the dispersion of the whole flock; therefore they redoubled their fury against the Prince of the Apostles, just as her modern enemies concentrate their shafts against the Pope, his successor. Does not this incident eloquently proclaim Peter's superior authority? In fact Peter figures so conspicuously in every page that his Primacy is not only admissible, but is forced on the judgment of the impartial reader.

What are the principal objections advanced against the Primacy of Peter? They are chiefly, I may say exclusively, confined to the three following: First—That our Lord rebuked Peter. Second— That St. Paul criticised his conduct on a point not affecting doctrine, but discipline. The Apostle of the Gentiles blames St. Peter because he withdrew for a time from the society of the Gentile converts, for fear of scandalizing the newly-converted Jews.[14] Third—That the supremacy of Peter conflicts with the supreme dominion of Christ.

For my part I cannot see how these objections can invalidate the claims of Peter. Was not Jesus Peter's superior? May not a superior rebuke his servant without infringing on the servant's prerogatives?

And why could not St. Paul censure the conduct of St. Peter without questioning that superior's authority? It is not a very uncommon thing for ecclesiastics occupying an inferior position in the Church to admonish even the Pope. St. Bernard, though only a monk, wrote a work in which, with Apostolic freedom, he administers counsel to Pope Eugenius III., and cautions him

[13] Acts xii.   [14] Gal. ii. 11.

against the dangers to which his eminent position exposes him. Yet no man had more reverence for any Pope than Bernard had for this great Pontiff. Cannot our Governor animadvert upon the President's conduct without impairing the President's jurisdiction?

Nay, from this very circumstance, I draw a confirming evidence of Peter's supremacy. St. Paul mentions it as a fact worthy of record that he actually *withstood Peter to his face*. Do you think it would be worth recording if Paul had rebuked James or John or Barnabas? By no means. If one brother rebukes another, the matter excites no special attention. But if a son rebukes his father, or if a Priest rebukes his Bishop to his face, we understand why he would consider it a fact worth relating. Hence, when St. Paul goes to the trouble of telling us that he took exception to Peter's conduct, he mentions it as an extraordinary exercise of Apostolic freedom, and leaves on our mind the obvious inference that Peter was his superior.

In the very same Epistle to the Galatians St. Paul plainly insinuates St. Peter's superior rank. "I went," he says, "to Jerusalem to see Peter, and I tarried with him fifteen days." [15] Saints Chrysostom and Ambrose tell us that this was not an idle visit of ceremony, but that the object of St. Paul in making the journey was to testify his respect and honor for the chief of the Apostles. St. Jerome observes in a humorous vein that "Paul went not to behold Peter's eyes, his cheeks or his countenance, whether he was thin or stout, with nose straight or twisted, covered with hair or bald, not to observe the outward man, *but to show honor to the first Apostle.*"

There are others who pretend, in spite of our Lord's declaration to the contrary, that loyalty to Peter is disloyalty to Christ, and that, by acknowledging Peter as the rock on which the Church is built, we set our Savior aside. So far from this being the case, we acknowledge Jesus Christ as the "chief cornerstone," as well as the Divine Architect of the building.

[15] Gal. i. 18.

The true test of loyalty to Jesus is not only to worship Him, but to venerate even the representatives whom He has chosen. Will anyone pretend to say that my obedience to the Governor's appointee is a mark of disrespect to the Governor himself? I think our State Executive would have little faith in the allegiance of any citizen who would say to him: "Governor, I honor you personally, but your official's order I shall disregard."

St. Peter is called the first Bishop of Rome because he transferred his see from Antioch to Rome, where he suffered martyrdom with St. Paul.

We are not surprised that modern skepticism, which rejects the Divinity of Christ and denies even the existence of God, should call in question the fact that St. Peter lived and died in Rome.

The reason commonly alleged for disputing this well-attested event is that the Acts of the Apostles make no mention of Peter's labors and martyrdom in Rome. For the same reason we might deny that St. Paul was beheaded in Rome; that St. John died in Ephesus, and that St. Andrew was crucified. The Scripture is silent regarding these historical records, and yet they are denied by no one.

The intrinsic evidence of St. Peter's first Epistle, the testimony of his immediate successors in the ministry, as well as the avowal of eminent Protestant commentators, all concur in fixing the See of Peter in Rome.

"Babylon," from which Peter addresses his first Epistle, is understood by learned annotators, Protestant and Catholic, to refer to Rome—the word Babylon being symbolical of the corruption then prevailing in the city of the Cæsars.

Clement, the fourth Bishop of Rome, who is mentioned in terms of praise by St. Paul; St. Ignatius, Bishop of Antioch, who died in 105; Irenæus, Origen, St. Jerome, Eusebius, the great historian, and other eminent writers testify to St. Peter's residence in Rome, while no ancient ecclesiastical writer has ever contradicted the statement.

John Calvin, a witness above suspicion; Cave, an able Anglican critic; Grotius and other distinguished Protestant writers, do not hesitate to re-echo the unanimous voice of Catholic tradition.

Indeed, no historical fact will escape the shafts of incredulity, if St. Peter's residence and glorious martyrdom in Rome are called in question.

CHAPTER X

THE SUPREMACY OF THE POPES

THE Church did not die with Peter. It was destined to continue till the end of time; consequently, whatever official prerogatives were conferred on Peter were not to cease at his death, but were to be handed down to his successors from generation to generation. The Church is in all ages as much in need of a Supreme Ruler as it was in the days of the Apostles. Nay, more; as the Church is now more widely diffused than it was then, and is ruled by frailer men, it is more than ever in need of a central power to preserve its unity of faith and uniformity of discipline.

Whatever privileges, therefore, were conferred on Peter which may be considered essential to the government of the Church are inherited by the Bishops of Rome, as successors of the Prince of the Apostles; just as the constitutional powers given to George Washington have devolved on the present incumbent of the Presidential chair.

Peter, it is true, besides the prerogatives inherent in his office, possessed also the gift of inspiration and the power of working miracles. These two latter gifts are not claimed by the Pope, as they were personal to Peter and by no means essential to the government of the Church. God acts toward His Church as we deal with a tender sapling. When we first plant it we water it and soften the clay about its roots. But when it takes deep root we leave it to the care of Nature's laws. In like manner, when Christ first planted His Church He nourished its infancy by miraculous agency; but when it grew to be a tree of fair proportions He left it to be governed by the general laws of His Providence.

From what I have said you can easily infer that the arguments in favor of Peter's Primacy have equal weight in demonstrating the supremacy of the Popes.

As the present question, however, is a subject of vast importance, I shall endeavor to show, from incontestable historical evidence, that the Popes have always, from the days of the Apostles, continued to exercise supreme jurisdiction not only in the Western Church till the Reformation, but also throughout the Eastern Church till the great schism of the ninth century.

First—Take the question of *appeals*. An appeal is never made from a superior to an inferior court, nor even from one court to another of co-ordinate jurisdiction. We do not appeal from Washington to Richmond, but from Richmond to Washington. Now, if we find the See of Rome from the foundation of Christianity entertaining and deciding cases of appeal from the Oriental churches; if we find that her decision was final and irrevocable, we must conclude that the supremacy of Rome over all the churches is an undeniable fact.

Let me give you a few illustrations:

To begin with Pope St. Clement, who was the third successor of St. Peter, and who is laudably mentioned by St. Paul in one of his Epistles. Some dissension and scandal having occurred in the church of Corinth, the matter is brought to the notice of Pope Clement. He at once exercises his supreme authority by writing letters of remonstrance and admonition to the Corinthians. And so great was the reverence entertained for these Epistles by the faithful of Corinth that, for a century later, it was customary to have them publicly read in their churches. Why did the Corinthians appeal to Rome, far away in the West, and not to Ephesus, so near home in the East, where the Apostle St. John still lived? Evidently because the jurisdiction of Ephesus was local, while that of Rome was universal.

About the year 190 the question regarding the proper day for celebrating Easter was agitated in the East, and referred to Pope

St. Victor I. The Eastern Church generally celebrated Easter on the day on which the Jews kept the Passover, while in the West it was observed then, as it is now, on the first Sunday after the full moon of the vernal equinox. St. Victor directs the Eastern churches, for the sake of uniformity, to conform to the practice of the West, and his instructions are universally followed.

St. Cyprian, Bishop of Carthage, was martyred in 258.

From his appeals to Pope St. Cornelius and to Pope St. Stephen, especially on the subject of baptism, from his writings and correspondence, as well as from the whole tenor of his administration, it is quite evident that Cyprian, as well as the African Episcopate, upheld the supremacy of the Bishop of Rome.

Dionysius, Bishop of Rome, about the middle of the third century, having heard that the Patriarch of Alexandria erred on some points of faith, demands an explanation of the suspected Prelate, who, in obedience to his superior, promptly vindicates his own orthodoxy.

St. Athanasius, the great patriarch of Alexandria, appeals in the fourth century to Pope Julius I. from an unjust decision rendered against him by the Oriental Bishops, and the Pope[1] reverses the sentence of the Eastern Council.

St. Basil, Archbishop of Cæsarea, in the same century has recourse in his afflictions to the protection of Pope Damasus.

St. John Chrysostom, Patriarch of Constantinople, appeals in the beginning of the fifth century to Pope Innocent I. for a redress of grievances inflicted on him by several Eastern Prelates, and by the Empress Eudoxia of Constantinople.

St. Cyril appeals to Pope Celestine against Nestorius; Nestorius, also, appeals to the same Pontiff, who takes the side of Cyril.

In a Synod held in 444, St. Hilary, Archbishop of Arles, in Gaul, deposed Celidonius, Bishop of Besancon, on the ground of an alleged canonical impediment to his consecration. The Bishop appealed to the Holy See, and both he and the Metropolitan personally repaired to Rome, to submit their cause to the judgment of Pope Leo the Great. After a careful investigation, the Pontiff

[1] Socrates' Ecclesiastical History, B. II., c. xv.

declared the sentence of the Synod invalid, revoked the censure, and restored the deposed Prelate to his See.

The same Pontiff also rebuked Hilary for having irregularly deposed Projectus from his See.

The judicial authority of the Pope is emphasized from the circumstance that Hilary was not an arrogant or a rebellious churchman, but an edifying and a zealous Prelate. He is revered by the whole Church as a canonized Saint, and after his death, Leo refers to him as Hilary of *happy memory.*

Theodoret, the illustrious historian and Bishop of Cyrrhus, is condemned by the pseudo-council of Ephesus in 449, and appeals to Pope Leo in the following touching language: "I await the decision of your Apostolic See, and I supplicate your Holiness to succor me, who invoke your righteous and just tribunal; and to order me to hasten to you, and to explain to you my teaching, which follows the steps of the Apostles. . . . I beseech you not to scorn my application. Do not slight my gray hairs. . . . Above all, I entreat you to teach me whether to put up with this unjust deposition or not; for I await your sentence. If you bid me rest in what has been determined against me, I will rest, and will trouble no man more. I will look for the righteous judgment of our God and Savior. To me, as Almighty God is my Judge, honor and glory are no object, but only the scandal that has been caused; for many of the simpler sort, especially those whom I have rescued from diverse heresies, considering *the See* which has condemned me, suspect that perhaps I really am a heretic, being incapable themselves of distinguishing accuracy of doctrine." [2] Leo declared the deposition invalid and Theodoret was restored to his See.

John, Abbot of Constantinople, appeals from the decision of the Patriarch of that city to Pope St. Gregory I., who reverses the sentence of the Patriarch.

In 859 Photius addressed a letter to Pope Nicholas I., asking the Pontiff to confirm his election to the Patriarchate of Constantinople. In consequence of the Pope's conscientious refusal Photius

[2] Epist. 113.

broke off from the communion of the Catholic Church and became the author of the Greek schism.

Here are a few examples taken at random from Church History. We see Prelates most eminent for their sanctity and learning occupying the highest position in the Eastern Church, and consequently far removed from the local influences of Rome, appealing in every period of the early Church from the decisions of their own Bishops and their Councils to the supreme arbitration of the Holy See. If this does not constitute superior jurisdiction, I have yet to learn what superior authority means.

Second—Christians of every denomination admit the orthodoxy of *the Fathers* of the first five centuries of the Church. No one has ever called in question the faith of such men as Basil, Chrysostom, Cyprian, Augustine, Jerome, Ambrose and Leo. They were the acknowledged guardians of pure doctrine, and the living representatives "of the faith once delivered to the Saints." They were to the Church in their generation what Peter and Paul and James were to the Church in its infancy. We instinctively consult them about the faith of those times; for, to whom shall we go for the Words of eternal life, if not to them?

Now, the Fathers of the Church, with one voice, pay homage to the Bishops of Rome as their superiors. The limited space I have allowed myself in this little volume will not permit me to give any extracts from their writings. The reader who may be unacquainted with the original language of the Fathers, or who has not their writings at hand, is referred to a work entitled, "Faith of Catholics," where he will find, in an English translation, copious extracts from their writings vindicating the Primacy of the Popes.

Third—*Ecumenical Councils* afford another eloquent vindication of Papal supremacy. An Ecumenical or General Council is an assemblage of Prelates representing the whole Catholic Church. A General Council is to the Church what the Executive and Legislative bodies in Washington are to the United States.

Up to the present time nineteen Ecumenical Councils have been convened, including the Council of the Vatican. The last

eleven were held in the West, and the first eight in the East. I
shall pass over the Western Councils, as no one denies that they
were subject to the authority of the Pope.

I shall speak briefly of the important influence which the Holy
See exercised in the eight Oriental Councils.

The first General Council was held in Nicæa, in 325; the second, in Constantinople, 381; the third, in Ephesus, in 431; the
fourth, in Chalcedon, in 451; the fifth, in Constantinople, in 553;
the sixth in the same city, in 680; the seventh, in Nicæa, in 787,
and the eighth, in Constantinople, in 869.

The Bishops of Rome convoked these assemblages, or at least
consented to their convocation; they presided by their legates over
all of them, except the first and second Councils of Constantinople, and they confirmed all these eight by their authority. Before becoming a law the Acts of the Councils required the Pope's
signature, just as our Congressional proceedings require the
President's signature before they acquire the force of law.

Is not this a striking illustration of the Primacy? The Pope
convenes, rules and sanctions the Synods, not by courtesy, but
by right. A dignitary who calls an assembly together, who pre-
sides over its deliberations, whose signature is essential for confirming its Acts has surely a higher authority than the other
members.

Fourth—I shall refer to one more historical point in support of
the Pope's jurisdiction over the whole Church. It is a most remarkable fact that *every nation hitherto converted from Paganism to Christianity since the days of the Apostles, has received the
light of faith from missionaries who were either especially commissioned by the See of Rome, or sent by Bishops in open communion with that See.* This historical fact admits of no exception.
Let me particularize.

Ireland's Apostle is St. Patrick. Who commissioned him? Pope
St. Celestine, in the fifth century.

St. Palladius is the Apostle of Scotland. Who sent him? The
same Pontiff, Celestine.

The Anglo-Saxons received the faith from St. Augustine, a

Benedictine monk, as all historians, Catholic and non-Catholic, testify. Who empowered Augustine to preach? Pope Gregory I., at the end of the sixth century.

St. Remigius established the faith in France, at the close of the fifth century. He was in active communion with the See of Peter.

Flanders received the Gospel in the seventh century from St. Eligius, who acknowledged the supremacy of the reigning Pope.

Germany and Bavaria venerate as their Apostle St. Boniface, who is popularly known in his native England by his baptismal name of Winfrid. He was commissioned by Pope Gregory II., in the beginning of the eighth century, and was consecrated Bishop by the same Pontiff.

In the ninth century two saintly brothers, Cyril and Methodius, evangelized Russia, Sclavonia, Moravia and other parts of Northern Europe. They recognized the supreme authority of Pope Nicholas I. and of his successors, Adrian II. and John VIII.

In the eleventh century Norway was converted by missionaries introduced from England by the Norwegian King, St. Olave.

The conversion of Sweden was consummated in the same century by the British Apostles Saints Ulfrid and Eskill. Both of these nations immediately after their conversion commenced to pay Romescot, or a small annual tribute to the Holy See—a clear evidence that they were in communion with the Chair of Peter.[3]

All the other nations of Europe, having been converted before the Reformation, received likewise the light of faith from Roman Catholic Missionaries, because Europe then recognized only one Christian Chief.

Passing from Europe to Asia and America, it is undeniable that St. Francis Xavier and the other Evangelists who, in the sixteenth century, extended the Kingdom of Jesus Christ through India and Japan, were in communion with the Holy See; and that those Apostles who, in the sixteenth and seventeenth centuries, converted the aboriginal tribes of South America and Mexico received their commission from the Chair of Peter.

But you will say: The people of the United States profess to be

[3] See Butler's Lives of the Saints—St. Olave, July 29th.

a Christian nation. Do you also claim them? Most certainly; for, even those American Christians who are unhappily severed from the Catholic Church are primarily indebted for their knowledge of the Gospel to missionaries in communion with the Holy See.

The white races of North America are descended from England, Ireland, Scotland and the nations of Continental Europe. Those European nations having been converted by missionaries in subjection to the Holy See, it follows that, from whatever part of Europe you are descended, whatever may be your particular creed, you are indebted to the Church of Rome for your knowledge of Christianity.

Do not these facts demonstrate the Primacy of the Pope? The Apostles of Europe and of other countries received their authority from Rome. Is not the power that sends an ambassador greater than he who is sent?

Thus we see that the name of the Pope is indelibly marked on every page of ecclesiastical history. The Sovereign Pontiff ever stands before us as commander-in-chief in the grand army of the Church. Do the bishops of the East feel themselves aggrieved at home by their Patriarchs or civil Rulers? They look for redress to Rome, as to the star of their hope. Are the Fathers and Doctors of the early Church consulted? With one voice they all pay homage to the Bishop of Rome as to their spiritual Prince. Is an Ecumenical Council to be convened in the East or West? The Pope is its leading spirit. Are new nations to be converted to the faith? There is the Holy Father clothing the missionaries with authority, and giving his blessing to the work. Are new errors to be condemned in any part of the globe? All eyes turn toward the oracle of Rome to await his anathema, and his solemn judgment reverberates throughout the length and breadth of the Christian world.

You might as well shut out the light of day and the air of heaven from your daily walks as exclude the Pope from his legitimate sphere in the hierarchy of the Church. The history of the United States with the Presidents left out would be more intelligible than the history of the Church to the exclusion of the

Vicar of Christ. How, I ask, could such authority endure so long if it were a usurpation?

But you will tell me: "The supremacy of the Pope has been disputed in many ages." So has the authority of God been called in question—nay, His very existence has been denied; for, "the fool hath said in his heart there is no God." [4] Does this denial destroy the existence and dominion of God? Has not parental authority been impugned from the beginning? But by whom? By unruly children. Was David no longer king because Absalom said so?

It is thus also with the Popes. Their parental sway has been opposed only by their undutiful sons who grew impatient of the Gospel yoke. Photius, the leader of the Greek schism, was an obedient son of the Pope until Nicholas refused to recognize his usurped authority. Henry VIII. was a stout defender of the Pope's supremacy until Clement VII. refused to legalize his adultery. Luther professed a most abject submission to the Pope till Leo X. condemned him.

You cannot, my dear reader, be a loyal citizen of the United States while you deny the constitutional authority of the President. You have seen that the Bishop of Rome is appointed not by man, but by Jesus Christ, President of the Christian commonwealth. You cannot, therefore, be a true citizen of the Republic of the Church so long as you spurn the legitimate supremacy of its Divinely constituted Chief. "He that is not with Me is against Me," says our Lord, "and he that gathereth not with Me scattereth." How can you be with Christ if you are against His Vicar?

The great evil of our times is the unhappy division existing among the professors of Christianity, and from thousands of hearts a yearning cry goes forth for unity of faith and union of churches.

It was, no doubt, with this laudable view that the Evangelical Alliance assembled in New York in the fall of 1873. The representatives of the different religious communions hoped to effect a reunion. But they signally and lamentably failed. Indeed, the

[4] Ps. lii.

only result which followed from the alliance was the creation of a new sect under the auspices of Dr. Cummins. That reverend gentleman, with the characteristic modesty of all religious reformers, was determined to have a hand in improving the work of Jesus Christ; and, like the other reformers, he said, with those who built the tower of Babel: "Let us make our name famous before"[5] our dust is scattered to the wind.

The Alliance failed, because its members had no common platform to stand on. There was no voice in that assembly that could say with authority: "Thus saith the Lord."

I heartily join in this prayer for Christian unity, and gladly would surrender my life for such a consummation. But I tell you that Jesus Christ has pointed out the only means by which this unity can be maintained, viz.: the recognition of Peter and his successors as the Head of the Church. Build upon this foundation and you will not erect a tower of Babel, nor build upon sand. If all Christian sects were united with the centre of unity, then the scattered hosts of Christendom would form an army which atheism and infidelity could not long withstand. Then, indeed, all could exclaim with Balaam: "How beautiful are thy tabernacles, O Jacob, and thy tents, O Israel!"[6]

Let us pray that the day may be hastened when religious dissensions will cease; when all Christians will advance with united front, under one common leader, to plant the cross in every region and win new kingdoms to Jesus Christ.

[5] Gen. xi. 4.
[6] Numb. xxiv. 5.

CHAPTER XI

INFALLIBILITY OF THE POPES

AS the doctrine of Papal Infallibility is strangely misapprehended by our separated brethren, because it is grievously misrepresented by those who profess to be enlightened ministers of the Gospel, I shall begin by stating what Infallibility does not mean, and shall then explain what it really is.

First—The infallibility of the Popes does not signify that they are inspired. The Apostles were endowed with the gift of inspiration, and we accept their writings as the revealed Word of God.

No Catholic, on the contrary, claims that the Pope is inspired or endowed with Divine revelation properly so called.

"For the Holy Spirit was not promised to the successors of Peter in order that they might spread abroad new doctrine which He reveals, but that, under His assistance, they might guard inviolably, and with fidelity explain, the revelation or deposit of faith handed down by the Apostles." [1]

Second—Infallibility does not mean that the Pope is impeccable or specially exempt from liability to sin. The Popes have been, indeed, with few exceptions, men of virtuous lives. Many of them are honored as martyrs. Seventy-nine out of the two hundred and fifty-nine that sat on the chair of Peter are invoked upon our altars as saints eminent for their holiness.

The avowed enemies of the Church charge only five or six Popes with immorality. Thus, even admitting the truth of the accusations brought against them, we have forty-three virtuous

[1] Conc. Vat. Const. *Pastor Æternus,* c. 4.

to one bad Pope, while there was a Judas Iscariot among the twelve Apostles.

But although a vast majority of the Soverign Pontiffs should have been so unfortunate as to lead vicious lives, this circumstance would not of itself impair the validity of their prerogatives, which are given not for the preservation of their morals, but for the guidance of their judgment; for, there was a Balaam among the Prophets, and a Caiphas among the High Priests of the Old Law.

The present illustrious Pontiff is a man of no ordinary sanctity. He has already filled the highest position in the Church for upwards of thirty years, "a spectacle to the world, to angels and to men," and no man can point out a stain upon his moral character.

And yet Pius IX., like his predecessors, confesses his sins every week. Each morning, at the beginning of Mass, he says at the foot of the altar, "I confess to Almighty God, and to His Saints, that I have sinned exceedingly in thought, word and deed." And at the Offertory of the Mass he says: "Receive, O Holy Father, almighty, everlasting God, this oblation which I, Thy unworthy servant, offer for my innumerable sins, offences and negligences."

With these facts before their eyes, I cannot comprehend how ministers of the Gospel betray so much ignorance, or are guilty of so much malice, as to proclaim from their pulpits, which ought to be consecrated to truth, that Infallibility means exemption from sin. I do not see how they can benefit their cause by so flagrant perversions of truth.

Third—Bear in mind, also, that this Divine assistance is guaranteed to the Pope not in his capacity as private teacher, but only in his official capacity, when he judges of faith and morals as Head of the Church. If a Pope, for instance, like Benedict XIV. were to write a treatise on Canon Law his book would be as much open to criticism as that of any Doctor of the Church.

Fourth—Finally, the inerrability of the Popes, being restricted to questions of faith and morals, does not extend to the natural sciences, such as astronomy or geology, unless where error is presented under the false name of science, and arrays itself against revealed truth.[2] It does not, therefore, concern itself about the nature and motions of the planets. Nor does it regard purely political questions, such as the form of government a nation ought to adopt, or for what candidates we ought to vote.

The Pope's Infallibility, therefore, does not in any way trespass on civil authority; for the Pope's jurisdiction belongs to spiritual matters, while the duty of the State is to provide for the temporal welfare of its subjects.

What, then, is the real doctrine of Infallibility? It simply means that the Pope, as successor of St. Peter, Prince of the Apostles, by virtue of the promises of Jesus Christ, is preserved from error of judgment when he promulgates to the Church a decision on faith or morals.

The Pope, therefore, be it known, is not the maker of the Divine law; he is only its expounder. He is not the author of revelation, but only its interpreter. All revelation came from God alone through His inspired ministers, and it was complete in the beginning of the Church. The Holy Father has no more authority than you or I to break one iota of the Scripture, and he is equally with us the servant of the Divine law.

In a word, the Sovereign Pontiff is to the Church, though in a more eminent degree, what the Supreme Court is to the United States. We have an instrument called the Constitution of the United States, which is the charter of our civil rights and liberties. If a controversy arise regarding a constitutional clause, the question is referred in the last resort, to the Supreme Court at Washington. The Chief Justice, with his associate judges, examines into the case and then pronounces judgment upon it; and this decision is final, irrevocable and practically infallible.

If there were no such court to settle constitutional questions, the Constitution itself would soon become a dead letter. Every litigant would conscientiously decide the dispute in his own favor and anarchy, separation and civil war would soon follow. But by means of this Supreme Court disputes are ended, and the

[2] Conc. Vat. Const. *Dei Filius*, cap 4; Coloss. ii. 8.

political union of the States is perpetuated. There would have been no civil war in 1861 had our domestic quarrel been submitted to the legitimate action of our highest court of judicature, instead of being left to the arbitrament of the sword.

The revealed Word of God is the constitution of the Church. This is the *Magna Charta* of our Christian liberties. The Pope is the official guardian of our religious constitution, as the Chief Justice is the guardian of our civil constitution.

When a dispute arises in the Church regarding the sense of Scripture the subject is referred to the Pope for final adjudication. The Sovereign Pontiff, before deciding the case, gathers around him his venerable colleagues, the Cardinals of the Church; or he calls a council of his associate judges of faith, the Bishops of Christendom; or he has recourse to other lights which the Holy Ghost may suggest to him. Then, after mature and prayerful deliberation, he pronounces judgment and his sentence is final, irrevocable and infallible.

If the Catholic Church were not fortified by this Divinely-established supreme tribunal, she would be broken up, like the sects around her, into a thousand fragments and religious anarchy would soon follow. But by means of this infallible court her marvelous unity is preserved throughout the world. This doctrine is the keystone in the arch of Catholic faith, and, far from arousing opposition, it ought to command the unqualified admiration of every reflecting mind.

These explanations being premised, let us now briefly consider the grounds of the doctrine itself.

The following passages of the Gospel, spoken at different times, were addressed exclusively to Peter: "Thou art Peter; and on this rock I will build My Church, and the gates of hell shall not prevail against it." [3] "I, the Supreme Architect of the universe," says our Savior, "will establish a Church which is to last till the end of time. I will lay the foundation of this Church so deep and strong on the rock of truth that the winds and storms of error shall not prevail against it. Thou, O Peter, shalt be the foundation

[3] Matt. xvi.

of this Church. It shall never fall, because thou shalt never be shaken; and thou shalt never be shaken, because thou shalt rest on Me, the rock of truth." The Church, of which Peter is the foundation, is declared to be impregnable—that is, proof against error. How can you suppose an immovable edifice built on a tottering foundation? For it is not the building that sustains the foundation, but it is the foundation that supports the building.

"And I will give to thee the keys of the Kingdom of Heaven." [4] Thou shalt hold the keys of truth with which to open to the faithful the treasures of heavenly science. "Whatsoever thou shalt bind on earth shall be bound also in Heaven." [5] The judgment which thou shalt pronounce on earth I will ratify in heaven. Surely the God of Truth is incapable of sanctioning an untruthful judgment.

"Behold, Satan hath desired to have you (My Apostles), that he may sift *you* as wheat. But I have prayed for *thee* (Peter) that thy faith fail not; and thou, being once converted, confirm thy brethren." [6] It is worthy of note that Jesus prays only for Peter. And why for Peter in particular? Because on his shoulders was to rest the burden of the Church. Our Lord prays for two things: First—That the faith of Peter and of his successors might not fail. Second—That Peter would confirm his brethren in the faith, "in order," as St. Leo says, "that the strength given by Christ to Peter should descend on the Apostles."

We know that the prayer of Jesus is always heard. Therefore the faith of Peter will always be firm. He was destined to be the oracle which all were to consult. Hence we always find him the prominent figure among the Apostles, the first to speak, the first to act on every occasion. He was to be the guiding star that was to lead the rest of the faithful in the path of truth. He was to be in the hierarchy of the Church what the sun is in the planetary system—the centre around which all would revolve. And is it not a beautiful spectacle, in harmony with our ideas of God's providence, to behold in His Church a counterpart of the starry system above us? There every planet moves in obedience to a

[4] Matt. xvi.   [5] Ibid.   [6] Luke xxii. 31, 32.

uniform law, all are regulated by one great luminary. So, in the spiritual order, we see every member of the Church governed by one law, controlled by one voice, and that voice subject to God.

"Feed My lambs; feed My sheep." [7] Peter is appointed by our Lord the universal shepherd of His flock—of the sheep and of the lambs—that is, shepherd of the Bishops and Priests as well as of the people. The Bishops are shepherds, in reference to their flocks; they are sheep, in reference to the Pope, who is the shepherd of shepherds. The Pope, as shepherd, must feed the flock not with the poison of error, but with the healthy food of sound doctrine; for he is not a shepherd, but a hireling, who administers pernicious food to his flock.

Among the General Councils of the Church already held I shall mention only three, as the acts of these Councils are amply sufficient to vindicate the unerring character of the See of Rome and the Roman Pontiffs. I wish also to call your attention to three facts: First—That none of these Councils was held in Rome; Second—That one of them assembled in the East, viz.: in Constantinople; and, Third—That in every one of them the Oriental and the Western Bishops met for the purpose of reunion.

The Eighth General Council, held in Constantinople in 869, contains the following solemn profession of faith: "Salvation primarily depends upon guarding the rule of right faith. And since we cannot pass over the words of our Lord Jesus Christ, who says, 'Thou art Peter, and on this rock I will build My Church,' what was said is confirmed by facts, because in the Apostolic See the Catholic religion has always been preserved immaculate, and holy doctrine has been proclaimed. Not wishing, then, to be separated from this faith and doctrine, we hope to merit to be in the one communion which the Apostolic See preaches, in which See is the full and true solidity of the Christian religion."

This Council clearly declares that *immaculate doctrine* has always *been preserved and preached in the Roman See.* But how could this be said of her, if the Roman See ever fell into error,

[7] John xxi. 16, 17.

and how could that See be preserved from error, if the Roman Pontiffs presiding over it ever erred in faith?

In the Second General Council of Lyons (1274), the Greek Bishops made the following profession of faith: "The holy Roman Church possesses full primacy and principality over the universal Catholic Church, which primacy, with the plenitude of power, she truly and humbly acknowledges to have received from our Lord Himself, in the person of Blessed Peter, Prince or Head of the Apostles, whose successor the Roman Pontiff is; and as the Roman See, above all others, is bound to defend the truth of faith, so, also, *if any questions on faith arise, they ought to be defined by her judgment."*

Here the Council of Lyons avows that the Roman Pontiffs have the power to determine definitely, and without appeal, any questions of faith which may arise in the Church; in other words, the Council acknowledges them to be the supreme and infallible arbiters of faith.

"We define," says the Council of Florence (1439), at which also were present the Bishops of the Greek and the Latin Church, "we define that the Roman Pontiff is the successor of the Blessed Peter, Prince of the Apostles, and *the true Vicar of Christ, the Head* of the whole Church, the Father and Doctor of all Christians, and we declare that to him, in the person of Blessed Peter, was given, by Jesus Christ our Savior, full power to feed, rule and govern the universal Church."

The Pope is here called the *true Vicar* or representative of Christ in this lower kingdom of His Church militant—that is, the Pope is the organ of our Savior, and speaks His sentiments in faith and morals. But if the Pope erred in faith and morals he would no longer be Christ's Vicar and true representative. Our minister in England, for instance, would not truly represent our Government if he was not the organ of its sentiments. The Roman Pontiff is called the *Head* of the whole Church—that is, the visible Head. Now the Church, which is the Body of Christ, is infallible. It is, as St. Paul says, "without spot or wrinkle, or any such thing." But how can you suppose an infallible body with a fallible head? How can an erring head conduct a body in the unerring ways of truth and justice?

He is declared by the same Council to be the *Father* and *Doctor* of all Christians. How can you expect an unerring family under an erring Father? The Pope is called the universal teacher or doctor. Teacher of what? Of truth, not of error. Error is to the mind what poison is to the body. You do not call poison food; neither can you call error doctrine. The Pope, as universal teacher, must always give to the faithful not the poisonous food of error, but the sound aliment of pure doctrine.

In fine, the Pope is also styled the *Chief Pilot* of the Church. It was not without a mysterious significance that our Lord entered Peter's bark instead of that of any of the other Apostles. This bark, our Lord has pledged Himself, shall never sink nor depart from her true course. How can you imagine a stormproof, never-varying bark under the charge of a fallible Pilot?

But did not the Vatican Council in promulgating the definition of Papal Infallibility in 1870, create a new doctrine of revelation? And did not the Church thereby forfeit her glorious distinction of being always unchangeable in her teaching?

The Council did not create a new creed, but rather confirmed the old one. It formulated into an article of faith a truth which in every age had been accepted by the Catholic world because it had been implicitly contained in the deposit of revelation.

I may illustrate this point by referring again to our Supreme Court. When the Chief Justice, with his colleagues, decides a constitutional question, his decision, though presented in a new shape, cannot be called a new doctrine, because it is based on the letter and spirit of the Constitution.

In like manner, when the Church issues a new dogma of faith, that decree is nothing more than a new form of expressing an old doctrine, because the decision must be drawn from the revealed Word of God.

The course pursued by the Church, regarding the infallibility of the Pope was practiced by her in reference to the Divinity of Jesus Christ. Our Savior was acknowledged to be God from the

beginning of the Church. Yet His Divinity was not formally defined till the Council of Nicæa in the fourth century, and it
would not have been defined even then had it not been denied
by Arius. And who will have the presumption to say that the
belief in the Divinity of our Lord had its origin in the fourth
century?

The following has always been the practice prevailing in the
Church of God from the beginning of her history. Whenever
Bishops or National Councils promulgated doctrines or condemned errors they always transmitted their decrees to Rome
for confirmation or rejection. What Rome approved, the universal
Church approved; what Rome condemned, the Church condemned.

Thus, in the third century, Pope St. Stephen reverses the decision of St. Cyprian, of Carthage, and of a council of African bishops regarding a question of baptism.

Pope St. Innocent I., in the fifth century, condemns the Pe-
lagian heresy, in reference to which St. Augustine wrote this
memorable sentence: "The acts of two councils were sent to the
Apostolic See, whence an answer was returned. The *question is
ended*. Would to God that the error also had ceased."

In the fourteenth century Gregory XI. condemns the heresy
of Wycliffe.

Pope Leo X., in the sixteenth, anathematizes Luther.

Innocent X., in the seventeenth, at the solicitation of the
French Episcopate, condemns the subtle errors of the Jansenists,
and in the nineteenth century Pius IX. promulgates the doctrine
of the Immaculate Conception.

Here we find the Popes in various ages condemning heresies
and proclaiming doctrines of faith; and they could not in a
stronger manner assert their infallibility than by so defining doctrines of faith and condemning errors. We also behold the Church
of Christendom ever saying Amen to the decisions of the Bishops
of Rome. Hence it is evident that, in every age, the Church recognized the Popes as infallible teachers.

Every independent government must have a supreme tribunal

regularly sitting to interpret its laws, and to decide cases of controversy likely to arise. Thus we have in Washington the Supreme Court of the United States.

Now the Catholic Church is a complete and independent organization, as complete in its spiritual sphere as the United States
Government is in the temporal order. The Church has its own
laws, its own autonomy and government.

The Church, therefore, like civil powers, must have a pu.
manent and stationary supreme tribunal to interpret its laws and
to determine cases of religious controversy.

What constitutes this permanent supreme court of the Church?
Does it consist of the Bishops assembled in General Council? No;
because this is not an ordinary but an extraordinary tribunal
which meets, on an average, only once in a hundred years.

Is it composed of the Bishops scattered throughout the world?
By no means, because it would be impracticable to consult all the
Bishops of Christendom upon every issue that might arise in the
Church. The poison of error would easily spread through the
body of the Church before a decision could be rendered by the
Prelates dispersed throughout the globe. The Pope, then, as Head
of the Catholic Church, constitutes, with just reason, this su-
preme tribunal.

And as the office of the Church is to guide men into all truth,
and to preserve them from all error, it follows that he who is appointed to watch over the constitution of the Church must be
infallible, or exempt from error in his official capacity as judge
of faith and morals. The prerogatives of the Pope must be commensurate with the nature of the constitution which he has to
uphold. The constitution is Divine and must have a Divinely
protected interpreter.

But you will tell me that infallibility is too great a prerogative
to be conferred on man. I answer: Has not God, in former times,
clothed His Apostles with powers far more exalted? They were
endowed with the gifts of working miracles, of prophecy and inspiration; they were the mouthpiece communicating God's revelation, of which the Popes are merely the custodians. If God could

make man the organ of His revealed Word, is it impossible for Him to make man its infallible guardian and interpreter? For, surely, greater is the Apostle who gives us the inspired Word than the Pope who preserves it from error.

If, indeed, our Saviour had visibly remained among us, no interpreter would be needed, since He would explain His Gospel to us; but as He withdrew His visible presence from us, it was eminently reasonable that He should designate someone to expound for us the meaning of His Word.

A Protestant Bishop, in the course of a sermon against Papal Infallibility, recently used the following language: "For my part, I have an infallible Bible, and this is the only infallibility that I require." This assertion, though plausible at first sight, cannot for a moment stand the test of sound criticism.

Let us see, sir, whether an infallible Bible is sufficient for you. Either you are infallibly certain that your interpretation of the Bible is correct or you are not.

If you are infallibly certain, then you assert for yourself, and of course for every reader of the Scripture, a personal infallibility which you deny to the Pope, and which we claim only for him. You make every man his own Pope.

If you are not infallibly certain that you understand the true meaning of the whole Bible—and this is a privilege you do not claim—then, I ask, of what use to you is the objective infallibility of the Bible without an infallible interpreter?

If God, as you assert, has left no infallible interpreter of His Word, do you not virtually accuse Him of acting unreasonably? for would it not be most unreasonable in Him to have revealed His truth to man without leaving him a means of ascertaining its precise import?

Do you not reduce God's word to a bundle of contradictions, like the leaves of the Sybil, which gave forth answers suited to the wishes of every inquirer?

Of the hundred and more Christian sects now existing in this country, does not each take the Bible as its standard of authority, and does not each member draw from it a meaning different from that of his neighbor? Now, in the mind of God the Scriptures can have but one meaning. Is not this variety of interpretations the bitter fruit of your principle: "An infallible Bible is enough for me," and does it not proclaim the absolute necessity of some authorized and unerring interpreter? You tell me to drink of the water of life; but of what use is this water to my parched lips, since you acknowledge that it may be poisoned in passing through the medium of your interpretation?

How satisfactory, on the contrary, and how reasonable is the Catholic teaching on this subject!

According to that system, Christ says to every Christian: Here, my child, is the Word of God, and with it I leave you an infallible interpreter, who will expound for you its hidden meaning and make clear all its difficulties.

Here are the waters of eternal life, but I have created a channel that will communicate these waters to you in all their sweetness without sediment of error.

Here is the written Constitution of My Church. But I have appointed over it a Supreme Tribunal, in the person of one "to whom I have given the keys of the Kingdom of Heaven," who will preserve that Constitution inviolate, and will not permit it to be torn into shreds by the conflicting opinions of men. And thus my children will be one, as I and the Father are one.

CHAPTER XII

TEMPORAL POWER OF THE POPES—HOW THEY ACQUIRED TEMPORAL POWER—VALIDITY AND JUSTICE OF THEIR TITLE—WHAT THE POPES HAVE DONE FOR ROME

I

HOW THE POPES ACQUIRED TEMPORAL POWER

FOR the clearer understanding of the origin and the gradual growth of the Temporal Power of the Popes, we may divide the history of the Church into three great epochs.

The first embraces the period which elapsed from the establishment of the Church to the days of Constantine the Great, in the fourth century; the second, from Constantine to Charlemagne, who was crowned Emperor in the year 800; the third, from Charlemagne to the present time.

When St. Peter, the first Pope in the long, unbroken line of Sovereign Pontiffs, entered Italy and Rome he did not possess a foot of ground which he could call his own. He could say with his Divine Master: "The foxes have holes and the birds of the air nests, but the Son of Man hath not whereon to lay his head."[1] The Apostle died as he had lived, a poor man, having nothing at his death save the affections of a grateful people.

But, although the Prince of the Apostles owned nothing that he could call his personal property, he received from the faithful large donations to be distributed among the needy. For in the

[1] Matt. viii. 20.

Acts of the Apostles we are told that "neither was anyone among them (the faithful) needy; for as many as were owners of lands or houses sold them, and brought the prices of the things which they sold and laid them before the feet of the Apostles, and distribution was made to everyone according as he had need." [2] Such was the filial attachment of the early Christians towards the Pontiffs of the Church; such was the confidence reposed in their personal integrity, and in their discretion in dispensing the charity of the faithful.

During the first three hundred years the Pastors of the Church were generally incapable of holding real estate in Rome; for Christianity was yet a proscribed religion, and the faithful were exposed to the most violent and unrelenting persecutions that have ever darkened the annals of history.

The Christians of Rome worshiped for the most part in the catacombs. These catacombs are subterranean chambers and passages under the city of Rome. They extend for miles in different directions, and are visited to this day by thousands of strangers. Here the primitive Christians prayed together, here they encouraged one another to martyrdom, here they died and were buried; so that these caverns served at the same time as temples of worship for the living and as tombs for the dead.

At last Constantine the Great brought peace to the Church. The long night of Pagan persecution was succeeded by the bright dawn of religious liberty, and as our Blessed Savior rose triumphant from the grave, after having lain there for three days, so did our early brethren in the faith emerge from the tombs of the catacombs, after having been buried, as it were, in the bowels of the earth for three centuries.

Constantine gave to the Roman Church munificent donations of money and real estate, which were augmented by additional grants contributed by subsequent emperors. Hence the patrimony of the Roman Pontiffs soon became very considerable. Voltaire himself tells us that the wealth which the Popes acquired was spent not in satisfying their own avarice and ambition, but in the

[2] Acts iv. 34, 35.

most laudable works of charity and religion. They expended their patrimony, he says, in sending missionaries to evangelize Pagan Europe, in giving hospitality to exiled Bishops at Rome and in feeding the poor. And I may here add that succeeding Popes have generously imitated the munificence of the early Pontiffs.

An event occurred in the reign of Constantine which paved the way for the partial jurisdiction which the Roman Pontiffs commenced to enjoy over Rome, and which they continued to exercise till they obtained full sovereignty in the days of King Pepin of France.

In the year 327 the Emperor Constantine transferred the seat of empire from Rome to Constantinople, the present capital of Turkey. The city was named after Constantine, who founded it. A subsequent emperor appointed a governor, or exarch, to rule Italy, who resided in the city of Ravenna. This new system, as is manifest, did not work well. The Emperor of Constantinople referred all matters to his deputy in Ravenna, and the deputy was more anxious to conciliate the Emperor than to satisfy the people of Rome. Italy and Rome were then in a political condition analogous to that in which the Irish were placed for several centuries.

Abandoned to itself, Rome became a tempting prey to those numerous hordes of Barbarians from the North that then devastated Italy. The city was successively attacked by the Goths under Alaric, and by the Vandals under Genseric, and was threatened by the Huns under Attila. Unable to obtain assistance from the Emperor in the East, or the Governor at Ravenna, the citizens of Rome looked up to the Popes as their only Governors and protectors, and their only salvation in the dangers which threatened them. The confidence which they reposed in the Pontiffs was not misplaced. The Popes were not only devoted spiritual Fathers, but firm and valiant civil Governors. When Attila, who was surnamed "the Scourge of God," approached the city with an army of 500,000 men, Pope Leo the Great went out to meet him unattended by troops. His mild eloquence disarmed the indomitable chieftain and induced him to retrace his steps. Thus he saved the city from pillage and the people from destruction. The same Pope Leo also confronted Genseric, the leader of the Vandals; and although he could not this time protect Rome from the plunder of the soldiers he saved the lives of the citizens from slaughter. Such acts as these were naturally calculated to bind the Roman people more strongly to the Popes and to alienate them from their nominal rulers.

In the early part of the eighth century Leo Isauricus, one of the successors of Constantine on the imperial throne, not content with his civil authority, endeavored, like Henry VIII., to usurp spiritual jurisdiction, and, like the same English monarch, sought to rob the people of their time-honored sacred traditions. A civil ruler dabbling in religion is as reprehensible as a clergyman dabbling in politics. Both render themselves odious as well as ridiculous. The Emperor commanded all paintings of our Savior and His saints to be removed from the churches on the assumption that such an exhibition was an act of idolatry. Pope Gregory II. wrote to the Emperor an energetic remonstrance, reminding him that "dogmas of faith are to be interpreted by the Pontiffs of the Church and not by emperors," and begging him to spare the sacred paintings. But the Pope's remonstrance and entreaties were in vain. This conduct of the Emperor tended to widen still more the breach between himself and the Roman people.

Soon after an event occurred which abolished forever the authority of the Byzantine Emperors in Italy, and established on a sure and lasting basis the temporal sovereignty of the Popes.

In 754 Astolphus, King of the Lombards, invaded Italy, captured some Italian cities and threatened to advance on Rome.

Pope Stephen III.,[3] who then ruled the Church, sent an urgent appeal to the Emperor Constantine Copronymus, successor of Leo the Isaurian, imploring him to come to the relief of Rome and his Italian provinces. The Emperor manifested his usual

[3] Sometimes called Stephen II., as Stephen, his predecessor, died three days after his election, whose name is omitted in some calendars.

apathy and indifference and received the message with coldness and neglect.

In this emergency Stephen, who sees that no time is to be lost, crosses the Alps in person, approaches Pepin, King of France, and begs that powerful monarch to protect the Italian people, who were utterly abandoned by those that ought to be their defenders. The pious King, after paying his homage to the Pope, sets out for Italy with his army, defeats the invading Lombards and places the Pope at the head of the conquered provinces.

Charlemagne, the successor of Pepin, not only confirms the grant of his father, but increases the temporal domain of the Pope by donating him some additional provinces.

This small piece of territory the Roman Pontiffs continued to govern from that time till 1870, with the exception of brief intervals of foreign usurpation. And certainly, if ever any Prince merited the appellation of legitimate sovereign, that title is eminently deserved by the Bishops of Rome.

II

THE VALIDITY AND JUSTICE OF THEIR TITLE

There are three titles which render the tenure of a Prince honest and incontestable, viz., *long possession, legitimate acquisition* and *a just use of the original grant confided to him*. The Bishop of Rome possessed his temporality by all these titles.

First—The temporal dominion of the Pope is most ancient in point of time. He commenced, as we have seen, to enjoy full sovereignty about the middle of the eighth century. The Pope was, consequently, a temporal ruler for upwards of 1,100 years. The Papal dynasty is, therefore, the oldest in Europe, and probably in the world. The Pope was the temporal ruler of Rome four hundred years before England subjugated Ireland, and seven hundred before the first European pressed his foot on the American continent.

Second—His civil authority was established not by the sword of conquest, nor the violence of usurpation. He did not mount the throne upon the ruins of outraged liberties or violated treaties; but he was called to rule by the unanimous voice of a grateful people. Always the devoted spiritual Father of Rome, he providentially became its civil defender; and the temporal power he had possessed already by popular suffrage was ratified and sanctioned by the sovereign act of the Frankish monarch. In a word, the ship of state was in danger of being engulfed beneath the fierce waves of foreign invasion. The captain, meantime, folded his arms and abandoned the ship to her fate. The Pope was called to the helm in the emergency, and he saved the vessel from shipwreck and the people from destruction. Hence, even Gibbon, the English historian, who cannot be suspected of partiality, has the candor to use the following language in discussing this subject: "Their (the Pope's) temporal dominion is now confirmed by the reverence of a thousand years, and their noblest title is the free choice of a people whom they had redeemed from slavery."

Third—What is the use or advantage of the temporal power? This is well worth considering, as many have erroneous notions on the subject.

The object is not to aggrandize or enrich the Pope. He ascends the Papal chair generally an old man, when human passion and human ambition, if any did exist, are on the wane. His personal expenses do not exceed a few dollars a day. He eats alone and very abstemiously. He has no wife, no children to enrich with the spoils of office, as he is an unmarried man. The Popedom is not hereditary, like the sovereignty of England, but elective, like the office of our President, and the Holy Father is succeeded by a Pontiff to whom he was bound by no family ties. What personal motive, therefore, can he have in desiring temporal sovereignty? I am sure, indeed, that if the Holy Father were to consult his own taste and feelings, he would much rather be free from the trammels of civil government. But he has higher interests to subserve. He must vindicate the eternal laws of justice which have been violated in his own person.

As the Popes were not actuated by a love of gain in possessing temporal dominion, neither had they any desire to enlarge their territory, small as it was. The temporalities of the Pope were not much larger than the State of Maryland before he was deprived of them by Victor Emmanuel a few years ago.

And this is the little slice of land which Victor Emmanuel wrested from the Holy Father. This is the vineyard which the modern King Achab wrung from the unoffending Naboth. But the Pontiff answers, like Naboth of old: "The Lord be merciful to me, and not let me give thee the inheritance of my fathers." [4]

This is the little ewe-lamb which the modern David has snatched from Uriah, its legitimate owner. The royal shepherd of Piedmont had already seized all the other lambs and sheep of his neighbors; but he was not satisfied till he added to his fold the solitary, tender lamb of the Pope. Let him take care, however, that the prophecy denounced by Nathan against David fall not upon himself and his posterity: "Why, therefore, hast thou despised the word of the Lord, to do evil in My sight? Therefore the sword shall never depart from thy house, because thou hast depised Me. Behold, I will raise up evil against thee out of thy own house." [5]

While the patrimony of the Pope was large enough to secure his independence, it was too small to provoke the fear and jealousy of foreign powers. The authority of the Roman Pontiffs in the Middle Ages was almost unbounded. Had they wished then, they could easily have increased their territory; yet they were content with what Providence placed originally in their hands. [6]

The sole end of the temporal power has been to secure for the

---

[4] III. Kings xxi. 3. [5] II. Kings xii.

[6] I dare say you could have found, a few years since, some persons in the United States who entertained a holy fear lest the Pope should one morning land upon our shores, and take forcible possession of our country. A venerable clergyman once informed me that when he went to pay his respects to President Pierce, who then occupied the White House, his Excellency remarked to him: "I had a visit from a nervous gentleman, who asked me whether I was making any preparations to resist the approach of the Pope. I replied that so far I had taken no steps, but that no doubt I would be prepared to meet the enemy when he arrived. The man retired more composed, though not fully satisfied."

Pope independence and freedom in the government of the Church. The Holy Father must be either a sovereign or a subject. There is no medium. If a subject, he might become either the pliant creature, if God would so permit, of his royal master, like the schismatic Patriarch of Constantinople, who, as Gibbon observed, was "a domestic slave under the eye of his master, at whose nod he passed from the convent to the throne, and from the throne to the convent." And, indeed, the Oriental schismatic Bishops are as subservient now as they were then to their temporal rulers. Or, what is far more probable, the Pope might become a virtual prisoner in his own house, as the present illustrious Pontiff is at this moment.

The Pope is the representative of Christ on earth. His office requires him to be in constant communication with prelates in every country in the world. Should the kingdom of Italy be embroiled in a war with any European Power—with Germany, for instance—it would be difficult, if not impossible, for the Holy Father and the German Bishops to confer with each other, and religion would suffer from the interruption of intercourse between the Head and the members.

The interests of Christianity demand that the Vicar of the Prince of Peace should possess one spot of territory which would be held inviolable, so that all nations and peoples could at all times, in war, as well as in peace, freely correspond with him. Nothing can be more revolting to our feelings than that the spiritual government of the Church should be constantly hampered by the hostile aggressions of ambitious rulers, an eventuality always likely to occur so long as the Pope remains the subject of any earthly potentate.[7]

---

[7] Some of the evils that were predicted to follow from the occupation of Rome by a foreign power have been too speedily realized. Already several convents and other ecclesiastical institutions have been seized and sold, and their inmates sent adrift. A number of colleges founded and endowed by the piety of foreign Catholics have been confiscated. Public religious processions through the streets of Rome have been prohibited. These and other outrages are perpetrated by a government which solemnly pledged itself to maintain inviolate the sovereign rights of the Holy Father when it took forcible possession of his city in 1870. From the

But we are told that the Roman people, by a *plebiscitum*, or popular vote, expressed their desire to be annexed to the Piedmontese Government. To this I answer, in the first place, that we ought to know what importance to attach to elections held under the shadow of the bayonet. It is well known that the Roman *plebiscitum* was undertaken by the authority and guided by the inspiration of the Italian troops. It is equally notorious that the numerous stragglers who accompanied the Italian army to Rome legalized the gigantic fraud of their master, as well as their own petty thefts, by voting in favor of annexation.

In the second place, the Roman people, even had they so desired, had no right to transfer, by *their* suffrage, the Patrimony of St. Peter to Victor Emmanuel. They could not give what did not belong to them. The Papal territory was granted to the Popes in trust, for the use and benefit of the Church—that is, for the use and benefit of the Catholics of Christendom. The Catholic world, therefore, and not merely a handful of Roman subjects, must give its consent before such a transfer can be declared legitimate. Rome is to Catholic Christendom what Washington is to the United States. As the citizens of Washington have no power, without the concurrence of the United States, to annex their city to Maryland or Virginia, neither can the citizens of Rome hand over their city to the Kingdom of Piedmont without the acquiescence of the faithful dispersed throughout the world.

We protest, therefore, against the occupation of Rome by foreign troops as a high-handed act of injustice, and a gross violation of the Commandment, "Thou shalt not steal."

We protest against it as a royal outrage, calculated to shock the public sense of honesty, and to weaken the sacred right of public and private property.

We protest against it as an unjustifiable violation of solemn treaties.

events that have already transpired, we shall not be surprised to see the Pope still more seriously hampered by a monarch who has unscrupulously violated his former guarantees.

We protest, in fine, against the spoliation as an impious sacrilege, because it is an unholy seizure of ecclesiastical property, and an attempt, as far as human agencies can accomplish it, to trammel and embarrass the free action of the Head of the Church.

III

WHAT THE POPES HAVE DONE FOR ROME

Although the temporal power of the Pope is a subject which concerns the universal Church, no nation has more reason to lament the loss of the Holy Father's temporalities than the Italians themselves, and particularly the inhabitants of Rome.

It is the residence of the Popes in Rome that has contributed to her material and religious grandeur. The Pontiffs have made her the Centre of Christendom, the Queen of religion, the Mistress of arts and sciences, the Depository of sacred learning.

By their creative and conservative spirit they have saved the illustrious monuments of the past, and, side by side with these, they have raised up Christian temples which surpass those of Pagan antiquity. In looking today at these old Roman monuments we know not which to admire more—the genius of those who designed and erected them, or the fostering care of the Popes who have preserved from destruction the venerable ruins. The residence of the Popes in Rome has made her what she is truly called, *"The Eternal City."*

Let the Popes leave Rome forever, and in five years grass will be growing on its streets.

Such was the case at the return of the Pope, in 1418, from Avignon, which had been the seat of the Sovereign Pontiffs during the preceding century. On the Pope's return the city of Rome had a population of only 17,000 [8] and Avignon, which, during the residence of the Popes in the fourteenth century contained a population of 100,000, has now a population of only 36,407 in-

[8] Memoir of Pope Sixtus V., by Baron Hübner, Vol. II., ch. 1.

habitants. Such, also, was the case in the beginning of the present century, when Pius VII. was an exile for four years from Rome, and a prisoner of the first Napoleon, in Grenoble, Savona and Fontainebleau. Grass then grew on the streets of Rome, and the city lost one-half of its population.

Rome has naturally no commercial attractions. It is only the presence of the Pope that keeps up her trade. Let the Popes abandon Rome, and her churches will soon be without worshipers; her artists without employment. Her glorious monuments will perish. Science and art and sacred literature will take their flight and perch upon some more favored spot. The hundred thousand and more strangers who annually flock to Rome from different parts of the world will shake off the dust from their feet and seek more congenial cities.

Let the Popes withdraw from Rome, and it may become almost as desolate as Jerusalem and Antioch are today.

Peter preached his first sermons in Jerusalem, but he did not select it as his See; and Jerusalem is today a Mahometan city, with its sacred places profaned by the foot of the Mussulman.

Peter occupied for a time the city of Antioch as his first See. But, in the mysterious providence of God, he abandoned Antioch and repaired to Rome; and now, little remains of the ancient Antioch of Peter's day except colossal ruins.

Had the Popes remained in Antioch, Syria would now very probably be, instead of Europe, the centre of Christianity and civilization. The immortal Dome of St. Peter's would, doubtless, overshadow the banks of the Orontes instead of the Tiber; and Antioch, not Rome, would be the focus of art, science, and sacred literature, and would be called today "The Eternal City."

Our present [9] beloved Pontiff, Pius IX., I need not inform you, is now treated with indignity in his own city. In his declining years, as well as in the early days of his Pontificate, he is made to drink deep of the chalice of affliction. His name is dear to us all. To many of us it is a name familiar from our youth; for

[9] When these lines were written, Pius IX. was the reigning Pontiff. He died February 7, 1878.

thirty-one years have now elapsed since he first assumed the reins of government; and it is a noteworthy fact that, since the days of Peter, no Pope has ever reigned so long as Pius IX.

The Pope in every age, like his Divine Master, has his period of persecution and his period of peace. Like Him, he has his days of sorrow and his days of joy, his days of humiliation and death, his days of exaltation and glory. Like Jesus Christ, he is one day greeted with acclamations as king, and another day crucified by his enemies.

But never does the Holy Father exhibit his title as Vicar of Christ more strikingly than in the midst of tribulations. If he did not suffer, he would bear no resemblance to his Divine Model and Master; and never does he more worthily deserve the filial homage of his children than when he is heavily laden with the cross.

I envy neither the heart nor the head of those men who are now gloating with fiendish joy over the calamities of the Pope; who are heaping insults and calumnies on his venerable head, while he is in the hands of his enemies,[10] and who are confidently predicting the downfall of the Papacy, from the present situation of the Head of the Church, as if the temporary privation of his dominions involved their irrevocable loss; or, as if even the perpetual destruction of the temporal power involved the destruction of the spiritual supremacy itself. "The Papacy," they say, "is gone. Its glory is vanished. Its sun is set. It is sunk below

---

[10] Some time ago, my attention was called to a certain excommunication or "curse," then widely circulated by the press of North Carolina. The "curse" is attributed to the Holy Father, and is fulminated against Victor Emmanuel. In this anathema, *cursing* and *damning* are heaped up in wild confusion. When this base forgery appeared, an article exposing the falsehood of the production was published. We fear, however, that many who read the slanderous charge did not read its refutation.

As to this "curse" against Victor Emmanuel so calumniously attributed to the Pope, I state here distinctly and positively that its author is not Pius IX., nor any other Roman Pontiff, nor any Catholic Priest or layman. It is to the Rev. Laurence Sterne, Minister of the Established Church of England, and to his romance of "Tristram Shandy," that the English-speaking world is indebted for this infamous compilation.

the horizon, never to rise again." Ill-boding prophets, will you never profit by the lessons of history? Have not numbers of Popes before Pius IX. been forcibly ejected from their See, and have they not been reinstated in their temporal authority? What has happened so often before may and will happen again.

For our part we have every confidence that ere long the clouds which now overshadow the civil throne of the Pope will be removed by the breath of a righteous God, and that his temporal power will be re-established on a more permanent basis than ever.

But whatever be the fate of the Pope's temporalities, we have no fears for the spiritual throne of the Papacy. The Pontiffs have received their earthly dominion from man, and what man gives man may take away. But the spiritual supremacy the Bishops of Rome have from God, and no man can destroy it. That Divine charter of their prerogatives, "Thou art Peter, and on this rock I will build My Church, and the gates of hell shall not prevail against it," [11] will ever shine forth as brightly as the sun, and it is as far as the sun above the reach of human aggression.

The Holy Father may live and die in the catacombs, as the early Pontiffs did for the first three centuries. He may be dragged from his See and perish in exile, like the Martins, the Gregories and the Piuses. He may wander a penniless pilgrim, like Peter himself. Rome itself may sink beneath the Mediterranean; but the chair of Peter will stand, and Peter will live in his successors.

[11] Matt. xvi. 18.

CHAPTER XIII

THE INVOCATION OF SAINTS

CHRISTIANS of most denominations are accustomed to recite the following article contained in the Apostles' Creed: "I believe in the communion of Saints." There are many, I fear, who have these words frequently on their lips, without an adequate knowledge of the precious meaning which they convey.

The true and obvious sense of the words quoted from the Creed is, that between the children of God, whether reigning in heaven or sojourning on earth, there exists an intercommunion, or spiritual communication by prayer; and, consequently, that our friends who have entered into their rest are mindful of us in their petitions to God.

In the exposition of her Creed the Catholic Church weighs her words in the scales of the sanctuary with as much precision as a banker weighs his gold. With regard to the Invocation of Saints the Church simply declares that it is "useful and salutary" to ask their prayers. There are expressions addressed to the Saints in some popular books of devotion which, to critical readers, may seem extravagant. But they are only the warm language of affection and poetry, to be regulated by our standard of faith, and notice that all the prayers of the Church end with the formula: "Through our Lord Jesus Christ," sufficiently indicating her belief that Christ is the Mediator of salvation. A heart tenderly attached to the Saints will give vent to its feelings in the language of hyperbole, just as an enthusiastic lover will call his future bride his adorable queen, without any intention of worshiping her as a goddess. This reflection should be borne in mind while reading such passages.

I might easily show, by voluminous quotations from ecclesiastical writers of the first ages of the Church, how conformable to the teaching of antiquity is the Catholic practice of invoking the intercession of the Saints. But as you, dear reader, may not be disposed to attach adequate importance to the writings of the Fathers, I shall confine myself to the testimony of Holy Scripture.

You will readily admit that it is a salutary custom to ask the prayers of the blessed in heaven, provided you have no doubt that they can *hear* your prayers, and that they have the *power* and the *will* to assist you. Now the Scriptures amply demonstrate the knowledge, the influence and the love of the Saints in our regard.

First—It would be a great mistake to suppose that the Angels and Saints reigning with God see and hear in the same manner that we see and hear on earth, or that knowledge is communicated to them as it is communicated to us. While we are confined in the prison of the body, we see only with our eyes and hear with our ears; hence our faculties of vision and hearing are very limited. Compared with the heavenly inhabitants, we are like a man in a darksome cell through which a dim ray of light penetrates. He observes but few objects, and these very obscurely. But as soon as our soul is freed from the body, soaring heavenward like a bird released from its cage, its vision is at once marvelously enlarged. It requires neither eyes to see nor ears to hear, but beholds all things in God as in a mirror. "We now," says the Apostle, "see through a glass darkly; but then face to face. Now, I know in part; but then I shall know even as I am known." [1] In our day we know what wonderful facility we have in communicating with our friends at a distance. A message to Berlin or Rome with the answer, which a century ago would require sixty days in transmission, can now be accomplished in sixty minutes.

I can hold a conversation with an acquaintance in San Fran-

[1] I. Cor. xiii. 12.

cisco, three thousand miles away, and can talk to him as easily and expeditiously as if he were closeted with me here in Baltimore.

Nay more, we can distinctly recognize one another by the sound of our voice.

If a scientist had predicted such events, a hundred years past, he would be regarded as demented. And yet he would not be a visionary, but a prophet.

Let us not be unwise in measuring Divine power by our finite reason.

If such revelations are made in the natural order, what may we not expect in the supernatural world? If science gives us such rapid and easy means of corresponding with our fellow beings on foreign shores, what methods may not the God of Sciences employ to enable us to communicate with our brethren on the shores of eternity?

"There are more things in heaven and earth, Horatio, than are dreamt of in your philosophy."

That the spirits of the just in heaven are clearly conversant with our affairs on earth is manifest from the following passages of Holy Writ. The venerable Patriarch Jacob, when on his deathbed, prayed thus for his two grandchildren: "May the angel that delivereth me from all evils bless these boys!" [2] Here we see a holy Patriarch—one singularly favored by Almighty God, and enlightened by many supernatural visions, the father of Jehovah's chosen people—asking the angel in heaven to obtain a blessing for his grandchildren. And surely we cannot suppose that he would be so ignorant as to pray to one that could not hear him.

The angel Raphael, after having disclosed himself to Tobias, said to him: "When thou didst pray with tears, and didst bury the dead, and didst leave thy dinner, I offered thy prayer to the Lord." [3] How could the angel, if he were ignorant of these petitions, have presented to God the prayers of Tobias?

To pass from the Old to the New Testament, our Savior declares that "there shall be joy before the angels of God upon one

[2] Gen. xlviii. 16.　　　　　　　[3] Tobias xii. 12.

sinner doing penance." [4] Then the angels are glad whenever you repent of your sins. Now, what is repentance? It is a change of heart. It is an interior operation of the will. The saints, therefore, are acquainted—we know not how—not only with your actions and words, but even with your very thoughts.

And when St. Paul says that "we are made a spectacle to the world, to angels, and to men," [5] what does he mean, unless that as our actions are seen by men even so they are visible to the angels in heaven?

The examples I have quoted refer, it is true, to the angels. But our Lord declares that the saints in heaven shall be like the angelic spirits, by possessing the same knowledge, enjoying the same happiness. [6]

We read in the Gospel that Dives, while suffering in the place of the reprobates, earnestly besought Abraham to cool his burning thirst. And Abraham, in his abode of rest after death, was able to listen and reply to him. Now, if communication could exist between the souls of the just and of the reprobate, how much easier is it to suppose that interchange of thought can exist between the saints in heaven and their brethren on earth?

These few instances are sufficient to convince you that the spirits in heaven hear our prayers.

Second—We have, also, abundant testimony from Scripture to show that the saints assist us by their prayers. Almighty God threatened the inhabitants of Sodom and Gomorrha with utter destruction on account of their crimes and abominations. Abraham interposes in their behalf and, in response to his prayer, God consents to spare those cities if only ten just men are found therein. Here the avenging hand of God is suspended and the fire of His wrath withheld, through the efficacy of the prayers of a single man. [7]

We read in the Book of Exodus that when the Amalekites were about to wage war on the children of Israel, Moses, the great servant and Prophet of the Lord, went upon a mountain to pray

[4] Luke xv. 10.
[6] Matt. xxii. 30.
[5] I. Cor. iv. 9.
[7] Gen. xxviii.

for the success of his people; and the Scriptures inform us that whenever Moses raised his hands in prayer the Israelites were victorious, but when he ceased to pray Amalek conquered. Could the power of intercessory prayer be manifested in a more striking manner? The silent prayer of Moses on the mountain was more formidable to the Amalekites than the sword of Josue and his armed hosts fighting in the valley.[8]

When the same Hebrew people were banished from their native country and carried into exile in Babylon, so great was their confidence in the prayers of their brethren in Jerusalem that they sent them the following message, together with a sum of money, that sacrifice might be offered up for them in the holy city: "Pray ye for us to the Lord our God, for we have sinned against the Lord our God." [9]

When the friends of Job had excited the indignation of the Almighty in consequence of their vain speech, God, instead of directly granting them the pardon which they sought, commanded them to invoke the intercession of Job: "Go," He says, "to My servant Job and offer for yourselves a holocaust, and My servant Job will pray for you and his face will I accept." [10] Nor did they appeal to Job in vain; for, "the Lord was turned at the penance of Job when he prayed for his friends." [11] In this instance we not only see the value of intercessory prayer, but we find God sanctioning it by His own authority.

But of all the sacred writers there is none that reposes greater confidence in the prayers of his brethren than St. Paul, although no one had a better knowledge than he of the infinite merits of our Savior's Passion, and no one could have more endeared himself to God by his personal labors. In his Epistles St. Paul repeatedly asks for himself the prayers of his disciples. If he wishes to be delivered from the hands of the unbelievers of Judea, and his ministry to be successful in Jerusalem, he asks the Romans to obtain these favors for him. If he desires the grace of

---

[8] Exod. xvii.
[10] Job xlii.
[9] Baruch i. 13.
[11] Ibid.

preaching with profit the Gospel to the Gentiles, he invokes the intercession of the Ephesians.

Nay, is it not a common practice among ourselves, and even among our dissenting brethren, to ask the prayers of one another? When a father is about to leave his house on a long journey the instinct of piety prompts him to say to his wife and children: "Remember me in your prayers."

Now I ask you, if our friends, though sinners, can aid us by their prayers, why cannot our friends, the saints of God, be able to assist us also? If Abraham and Moses and Job exercised so much influence with the Almighty while they lived in the flesh, is their power with God diminished now that they reign with Him in heaven?

We are moved by the children of Israel sending their pious petitions to their brethren in Jerusalem. They recalled to mind, no doubt, what the Lord said to Solomon after he had completed the temple: "My eyes shall be open and My ears attentive to the prayer of him that shall pray in this place." [12] If the supplications of those that prayed in the earthly Jerusalem were so efficacious, what will God refuse to those who pray to Him face to face in the heavenly Jerusalem?

Third—But you will ask, are the saints in heaven so interested in our welfare as to be mindful of us in their prayers? Or, are they so much absorbed in the contemplation of God, and in the enjoyment of celestial bliss, as to be altogether regardless of their friends on earth? Far from us the suspicion that the saints reigning with God ever forget us. In heaven, charity is triumphant. And how can the saints have love, and yet be unmindful of their brethren on earth? If they have one desire greater than another, it is to see us one day wearing the crowns that await us in heaven. If they were capable of experiencing sorrow, their grief would spring from the consideration that we do not always walk in their footsteps here, so as to make sure our election to eternal glory hereafter.

[12] II. Paralip. vii. 15.

The Hebrew people believed, like us, that the saints after death were occupied in praying for us. We read in the Book of Maccabees that Judas Maccabeus, the night before he engaged in battle with the army of the impious Nicanor, had a supernatural dream, or vision, in which he beheld Onias, the High-Priest, and the prophet Jeremiah, both of whom had been long dead. Onias appeared to him with outstretched arms, praying for the people of God. Pointing to Jeremiah, he said to Judas Maccabeus: "This is a lover of his brethren and the people of Israel. This is he that prayeth much for the people and for all the holy city, Jeremiah, the Prophet of God." [13] Then Jeremiah, as is related in the sequel of the vision, handed a sword to Judas, with which the prophet predicted that Judas would conquer his enemies. The soldiers, animated by the relation of Judas, fought with invincible courage and overcame the enemy. The Book of Maccabees, though not admitted by our dissenting brethren to be inspired, must, at least, be acknowledged by them to be a faithful historical record. It is manifest, therefore, from this narrative that the Hebrew people believed that the saints in heaven pray for their brethren on earth.

St. John in his Revelation describes the Saints before the throne of God praying for their earthly brethren: "The four and twenty ancients fell down before the Lamb, having every one of them harps and golden vials full of odors, which are the prayers of the saints." [14]

The prophet Zachariah records a prayer that was offered by the angel for the people of God, and the favorable answer which came from heaven: "How long, O Lord, wilt Thou not have mercy on Jerusalem, and on the cities of Juda, with which Thou hast been angry? . . . And the Lord answered the angel . . . good words, comfortable words." [15]

Nor can we be surprised to learn that the angels labor for our salvation, since we are told by St. Peter that "the devil goeth about like a roaring lion, seeking whom he may devour;" for, if hate impels the demons to ruin us, surely love must inspire

[13] II. Mac. xv. 14.   [14] Revel. v. 8.   [15] Zach. i. 12, 13.

the angels to help us in securing the crown of glory. And if the angels, though of a different nature from ours, are so mindful of us, how much more interest do the saints manifest in our welfare, who are bone of our bone and flesh of our flesh?

To ask the prayers of our brethren in heaven is not only conformable to Holy Scripture, but is prompted by the instincts of our nature. The Catholic doctrine of the Communion of Saints robs death of its terrors, while the Reformers of the sixteenth century, in denying the Communion of Saints, not only inflicted a deadly wound on the Creed, but also severed the tenderest chords of the human heart. They broke asunder the holy ties that unite earth with heaven—the soul in the flesh with the soul released from the flesh. If my brother leaves me to cross the seas I believe that he continues to pray for me. And when he crosses the narrow sea of death and lands on the shores of eternity, why should he not pray for me still? What does death destroy? The body. The soul still lives and moves and has its being. It thinks and wills and remembers and loves. The dross of sin and selfishness and hatred are burned by the salutary fires of contrition, and nothing remains but the pure gold of charity.

O far be from us the dreary thought that death cuts off our friends entirely from us! Far be from us the heartless creed which declares a perpetual divorce between us and the just in heaven! Do not imagine when you lose a father or mother, a tender sister or brother, who die in the peace of Christ, that they are forgetful of you. The love they bore you on earth is purified and intensified in heaven. Or if your innocent child, regenerated in the waters of baptism, is snatched from you by death, be assured that, though separated from you in body, that child is with you in spirit and is repaying you a thousand-fold for the natural life it received from you. Be convinced that the golden link of prayer binds you to that angelic infant, and that it is continually offering its fervent petitions at the throne of God for you, that you may both be reunited in heaven. But I hear men cry out with Pharisaical assurance, "You dishonor God, sir, in praying to the saints. You make void the mediatorship of Jesus Christ. You put the creature above the Creator." How utterly groundless is this objection! We do not dishonor God in praying to the saints. We should, indeed, dishonor Him if we consulted the saints *independently* of God. But such is not our practice. The Catholic Church teaches, on the contrary, that God alone is the Giver of all good gifts; that He is the Source of all blessings, the Fountain of all goodness. She teaches that whatever happiness or glory or *influence* the saints possess, all comes from God. As the moon borrows her light from the sun, so do the blessed borrow their light from Jesus, "the Sun of Justice," the one Mediator (of redemption) of God and men." [16] Hence, when we address the saints, we beg them to pray for us through the merits of Jesus Christ, while we ask Jesus to help up through His own merits.

But what is the use of praying to the saints, since God can hear us. If it is vain and useless to pray to the saints because God can hear us, then Jacob was wrong in praying to the angel; the friends of Job were wrong in asking him to pray for them, though God commanded them to invoke Job's intercession; the Jews exiled in Babylon were wrong in asking their brethren in Jerusalem to pray for them; St. Paul was wrong in beseeching his friends to pray for him; then we are all wrong in praying for each other. You deem it useful and pious to ask your pastor to pray for you. Is it not, at least, equally useful for me to invoke the prayers of St. Paul, since I am convinced that he can hear me?

God forbid that our supplications to our Father in heaven should diminish in proportion as our prayers to the Saints increase; for, after all, we must remember that, while the Church declares it necessary for salvation to pray to God, she merely asserts that it is "good and useful to invoke the saints." [17] To ask the prayers of the saints, far from being useless, is most profitable. By invoking their intercession, instead of one we have many praying for us. To our own tepid petitions we unite the fervent

[16] I. Tim. ii. 5.
[17] Council of Trent, Sess. xxv.

supplications of the blessed and "the Lord will hear the prayers of the just." [18] To the petitions of us, poor pilgrims in this vale of tears, are united those of the citizens of heaven. We ask them to pray to their God and to our God, to their Father and to our Father, that we may one day share their delights in that blessed country in company with our common Redeemer, Jesus Christ, with whom to live is to reign.

[18] Prov. xv. 20.

CHAPTER XIV

IS IT LAWFUL TO HONOR THE BLESSED VIRGIN MARY AS A SAINT, TO INVOKE HER AS AN INTERCESSOR, AND TO IMITATE HER AS A MODEL

I

IS IT LAWFUL TO HONOR HER?

THE sincere adorers and lovers of our Lord Jesus Christ look with reverence on every object with which He was associated, and they conceive an affection for every person that was near and dear to Him on earth. The closer the intimacy of those persons with our Savior, the holier do they appear in our estimation, just as those planets which revolve the nearest around the sun partake most of its light and heat.

There is something hallowed to the eye of the Christian in the very soil of Judea, because it was pressed by the footprints of our Blessed Redeemer. With what reverent steps we would enter the cave of Bethlehem because *there* was born the Savior of the world. With what religious demeanor we would tread the streets of Nazareth when we remembered that *there* were spent the days of His boyhood. What profound religious awe would fill our hearts on ascending Mount Calvary, where He paid by his blood the ransom of our souls.

But if the *lifeless* soil claims so much reverence, how much more veneration would be enkindled in our hearts for the *living* persons who were the friends and associates of our Savior on earth! We know that He exercised a certain salutary and magnetic influence on those whom He approached. "All the multitude sought to touch Him, for virtue went out from Him and healed all,"[1] as happened to the woman who had been troubled with an issue of blood.[2]

We would seem, indeed, to draw near to Jesus, if we had the happiness of only conversing with the Samaritan woman, or of eating at the table of Zaccheus, or of being entertained by Nicodemus. But if we were admitted into the inner circle of His friends—of Lazarus, Mary and Martha for instance—the Baptist or the Apostles, we would be conscious that in their company we were drawing still nearer to Jesus and imbibing somewhat of that spirit which they must have largely received from their familiar relations with Him.

Now, if the land of Judea is looked upon as hallowed ground because Jesus dwelt there; if the Apostles were considered as models of holiness because they were the chosen companions and pupils of our Lord in His latter years, how peerless must have been the sanctity of Mary, who gave Him birth, whose breast was His pillow, who nursed and clothed Him in infancy, who guided His early steps, who accompanied Him in His exile to Egypt and back, who abode with Him from infancy to boyhood, from boyhood to manhood, who during all that time listened to the words of wisdom which fell from His lips, who was the first to embrace Him at His birth, and the last to receive His dying breath on Calvary. This sentiment is so natural to us that we find it bursting forth spontaneously from the lips of the woman of the Gospel, who, hearing the words of Jesus full of wisdom and sanctity, lifted up her voice and said to Him: "Blessed is the womb that bore Thee and the paps that gave Thee suck."

It is in accordance with the economy of Divine Providence that, whenever God designs any person for some important work, He bestows on that person the graces and dispositions necessary for faithfully discharging it.

[1] Luke vi. 19. [2] Matt. ix. 20.

When Moses was called by heaven to be the leader of the Hebrew people he hesitated to assume the formidable office on the plea of "impediment and slowness of tongue." But Jehovah reassured him by promising to qualify him for the sublime functions assigned to him: "I will be in thy mouth, and I will teach thee what thou shalt speak." [3]

The Prophet Jeremiah was sanctified from his very birth because he was destined to be the herald of God's law to the children of Israel: "Before I formed thee in the bowels of thy mother I knew thee, and before thou camest forth out of the womb I sanctified thee." [4]

"Elizabeth was filled with the Holy Ghost," [5] that she might be worthy to be the hostess of our Lord during the three months that Mary dwelt under her roof.

John the Baptist was "filled with the Holy Ghost even from his mother's womb." [6] "He was a burning and a shining light" [7] because he was chosen to prepare the way of the Lord.

The Apostles received the plenitude of grace; they were endowed with the gift of tongue and other privileges[8] before they commenced the work of the ministry. Hence St. Paul says: "Our sufficiency is from God, who hath made us *fit* ministers of the New Testament." [9]

Now of all who have participated in the ministry of the Redemption there is none who filled any position so exalted, so sacred, as is the incommunicable office of Mother of Jesus; and there is no one, consequently, that *needed* so high a degree of holiness as she did.

For, if God thus sanctified His Prophets and Apostles as being destined to be the bearers of the Word of life, how much more sanctified must Mary have been, who was to bear the Lord and "Author of life." [10] If John was so holy because he was chosen as the pioneer to prepare the way of the Lord, how much more holy was she who ushered Him into the world. If holiness became John's mother, surely a greater holiness became the mother

---

[3] Exod. iv. 12.   [4] Jer. i. 5.   [5] Luke i. 41.   [6] Ibid. i. 15.
[7] John v. 35.   [8] Acts ii.   [9] II. Cor. iii. 6.   [10] Acts iii. 15.

of John's Master. If God said to His Priests of old: "Be ye clean, you that carry the vessels of the Lord;" [11] nay, if the vessels themselves used in the divine service and churches are set apart by special consecration, we cannot conceive Mary to have been ever profaned by sin, who was the chosen vessel of election, even the Mother of God.

When we call the Blessed Virgin the Mother of God, we assert our belief in two things: First—That her Son, Jesus Christ, is true man, else she were not a *mother*. Second—That He is true God, else she were not the *Mother of God*. In other words, we affirm that the Second Person of the Blessed Trinity, the Word of God, who in His divine nature is from all eternity begotten of the Father, consubstantial with Him, was in the fulness of time again begotten, by being born of the Virgin, thus taking to Himself, from her maternal womb, a human nature of the same substance with hers.

But it may be said the Blessed Virgin is not the Mother of the Divinity. She had not, and she could not have, any part in the generation of the Word of God, for that generation is eternal; her maternity is temporal. He is her Creator; she is His creature. Style her, if you will, the Mother of the man Jesus or even of the human nature of the Son of God, but not the Mother of God.

I shall answer this objection by putting a question. Did the mother who bore us have any part in the production of our *soul?* Was not this nobler part of our being the work of God alone? And yet who would for a moment dream of saying "the mother of my body," and not *"my* mother?"

The comparison teaches us that the terms parent and child, mother and son, refer to the persons and not to the parts or elements of which the persons are composed. Hence no one says: "The mother of my *body,*" "the mother of my *soul;*" but in all propriety "my mother," the mother of me who live and breathe, think and act, *one* in my personality, though uniting in it a soul directly created by God, and a material body directly derived from the maternal womb. In like manner, as far as the

[11] Isaiah iii. 11.

sublime mystery of the Incarnation can be reflected in the natural order, the Blessed Virgin, under the overshadowing of the Holy Ghost, by communicating to the Second Person of the Adorable Trinity, as mothers do, a true human nature of the same substance with her own, is thereby really and truly His Mother.

It is in this sense that the title of *Mother of God*, denied by Nestorius, was vindicated to her by the General Council of Ephesus, in 431; in this sense, and in no other, has the Church called her by that title.

Hence, by immediate and necessary consequence, follow her surpassing dignity and excellence, and her special relationship and affinity, not only with her Divine Son, but also with the Father and the Holy Ghost.

Mary, as Wordsworth beautifully expressed it, united in her person "a mother's love with maiden purity." The Church teaches us that she was always a Virgin—a Virgin before her espousals, during her married life and after her spouse's death. "The Angel Gabriel was sent from God . . . to a Virgin espoused to a man whose name was Joseph, . . . and the Virgin's name was Mary." [12]

That she remained a Virgin till after the birth of Jesus is expressly stated in the Gospel.[13] It is not less certain that she continued in the same state during the remainder of her days; for in the Apostles' and the Nicene Creed she is called a Virgin, and that epithet cannot be restricted to the time of our Saviour's birth. It must be referred to her whole life, inasmuch as both creeds were compiled long after she had passed away.

The Canon of the Mass, which is very probably of Apostolic antiquity, speaks of her as the "glorious *ever Virgin*," and in this sentiment all Catholic tradition concurs.

There is a propriety which suggests itself to every Christian in Mary's remaining a Virgin after the birth of Jesus, for, as Bishop Bull of the Protestant Episcopal Church of England re-

[12] Luke i. 26, 27.
[13] Matt. i. 25.

marks, "It cannot with decency be imagined that the most holy vessel which was once consecrated to be a receptacle of the Deity should be afterwards desecrated and profaned by human use." The learned Grotius, Calvin and other eminent Protestant writers hold the same view.

The doctrine of the perpetual virginity of Mary is now combated by Protestants, as it was in the early days of the Church by Helvidius and Jovinian, on the following grounds:

First—The Evangelist says that "Joseph took unto him his wife, and he knew her not *till* she brought forth her first-born son." [14] This sentence suggests to dissenters that other children besides Jesus were born to Mary. But the qualifying word *till* by no means implies that the chaste union which had subsisted between Mary and Joseph up to the birth of our Lord was subsequently altered. The Protestant Hooker justly complains of the early heretics as having "abused greatly these words of Matthew, gathering against the honor of the Blessed Virgin, that a thing denied with special circumstance doth import an opposite affirmation when once that circumstance is expired." [15] To express Hooker's idea in plainer words, when a thing is said not to have occurred until another event had happened, it does not necessarily follow that it did occur after that event took place.

The Scripture says that the raven went forth from the ark, "and did not return *till* the waters were dried up upon the earth" [16]—that is, it never returned. "Samuel saw Saul no more *till* the day of his death." [17] He did not, of course, see him after death. "The Lord said to my Lord: Sit thou at my right hand *until* I make thy enemies thy footstool." [18] These words apply to our Savior, who did not cease to sit at the right of God after His enemies were subdued.

Second—But Jesus is called Mary's *first-born* Son, and does not a first-born always imply the subsequent birth of other children to the same mother? By no means; for the name of first-born was given to the first son of every Jewish mother, whether

[14] Matt. i. 25.   [15] Book V., ch. xlv.   [16] Gen. viii. 7.
[17] Kings xv. 35.   [18] Ps. cix.

other children followed or not. We find this epithet applied to Machir, for instance, who was the only son of Manasses.[19]

Third—But is not mention frequently made of the brethren of Jesus?[20] Fortunately the Gospels themselves will enable us to trace the maternity of those who are called His brothers, not to the Blessed Virgin, but to another Mary. St. Matthew mentions, by name, James and Joseph among the brethren of Jesus;[21] and the same Evangelist and also St. Mark tell us that among those who were present at the Crucifixion were Mary Magdalen and Mary the mother of James and Joseph.[22] And St. John, who narrates with more detail the circumstances of the Crucifixion, informs us who this second Mary was, for he says that there stood by the cross of Jesus His mother and His Mother's sister, Mary of Cleophas, and Mary Magdalen.[23] There is no doubt that Mary of Cleophas is identical with Mary, who is called by Matthew and Mark the mother of James and Joseph. And as Mary of Cleophas was the kinswoman of the Blessed Virgin, James and Joseph are called the brothers of Jesus, in conformity with the Hebrew practice of giving that appellation to cousins or near relations. Abraham, for instance, was the uncle of Lot, yet he calls him brother.[24]

Mary is exalted above all other women, not only because she united "a mother's love with maiden purity," but also because she was conceived without original sin. The dogma of the Immaculate Conception is thus expressed by the Church: "We define that the Blessed Virgin Mary in the first moment of her conception, by the singular grace and privilege of Almighty God, in virtue of the merits of Jesus Christ, the Savior of the human race, was preserved free from every stain of original sin."[25]

Unlike the rest of the children of Adam, the soul of Mary was never subject to sin, even in the first moment of its infusion into the body. She alone was exempt from the original taint. This im-

---

[19] Josue xvii. 1.   [20] Matt. xii. 46; xiii. 55, 56.
[21] Ibid.   [22] Matt. xxvii.; Mark xv.   [23] John xix. 25.
[24] Gen. xiii. 8.   [25] Bulla Dogmat. Pii Papæ IX.

munity of Mary from original sin is exclusively due to the merits of Christ, as the Church expressly declares. She needed a Redeemer as well as the rest of the human race and therefore was "redeemed, but in a more sublime manner." [26] Mary is as much indebted to the precious blood of Jesus for having been *preserved* as we are for having been *cleansed* from original sin.

Although the Immaculate Conception was not formulated into a dogma of faith till 1854, it is at least implied in Holy Scripture. It is in strict harmony with the place which Mary holds in the economy of Redemption, and has virtually received the pious assent of the faithful from the earliest days of the Church.

In Genesis we read: "I will put enmities between thee and the woman, and thy seed and her seed; she shall crush thy head." [27] All Catholic commentators, ancient and modern, recognize in the Seed, the Woman and the serpent types of our Savior, of Mary and the devil. God here declares that the enmity of the Seed and that of the Woman toward the tempter were to be identical. Now the enmity of Christ, or the Seed, toward the evil one was absolute and perpetual. Therefore the enmity of Mary, or the Woman, toward the devil never admitted of any momentary reconciliation which would have existed if she were ever subject to original sin.

It is worthy of note that as three characters appear on the scene of our fall—Adam, Eve and the rebellious Angel—so three corresponding personages figure in our redemption—Jesus Christ, who is the second Adam;[28] Mary, the second Eve, and the Archangel Gabriel. The second Adam was immeasurably superior to the first, Gabriel was superior to the fallen Angel, and hence we are warranted by analogy to conclude that Mary was superior to Eve. But if she had been created in original sin, instead of being superior, she would be inferior to Eve, who was certainly created immaculate. We cannot conceive that the mother of Cain was created superior to the mother of Jesus. It would have been unworthy of a God of infinite purity to have been born of a woman that was even for an instant under the dominion of Satan.

[26] Ibid.   [27] Gen. iii. 15.   [28] Cor. xv. 45.

The liturgies of the Church, being the established formularies of her public worship, are among the most authoritative documents that can be adduced in favor of any religious practice.

In the liturgy ascribed to St. James, Mary is commemorated as "our most holy, immaculate and most glorious Lady, Mother of God and ever Virgin Mary." [29]

In the Maronite Ritual she is invoked as "our holy, praiseworthy and immaculate Lady." [30]

In the Alexandrian liturgy of St. Basil, she is addressed as "most holy, most glorious, immaculate." [31]

The Feast of Mary's Conception commenced to be celebrated in the East in the fifth, and in the West in the seventh centuries. It was not introduced into Rome till probably towards the end of the fourteenth century. Though Rome is always the first that is called on to sanction a new festival, she is often the last to take part in it. She is the first that is expected to give the keynote, but frequently the last to join in the festive song. While she is silent, the notes are faint and uncertain; when her voice joins in the chant, the song of praise becomes constant and universal.

It is scarcely necessary for me to add that the introduction of the festival of the Conception after the lapse of so many centuries from the foundation of Christianity no more implies a novelty of doctrine than the erection of a monument in 1875 to Arminius, the German hero who flourished in the first century, would be an evidence of his recent exploits. The Feast of the Blessed Trinity was not introduced till the fifth century, though it commemorates a fundamental mystery of the Christian religion.

It is interesting to us to know that the Immaculate Conception of Mary has been interwoven in the earliest history of our own country. The ship that first bore Columbus to America was named Mary of the Conception. This celebrated navigator gave the same name to the second island which he discovered. The first chapel erected in Quebec, when that city was founded in the

---

[29] Bibliotheca Max. Patrum, t. 2, p. 3.
[30] De sac ordinat., p. 313.
[31] Renaudot. Lit. Orient.

early part of the seventeenth century was dedicated to God under the invocation of Mary Immaculate.

In view of these three great prerogatives of Mary—her divine maternity, her perpetual virginity and her Immaculate Conception—we are prepared to find her blessedness often and expressly declared in Holy Scripture.

The Archangel Gabriel is sent to her from heaven to announce to her the happy tidings that she was destined to be the mother of the world's Redeemer. No greater favor was ever before or since conferred on woman, whether we consider the dignity of the messenger, or the momentous character of the message, or the terms of respect in which it is conveyed.

"The Angel Gabriel was sent from God into a city of Galilee called Nazareth to a virgin . . . and the virgin's name was Mary. And the Angel being come in said unto her: Hail, full of grace, the Lord is with thee; blessed art thou among women. Who, having heard, was troubled at his saying and thought with herself what manner of salutation this should be. And the Angel said to her: Fear not, Mary, for thou hast found grace with God. Behold, thou shalt conceive in thy womb, and shalt bring forth a son, and thou shalt call his name Jesus. . . . The Holy Ghost shall come upon thee, and the power of the most high shall overshadow thee, and therefore, also, the Holy which shall be born of thee shall be called the Son of God." [32] The Almighty does not send to Mary, a prophet or priest, or any other earthly ambassador, nor even one of the lower choirs of angels, but He commissions an Archangel to confer with her.

"Hail full of grace!" Gabriel does not congratulate her on her personal charms, though she is the fairest daughter of Israel. He does not praise her for her exalted ancestry, though she is descended from the Kings of Juda. But he commends her because she is the chosen child of benediction. He admires the hidden virtues of her soul, brighter than the sun, fairer than the moon, purer than angels, he sees before him,

"Our tainted nature's solitary boast,"

[32] Luke i. 26-35.

one that alone escaped the taint of Adam's disobedience. As the precious diamond reflects various colors according as it is exposed to the sun's rays, so did the soul of Mary, from the moment that the "Sun of Justice" shone upon her, exhibit every grace that was prompted by the occasion.

St. Stephen and the Apostles were also said to be full of the Spirit of God. By this, however, we are not to understand that the same measure of grace was imparted to them which was given to Mary. On each one it is bestowed according to his merits and needs. "One is the glory of the sun, another the glory of the moon, and another the glory of the stars, for star differeth from star in glory;"[33] and as Mary's office of Mother of God immeasurably surpassed in dignity that of the proto-martyr and of the Apostles, so did her grace superabound over theirs.

"The Lord is with thee." "He exists in His creatures in different ways; in those that are endowed with reason in one way, in irrational creatures in another. His irrational creatures have no means of apprehending or possessing Him. All rational creatures may indeed apprehend Him by knowledge, but only the good by love. Only in the good does He so exist as to be with them as well as in them; with them by a certain harmony and agreement of will, and in this way God is with all His Saints. But He is with Mary in a yet more special manner, for in her there was so great an agreement and union with God that not her will only, but her very flesh was to be united to him."[34]

"Blessed art Thou among women." The same expression is applied to two other women in the Holy Scripture—viz., to Jahel and Judith. The former was called blessed after she had slain Sisara,[35] and the latter after she had slain Holofernes,[36] both of whom had been enemies of God's people. In this respect these two women are true types of Mary, who was chosen by God to crush the head of the serpent, the infernal enemy of mankind. And if they deserved the title of blessed for being the instruments of God in rescuing Israel from temporal calamities, how

---

[33] I. Cor. xv. 41.
[35] Judges, v.

[34] St. Bernard.
[36] Judith, xiii.

much more does Mary merit that appellation, who co-operated so actively in the salvation of the human race!

The Evangelist proceeds: "And Mary, rising up in those days, went . . . into a city of Juda; and she entered into the house of Zachary and saluted Elizabeth. And it came to pass that when Elizabeth heard the salutation of Mary the infant leapt in her womb. And Elizabeth was filled with the Holy Ghost, and she cried out with a loud voice and said: Blessed art thou among women, and blessed is the fruit of thy womb. And whence is this to me that the mother of my Lord should come to me? For behold, as soon as the voice of thy salutation sounded in my ears, the infant in my womb leaped for joy. And blessed art thou that hast believed, because those things shall be accomplished that were spoken to thee by the Lord." [37]

There is joy in Mary's heart in being chosen to become the mother of the world's Redeemer. She wishes by her visit to communicate that joy to her cousin. The Sun of Justice is shining within her. She desires to diffuse His rays through Elizabeth's household. She is laden with spiritual treasures. She must share them with her kinswoman, especially as she is none the poorer in making others richer.

The usual order of salutation is here reversed. Age pays reverence to youth. A lady who is revered by the whole community honors a lowly maiden. An inspired matron expresses her astonishment that her young kinswoman should deign to visit her. She extols Mary's faith and calls her blessed. She blends the praise of Mary with the praise of Mary's Son, and even the infant John testifies his reverential joy by leaping in his mother's womb. And we are informed that during this interview Elizabeth was filled with the Holy Ghost, to remind us that the veneration she paid to her cousin was not prompted by her own feelings, but was dictated by the Spirit of God.

Then Mary breaks out into that sublime canticle, the Magnificat: "My soul doth magnify the Lord, and my spirit hath rejoiced in God my Savior, because He hath regarded the humility

[37] Luke i. 39-45.

of his handmaid, for behold from henceforth all generations shall call me blessed." [38] On these words I shall pause to make one reflection.

The Holy Ghost, through the organ of Mary's chaste lips, prophesies that all generations shall call her blessed, with evident approval of the praise she should receive.

What a daring prophecy is this! Among the wonderful predictions recorded in Holy Scripture, I can recall none that more strongly commands my admiration. Here is a modest, retiring maiden, living in an obscure village in a remote quarter of the civilized world, openly announcing that every age till the end of time, should pronounce her hallowed. We have no reason to question this prophecy, for it is recorded in the inspired pages of the Gospel. And we know also without the shadow of a doubt that the prophecy has been literally fulfilled. For, in every epoch, and in every Christian land from the rising to the setting sun, her *Magnificat* has daily resounded.

Now the Catholic is the only Church whose children, generation after generation, from the first to the present century, have pronounced her blessed; of all Christians in this land, they alone contribute to the fulfilment of the prophecy.

Therefore, it is only Catholics that earn the approval of Heaven by fulfilling the prediction of the Holy Ghost.

Protestants not only concede that we bless the name of Mary, but they even reproach us with being too lavish in our praises of her.

On the other hand, they are careful to exclude themselves from the "generations" that were destined to call her blessed, for, in speaking of her, they almost invariably withhold from her the title of *blessed,* preferring to call her *the Virgin,* or *Mary the Virgin,* or *the Mother of Jesus.* And while Protestant churches will resound with the praises of Sarah and Rebecca and Rachel, of Miriam and Ruth, of Esther and Judith of the Old Testament, and of Elizabeth and Anna, of Magdalen and Martha of the New, the name of Mary the Mother of Jesus is uttered with bated

[38] Luke i. 46-48.

breath, lest the sound of her name should make the preacher liable to the charge of superstition.

The piety of a mother usually sheds additional lustre on the son, and the halo that encircles her brow is reflected upon his. The more the mother is extolled, the greater honor redounds to the son. And if this is true of all men who do not choose their mothers, how much more strictly may it be affirmed of Him who chose His own Mother, and made her Himself such as He would have her, so that all the glories of His Mother are essentially His own. And yet we daily see ministers of the Gospel ignoring Mary's exalted virtues and unexampled privileges and parading her alleged imperfections; nay, sinfulness, as if her Son were dishonored by the piety, and took delight in the defamation of His Mother.

Such defamers might learn a lesson from one who made little profession of Christianity.

> "Is thy name Mary, maiden fair?
>   Such should, methinks, its music be.
> The sweetest name that mortals bear,
>   Were best befitting thee.
> And she to whom it once was given
> *Was half of earth and half of heaven.*" [39]

Once more the title of *blessed,* is given to Mary. On one occasion a certain woman, lifting up her voice, said to Jesus: "Blessed is the womb that bore thee and the paps that gave thee suck." [40] It is true that our Lord replied: "Yea, rather (or yea, likewise), blessed are they who hear the word of God and keep it." It would be an unwarrantable perversion of the sacred text to infer from this reply that Jesus intended to detract from the praise bestowed on His Mother. His words may be thus correctly paraphrased: She is blessed indeed in being the chosen instrument of My incarnation, but more blessed in keeping My word. Let others be comforted in knowing that though they cannot share with My Mother in the privilege of her maternity, they can participate

[39] Oliver W. Holmes.
[40] Luke xi. 27.

with her in the blessed reward of them who hear My word and keep it.

In the preceding passages we have seen Mary declared blessed on four different occasions, and hence, in proclaiming her blessedness, far from paying her unmerited honor, we are but re-echoing the Gospel verdict of saint and angel and of the Spirit of God Himself.

Wordsworth, though not nurtured within the bosom of the Catholic Church, conceives a true appreciation of Mary's incomparable holiness in the following beautiful lines:

> "Mother! whose virgin bosom was uncrossed
> With the least shade of thought to sin allied;
> Woman! above all women glorified,
> Our tainted nature's solitary boast;
> Purer than foam on central ocean tost,
> Brighter than eastern skies at daybreak strewn
> With fancied roses, than the unblemished moon
> Before her wane begins on heaven's blue coast,
> Thy image falls to earth. Yet some, I ween,
> Not unforgiven, the suppliant knee might bend
> As to a visible power, in which did blend
> All that was mixed and reconciled in thee
> Of mother's love with maiden purity,
> Of high with low, celestial with serene."

To honor one who has been the subject of divine, angelic and saintly panegyric is to use a privilege, and the privilege is heightened into a sacred duty when we remember that the spirit of prophecy foretold that she should ever be the unceasing theme of Christian eulogy as long as Christianity itself would exist.

"Honor he is worthy of, whom the king hath a mind to honor." [41] The King of kings hath honored Mary; His divine Son did not disdain to be subject to her, therefore should we honor her, especially as the honor we pay to her redounds to God, the source of all glory. The Royal Prophet, than whom no man paid higher praise to God, esteemed the friends of God worthy of all honor: "To me Thy friends, O God, are made exceedingly honorable." [42] Now the dearest friends of God are they

[41] Esther vi. 11.   [42] Ps. cxxxviii. (In Protestant version, Ps. cxxxix.)

who most faithfully keep His precepts: "You are My friends, if you do the things that I command you." [43] Who fulfilled the divine precepts better than Mary, who kept all the words of her Son, pondering them in her heart? "If any man minister to me," says our Savior, "him will My Father honor." [44] Who ministered more constantly to Jesus than Mary, who discharged towards Him all the offices of a tender mother?

Heroes and statesmen may receive the highest military and civic honors which a nation can bestow without being suspected of invading the domain of the glory which is due to God. Now is not heroic sanctity more worthy of admiration than civil service and military exploits, inasmuch as religion ranks higher than patriotism and valor? And yet the admirers of Mary's exalted virtues can scarcely celebrate her praises without being accused in certain quarters of Mariolatry.

When a nation wishes to celebrate the memory of its distinguished men its admiration is not confined to words, but vents itself in a thousand different shapes. See in how many ways we honor the memory of Washington. Monuments on which his good deeds are recorded are erected to his name. The grounds in which his remains repose on the banks of the Potomac are kept in order by a volunteer band of devoted ladies, who adorn the place with flowers. And this cherished spot is annually visited by thousands of pilgrims from the most remote sections of the country. These visitors will eagerly snatch a flower or a leaf from a shrub growing near Washington's tomb, or will strive even to clip off a little shred from one of his garments, still preserved in the old mansion, to bear home with them as precious relics.

I have always observed when traveling on the missions up and down the Potomac, that whenever the steamer came to the point opposite Mount Vernon the bell was tolled, and every eye was directed toward Washington's grave.

The 22nd of February, Washington's birthday, is kept as a national holiday, at least in certain portions of the country. I well remember that formerly military and fire companies paraded

[43] John xv. 14.   [44] John xii. 26.

the streets, and that patriotic speeches recounting the heroic deeds of the first President were delivered, the festivities of the day closing with a social banquet.

As the citizens of the United States manifest in divers ways their admiration for Washington, so do the citizens of the republic of the Church love to exhibit in corresponding forms their veneration for the Mother of Jesus.

Monuments and statues are erected to her. Thrice each day— at morn, noon and even—the Angelus bells are rung, to recall to our mind the Incarnation of our Lord, and the participation of Mary in this great mystery of love.

Her shrines are tastefully adorned by pious hands and visited by devoted children, who wear her relics or any object which bears her image, or which is associated with her name.

Her natal day and other days of the year, sacred to her memory, are appropriately commemorated by processions, by participation in the banquet of the Eucharist, and by sermons enlarging on her virtues and prerogatives.

As no one was ever suspected of loving his country and her institutions less because of his revering Washington, so no one can reasonably suppose that our homage to God is diminished by our fostering reverence for Mary. As our object in eulogizing Washington is not so much to honor the man as to vindicate those principles of which he was the champion and exponent, and to express our gratitude to God for the blessings bestowed on our country through him, even so our motive in commemorating Mary's name is not merely to praise her, but still more to keep us in perpetual remembrance of our Lord's Incarnation, and to show our thankfulness to Him for the blessings wrought through that great mystery in which she was so prominent a figure. There is not a grain of incense offered to Mary which does not ascend to the throne of God Himself.

Experience sufficiently demonstrates that the better we understand the part which Mary has taken in the work of redemption, the more enlightened becomes our knowledge of our Redeemer Himself, and that the greater our love for her, the deeper and

broader is our devotion to Him; while experience also testifies
that our Savior's attributes become more confused and warped
in the minds of a people in proportion as they ignore Mary's
relations to Him.

The defender of a beleaguered citadel concentrates his forces
on the outer fortifications and towers, knowing well that the
capture of these outworks would endanger the citadel itself, and
that *their* safety involves *its* security.

Jesus Christ is the citadel of our faith, the stronghold of our
soul's affections. Mary is called the "Tower of David," and the
gate of Sion which the Lord loveth more than all the tabernacles
of Jacob,[45] and which He entered at His Incarnation.

So intimately is this living gate of Sion connected with Jesus,
the Temple of our faith, that no one has ever assailed the former
without invading the latter. The Nestorian would have Mary
to be only an ordinary mother because he would have Christ to
be a mere man.

Hence, if we rush to the defence of the gate of Sion, it is because we are more zealous for the city of God. If we stand as
sentinels around the tower of David, it is because we are more
earnest in protecting Jerusalem from invasion. If we forbid profane hands to touch the ark of the covenant, it is because we are
anxious to guard from profanation the Lord of the ark. If we
are so solicitous about Mary's honor, it is because "the love of
Christ" presseth us. If we will not permit a single wreath to be
snatched from her fair brow, it is because we are unwilling that
a single feature of Christ's sacred humanity should be obscured,
and because we wish that He should ever shine forth in all the
splendor of His glory, and clothed in all the panoply of His
perfections.

But you will ask: Why do you so often blend together the
worship of God and the veneration of the Blessed Virgin? Why
such exclamations as *Blessed be Jesus and Mary?* Why do you
so often repeat in succession the Lord's prayer and the Angelical
salutation? Is not this practice calculated to level all distinctions

[45] Ps. lxxxvi.

between the Creator and His creature, and to excite the displeasure of a God ever jealous of His glory?

Those who make this objection should remember that the praises of the Lord and His Saints are frequently combined in Holy Scripture itself.

Witness Judith. On returning from the tent of Holofernes, she sang: *"Praise ye the Lord, our God,* who hath not forsaken them that hope in Him, *and by me His handmaid,* He hath fulfilled His mercy which He promised to the house of Israel. . . . And Ozias, the prince of the people of Israel, said to her: *Blessed art thou, O daughter,* by the Lord the Most High God, above all women upon the earth, *Blessed be the Lord* who made heaven and earth . . . because He hath so magnified thy name this day, that thy praise shall not depart out of the mouth of men." [46]

Witness Ecclesiasticus. After glorifying God for His mighty works, he immediately sounds the praises of Enoch and Noe, of Abraham, Isaac and Jacob, of Moses and Aaron, of Samuel and Nathan, of David and Josias, of Isaiah and Jeremiah, and other kings and prophets of Israel.[47]

Elizabeth, in the same breath, exclaims: "Blessed art thou among women, and blessed is the fruit of thy womb." [48]

And Mary herself, under the inspiration of Heaven, cries out: "My soul *doth magnify the Lord,* and my spirit hath rejoiced in God my Savior. . . . For, behold from henceforth all generations *shall call me blessed."* [49]

Here are the names of Creator and creature interwoven like threads of gold and silver in the same woof, without provoking the jealousy of God.

God jealous of the honor paid to Mary! Will a father be jealous of the honor paid to his child, especially of a child who reflects his own image and likeness, and exhibits those virtues which he had inculcated on her tender mind? And is not Mary God's child of predilection? Will an architect be envious of the praise bestowed on a magnificent temple which his genius planned and

---

[46] Judith xiii.
[48] Luke i.

[47] Eccles. xliii. *et seq.*
[49] Ibid.

reared? Is not the living temple of Mary's heart the work of the Supreme Architect? Must she not say with all of God's creatures: "Thy hands (O Lord) have made me and formed me." Is it not He who has adorned that living temple with those rare beauties which we so much admire? Has she not declared so when she exclaimed: "He that is mighty hath done great things to me, and holy is His name!" [50]

God jealous of the honor paid to Mary! As well might we imagine that the sun, if endowed with intelligence, would be jealous of the mellow, golden cloud which encircles him, which reflects his brightness and presents in bolder light his inaccessible splendor. As well imagine that the same luminary would be jealous of our admiration for the beautiful rose, whose opening petals and rich color and delicious fragrance are the fruit of his beneficent rays.

Hence in uniting Mary's praise with that of Jesus we are strictly imitating the sacred Text. We are imitating Joachim, the High Priest, and the people of God in Bethulia, who unite the praises of Judith with the praises of Jehovah.

We are imitating the sacred writer of Ecclesiasticus who, after extolling God for His mighty works, sounds the praises of Enoch and Noe, of Abraham, Isaac and Jacob, of David and Josiah, of Isaiah and Jeremiah, and other Kings and Prophets of Israel.

We are imitating Elizabeth, who exclaimed in one breath: "Blessed art thou (Mary) among women and blessed is (Jesus) the fruit of thy womb."

And as no one ever suspected that the encomiums pronounced on Judith and the virtuous Kings and Prophets of Israel detracted from God's honor, so neither do we lessen His glory in exalting the Blessed Virgin. I find Jesus and Mary together at the manger, together in Egypt, together in Nazareth, together in the temple, together at the cross. I find their names side by side in the Apostles' and the Nicene Creed. It is fitting that both should find a place in my heart, and that both names should

[50] Luke i. 49.

often flow successively from my lips. Inseparable in life and in death, they should not be divorced in my prayer. "What God hath joined together, let not man put asunder."

II

IS IT LAWFUL TO INVOKE HER?

The Church exhorts her children not only to honor the Blessed Virgin, but also to invoke her intercession. It is evident from Scripture that the Angels and Saints in heaven can hear our prayers and that they have the power and the will to help us.[51] Now, if the angels are conversant with what happens on earth; if the Prophets, even while clothed in the flesh, had a clear vision of things which were transpiring at a great distance from them; if they could penetrate into the future and foretell events which were then hidden in the womb of time, shall we believe that God withholds a knowledge of our prayers from Mary, who is justly styled the Queen of Angels and Saints? For, as Mary's sanctity surpasses that of all other mortals, her knowledge must be proportionately greater than theirs, since knowledge constitutes one of the sources of celestial bliss.

If Stephen, while his soul was still in the prison of the body, "*saw* the glory of God, and Jesus standing on the right hand of God;"[52] if Paul "*heard* secret words"[53] spoken in paradise, is it surprising that Mary hears and sees us, now that she is elevated to heaven and stands "face to face" before God, the perfect Mirror of all knowledge? It is as easy for God to enable His Saints to see things terrestrial from heaven as things celestial from earth.

The influence of Mary's intercession exceeds that of the angels, patriarchs and prophets in the same degree that her sanctity surpasses theirs. If our heavenly Father listens so propitiously to the voice of His servants, what will He refuse to her who is His chosen daughter of predilection, chosen among thousands to be

[51] Gen. xlviii. 16; Tobias xii. 12; Luke xv. 10; Zach. i. 12, 13.
[52] Acts vii. 55.   [53] II. Cor. xii. 4.

the Mother of His beloved Son? If we ourselves, though sinners, can help one another by our prayers, how irresistible must be the intercession of Mary, who never grieved Almighty God by sin, who never tarnished her white robe of innocence by the least defilement, from the first moment of her existence till she was received by triumphant angels into heaven.

In speaking of the patronage of the Blessed Virgin, we must never lose sight of her title of Mother of our Redeemer nor of the great privileges which that prerogative implies. Mary was the Mother of Jesus. She exercised toward Him all the influence that a prudent mother has over an affectionate child. "Jesus," says the Gospel, "was subject to them," [54] that is, to Mary and Joseph. We find this obedience of our Lord toward His Mother forcibly exemplified at the marriage feast of Cana. Her wishes are delicately expressed in these words: "They have no wine." He instantly obeys her by changing water into wine, though the time for exercising His public ministry and for working wonders had not yet arrived.

Now, Mary has never forfeited in heaven the title of Mother of Jesus. She is still His Mother, and while adoring Him as her God she still retains her maternal relations, and He exercises toward her that loving willingness to grant her request which the best of sons entertains for the best of mothers.

Never does Jesus appear to us so amiable and endearing as when we see Him nestled in the arms of His Mother. We love to contemplate Him, and artists love to represent Him, in that situation. It appears to me that had we lived in Jerusalem in His day and recognized, like Simeon, the Lord of majesty in the form of an Infant, and had we a favor to ask Him, we would present it through Mary's hands while the Divine eyes of the Babe were gazing on her sweet countenance. And even so now. Never will our prayers find a readier acceptance than when offered through her.

In invoking Our Lady's patronage we are actuated by a triple sense of the majesty of God, our own unworthiness and of

[54] Luke ii. 51.

Mary's incomparable influence with her Heavenly Father. Conscious of our natural lowliness and sins, we have frequent recourse to her intercession in the assured hope of being more favorably heard.

> "And even as children who have much offended
> A too indulgent father, in great shame,
> Penitent, and yet not daring unattended
> To go into his presence, at the gate
> Speak to their sister and confiding wait
> Till she goes in before and intercedes;
> So men, repenting of their evil deeds,
> And yet not venturing rashly to draw near
> With their requests, an angry Father's ear,
> Offer to her their prayers and their confession,
> And she in heaven for them makes intercession." [55]

Do you ask me, is Mary willing to assist you? Does she really take an interest in your welfare? Or is she so much absorbed by the fruition of God as to be indifferent to our miseries? "Can a woman forget her infant so as not to have pity on the fruit of her womb?" [56] Even so Mary will not forget us.

The love she bears us, her children by adoption, can be estimated only by her love for her Son by nature. It was Mary that nursed the Infant Savior. It was her hands that clothed Him. It was her breast that sheltered Him from the rude storm and from the persecution of Herod. She it was that wiped the stains from His brow when taken down from the cross. Now we are the brothers of Jesus. He is not ashamed, says the Apostle, to call us His brethren.[57] Neither is Mary ashamed to call us her children by adoption. At the foot of the cross she adopted us in the person of St. John. She is anxious to minister to our souls as she ministered to the corporal wants of her Son. She would be the instrument of God in feeding us with Divine grace, in clothing us with the garments of innocence, in sheltering us from the storms of temptations, in wiping away the stains of sin from our soul.

[55] Longfellow's "Golden Legend."
[56] Isaiah xlix. 15.   [57] Heb. ii. 11.

If the angels, though of a different nature from ours, have so much sympathy for us as to rejoice in our conversion,[58] how great must be the interest manifested toward us by Mary, who is of a common nature with us, descended from the same primitive parents, being bone of our bone, and flesh of our flesh, and who once trod the thorny path of life that we now tread!

Though not of the household of the faith, Edgar A. Poe did not disdain to invoke Our Lady's intercession, and to acknowledge the influence of her patronage in heaven.

"At morn—at noon—at twilight dim—
Maria! thou hast heard my hymn;
In joy and woe—in good and ill—
Mother of God, be with me still!
When the hours flew brightly by,
And not a cloud obscured the sky,
My soul, lest it should truant be,
Thy grace did guide to thine and thee;
Now, when storms of fate o'ercast
Darkly my present and my past,
Let my future radiant shine,
With sweet hopes of thee and thine."

Some persons not only object to the invocation of Mary as being unprofitable, but they even affect to be scandalized at the confidence we repose in her intercession, on the groundless assumption that by praying to her we ignore and dishonor God, and that we put the creature on a level with the Creator.

Every Catholic child knows from the catechism that to give to any creature the supreme honor due to God alone is idolatry. How can we be said to dishonor God, or bring Him down to a level with His creature by invoking Mary, since we acknowledge her to be a pure creature indebted like ourselves to Him for every gift and influence that she possesses? This is implied in the very form of our petitions.

When we address our prayers to her we say: *Pray for us sinners,* implying by these words that she herself is a petitioner at the throne of Divine mercy. To God we say: *Give us our daily*

[58] Luke xv. 7.

bread, thereby acknowledging Him to be the source of all bounty.
This principle being kept in view, how can we be justly ac-
cused of slighting God's majesty by invoking the intercession of
His handmaid?

If a beggar asks and receives alms from me through my servant, should I be offended at the blessings which he invokes upon
her? Far from it. I accept them as intended for myself, because
she bestowed what was mine, and with my consent.

Our Lord says to His Apostles: "I dispose to you a kingdom,
that you may eat and drink at My table in My kingdom and may
sit upon thrones, judging the twelve tribes of Israel." [59] And St.
Paul says: "Know you not that we shall judge angels, how much
more things of this world?" [60] If the Apostles may sit at the table
of the Lord in heaven without prejudice to His majesty, surely
Our Lady can stand as an advocate before Him without infringing on His rights. If they can exercise the dread prerogative of
judges of angels and of men without trespassing on the Divine
judgeship of Jesus, surely Mary can fulfil the more modest function of intercessor with her Son without intruding on His supreme mediatorship, for higher is the office of judge than that
of advocate. And yet, while no one is ever startled at the power
given to the Apostles, many are impatient of the lesser privilege
claimed for Mary.

III

IS IT LAWFUL TO IMITATE HER AS A MODEL?

But while the exalted privileges of Mary render her worthy of
our veneration, while her saintly influence renders her worthy
of our invocation, her personal life is constantly held up to us as
a pattern worthy of our imitation. If she occupies so prominent a
place in our pulpits, this prominence is less due to her prerogatives as a mother, or to her intercession as a patroness, than to
her example as a Saint.

[59] Luke xxii. 29, 30.   [60] I. Cor. vi.

After our Lord Jesus Christ, no one has ever exercised so salutary and so dominant an influence as the Blessed Virgin on society, on the family and on the individual.

The Mother of Jesus exercises throughout the Christian commonwealth that hallowing influence which a good mother wields over the Christian family.

What temple or chapel, how rude soever it may be, is not adorned with a painting or a statue of the Madonna? What house is not embellished with an image of Mary? What Catholic child is a stranger to her familiar face?

The priest and the layman, the scholar and the illiterate, the prince and the peasant, the mother and the maid, acknowledge her benign sway.

And if Christianity is so fruitful in comparison with Paganism, in conjugal fidelity, in female purity and in the respect paid to womanhood, these blessings are in no small measure due to the force of Mary's all-pervading influence and example. Ever since the Son of God chose a woman to be His mother man looks up to woman with a homage akin to veneration.

The poet Longfellow pays the following tribute to Mary's sanctifying influence:

"This is indeed the blessed Mary's land,
Virgin and mother of our dear Redeemer!
All hearts are touched and softened at her name
Alike the bandit with the bloody hand,
The priest, the prince, the scholar and the peasant
The man of deeds, the visionary dreamer
Pay homage to her as one ever present!

And if our faith had given us nothing more
Than this example of all womanhood,
So mild, so merciful, so strong, so good,
So patient, peaceful, loyal, loving, pure,
This were enough to prove it higher and truer
Than all the creeds the world had known before." [61]

St. Ambrose gives us the following beautiful picture of Mary's life before her espousals: "Let the life," he says, "of the Blessed

[61] Longfellow's "Golden Legend."

Mary be ever present to you in which, as in a mirror, the beauty of chastity and the form of virtue shine forth. She was a virgin not only in body, but in mind, who never sullied the pure affection of her heart by unworthy feelings. She was humble of heart, serious in her conversation, fonder of reading than of speaking. She placed her confidence rather in the prayer of the poor than in the uncertain riches of this world. She was ever intent on her occupation, . . . and accustomed to make God rather than man the witness of her thoughts. She injured no one, wished well to all, reverenced age, yielded not to envy, avoided all boasting, followed the dictates of reason and loved virtue. When did she sadden her parents even by a look? . . . There was nothing forward in her looks, bold in her words or unbecoming in her actions. Her carriage was not abrupt, her gait not indolent, her voice not petulant, so that her very appearance was the picture of her mind and the figure of piety."

Her life as a spouse and as a mother was a counterpart of her earlier years. The Gospel relates one little circumstance which amply suffices to demonstrate Mary's super-eminent holiness of life, and to exhibit her as a beautiful pattern to those who are called to rule a household. The Evangelist tells us that Jesus "was subject to them" [62]—that is, to Mary and Joseph. He obeyed all her commands, fulfilled her behests, complied with her smallest injunctions; in a word, He discharged toward her all the filial observances which a dutiful son exercises toward a prudent mother. These relations continued from His childhood to His public life, nor did they cease even then.

Now Jesus being the Son of God, "the brightness of His glory and the figure of His substance," [63] could not sin. He was incapable of fulfilling an unrighteous precept. The obvious conclusion to be drawn from these facts is, that Mary never sinned by commanding, as Jesus could not sin by obeying; that all her precepts and counsels were stamped with the seal of Divine approbation, and that the Son never fulfilled any injunction of His

[62] Luke ii. 51.
[63] Heb. i. 3.

earthly Mother which was not ratified by His Eternal Father in heaven.

Such is the beautiful portrait which the Church holds up to the contemplation of her children, that studying it they may admire the original, admiring they may love, loving they may imitate, and thus become more dear to God by being made "conformable to the image of His Son," [64] of whom Mary is the most perfect mirror.

[64] Rom. viii. 29.

CHAPTER XV

SACRED IMAGES

THE veneration of the images of Christ and His saints is a cherished devotion in the Catholic Church, and this practice will be vindicated in the following lines.

It is true, indeed, that the making of holy images was not so general among the Jews as it is among us, because the Hebrews themselves were prone to idolatry, and because they were surrounded by idolatrous people, who might misconstrue the purpose for which the images were intended. For the same prudential reasons the primitive Christians were very cautious in making images, and very circumspect in exposing them to the gaze of the heathen among whom they lived, lest Christian images should be confounded with Pagan idols.

The catacombs of Rome, to which the faithful alone were admitted, abounded, however, in sacred emblems and pious representations, which are preserved even to this day and attest the practice of the early Christian Church. We see there painted on the walls or on vases of glass the Dove, the emblem of the Holy Ghost, Christ carrying His cross, or bearing on His shoulders the lost sheep. We meet also the Lamb, an anchor and a ship—appropriate types of our Lord, of hope and of the Church.

The first crusade against images was waged in the eighth century by Leo the Isaurian, Emperor of Constantinople. He commanded the paintings of our Lord and His Saints to be torn down from the church walls and burned. He even invaded the sanctuary of home, and snatched thence the sacred emblems which adorned private residences. He caused statues of bronze, silver and gold to be melted down and conveniently converted them into coins, upon which his own image was stamped. Like Henry VIII. and Cromwell, this royal Iconoclast affected to be moved by a zeal for purity of worship, while avarice was the real motive of his action.

The Emperor commanded the learned librarians of his imperial library to give public approbation to his decrees against images, and when those conscientious men refused to endorse his course they were all confined in the imperial library, the building was set on fire and thirty thousand volumes, the splendid basilica which contained them, innumerable paintings and the librarians themselves were involved in one common destruction.

Constantine Copronymus prosecuted the vandalism of Leo, his predecessor. Stephen, an intrepid monk, presented to the Emperor a coin bearing that tyrant's effigy, with these words: "Sire, whose image is this?" "It is mine," replied the Emperor. The monk then threw down the piece of money and trampled it. He was instantly seized by the imperial attendants and soon after put to a painful death. "Alas!" cried the holy man to the Emperor, "if I am punished for dishonoring the image of a mortal monarch, what punishment do they deserve who burn the image of Jesus Christ?"

The demolition of images was revived by the Reformers of the sixteenth century. Paintings and statues were ruthlessly destroyed, chiefly in the British Isles, Germany and Holland, under the pretext that the making of them was idolatrous. But as the Iconoclasts of the eighth century had no scruple about appropriating to their own use the gold and silver of the statues which they melted, neither had the Iconoclasts of the sixteenth century any hesitation in confiscating and worshiping in the idolatrous churches whose statues and paintings they broke and disfigured.

A stranger who visits some of the desecrated Catholic churches of Great Britain and the Continent which are now used as Protestant temples cannot fail to notice the mutilated statues of the Saints still standing in their niches.

This barbaric warfare against religious memorials was not

only a grievous sacrilege, but an outrage against the fine arts; and had the destroying angels extended their ravages over Europe the immortal works of Michael Angelo and Raphael would be lost to us today.

The doctrine of the Catholic Church regarding the use of sacred images is clearly and fully expressed by the General Council of Trent in the following words: "The images of Christ, and of His Virgin Mother, and of other Saints, are to be had and retained, especially in churches; and a due honor and veneration is to be given to them; not that any divinity or virtue is believed to be in them for which they are to be honored, or that any prayer is to be made to them, or that any confidence is to be placed in them, as was formerly done by the heathens, who placed their hopes in idols; but because the honor which is given them is referred to the originals which they represent, so that by the images which we kiss, and before which we uncover our heads or kneel, we adore Christ and venerate His Saints, whose likeness they represent." [1]

Every Catholic child clearly comprehends the essential difference which exists between a Pagan idol and a Christian image. The Pagans looked upon an idol as a god endowed with intelligence and the other attributes of the Deity. They were therefore idolaters, or *image worshipers.* Catholic Christians know that a holy image has no intelligence or power to hear and help them. They pay it a relative respect—that is, their reverence for the copy is proportioned to the veneration which they entertain for the heavenly original to which it is also referred.

For the sake of my Protestant readers I may here quote their own great Leibnitz on the reverence paid to sacred images. He says, in his *Systema Theologicum,* p. 142: "Though we speak of the honor paid to images, yet this is only a manner of speaking, which really means that we honor not the senseless thing which is incapable of understanding such honor, but the prototype, which receives honor through its representation, according to the teaching of the Council of Trent. It is in this sense, I take it,

[1] Sess. xxv.

that scholastic writers have spoken of the same worship being paid to images of Christ as to Christ our Lord Himself; for the act which is called the worship of an image is really the worship of Christ Himself, through and in the presence of the image and by occasion of it; by the inclination of the body toward it as to Christ Himself, as rendering Him more manifestly present, and raising the mind more actively to the contemplation of Him. Certainly, no sane man thinks, under such circumstances, of praying in this wise: 'Give me, O image, what I ask; to thee, O marble or wood, I give thanks;' but 'Thee, O Lord, I adore; to Thee I give thanks and sing songs of praise.' Given, then, that there is no other veneration of images than that which means veneration of their prototype, there is surely no more idolatry in it than there is in the respect shown in the utterance of the Most Holy Names of God and Christ; for, after all, names are but signs or symbols, and even as such inferior to images, for they represent much less vividly. So that when there is question of honoring images, this is to be understood in the same way as when it is said that at the name of Jesus every knee shall bend, or that the name of the Lord is blessed, or that glory be given to His Name. Thus, the bowing before an image outside of us is no more to be reprehended than the worshiping before an external image in our own minds; for the external image does but serve the purpose of expressing visibly that which is internal."

In the Book of Exodus we read: "Thou shalt not make to thyself a graven thing, nor the likeness of anything that is in heaven above, or in the earth beneath, or of those things that are in the waters under the earth. Thou shalt not adore them nor serve them." [2] Protestants contend that these words contain an absolute prohibition against the making of images, while the Catholic Church insists that the commandment referred to merely prohibits us from worshiping them as gods.

The text cannot mean the absolute prohibition of making images; for in that case God would contradict Himself by commanding in one part of Scripture what He condemns in another.

[2] Chap. xx.

In Exodus (xxv. 18), for instance, He commands two cherubim of beaten gold to be made and placed on each side of the oracle; and in Numbers (xxi. 8) He commands Moses to make a brazen serpent, and to set it up for a sign, that "whosoever being struck by the fiery serpents shall look upon it, shall live." Are not cherubim and serpents the likenesses of creatures in heaven above, in the earth beneath and in the waters under the earth? for cherubim dwell in heaven and serpents are found on land and sea.

We should all, without exception, break the commandment were we to take it in the Protestant sense. Have you not at home the portraits of living and departed relatives? And are not these the likenesses of persons in heaven above and on the earth beneath?

Westminster Abbey, though once a Catholic Cathedral, is now a Protestant house of worship. It is filled with the statues of illustrious men; yet no one will accuse the English church of idolatry in allowing those statues to remain there. But you will say: The worshipers in Westminster have no intention of adoring these statues. Neither have we any intention of worshiping the statues of the Saints. An English parson once remarked to a Catholic friend: "Tom, don't you pray to images?" "We pray before them," replied Tom; "but we have no intention of praying to them." "Who cares for your intention," retorted the parson. "Don't you pray at night?" observed Tom. "Yes," said the parson; "I pray at my bed." "Yes; you pray to the bed-post." "Oh, no!" said the reverend gentleman; "I have no intention of doing that." "Who cares," replied Tom, "for your intention."

The moral rectitude or depravity of our actions cannot be determined without taking into account the intention.

There are many persons who have been taught in the nursery tales, that Catholics worship idols. These persons, if they visit Europe and see an old man praying before an image of our Lord or a Madonna which is placed along the wayside, are at once confirmed in their prejudices. Their zeal against idols takes fire and they write home, adding one more proof of idolatry against

the benighted Romanists. If these superficial travelers had only
the patience to question the old man he would tell them, with
simplicity of faith, that the statue had no life to hear or help him,
but that its contemplation inspired him with greater reverence
for the original.

As I am writing for the information of Protestants, I quote
with pleasure the following passage, written by one of their own
theologians, in the *Encyclopédie* (Edit. d'Yverdun, tom. 1, art.
Adorer):

"When Lot prostrates himself before the two angels it is an act
of courtesy towards honored guests; when Jacob bows down
before Esau it is an act of deference from a younger to an elder
brother; when Solomon bows low before Bethsabee it is the
honor which a son pays to his mother; when Nathan, coming in
before David, 'had worshiped, bowing down to the ground,' it
is the homage of a subject to his prince. But when a man prostrates himself in prayer to God it is the creature adoring the
Creator. And if these various actions are expressed—sometimes
by the word *adore,* sometimes by *worship* or *prostration*—it is not
the bare meaning of the word which has guided interpreters in
rendering it, but the nature of the case. When an Israelite pros-
trated himself before the king no one thought of charging him
with idolatry. If he had done the same thing in the presence of
an idol, the very same bodily act would have been called idolatry.
And why? Because all men would have judged by his action that
he regarded the idol as a real Divinity and that he would express,
in respect to it, the sentiments manifested by adoration in the
limited sense which we give to the word. What shall we think,
then, of what Catholics do to show honor to Saints, to relics, to
the wood of the cross? They will not deny that their acts of
reverence, in such cases, are very much like those by which they
pay outward honor to God. But have they the same ideas about
the Saints, the relics and the cross as they have about God? I believe that we cannot fairly accuse them of it."

A gentleman who was present at the unveiling of Clay's statue
in the city of Richmond informed me that as soon as the curtain

was uplifted, and the noble form of the Kentucky statesman appeared in full view, the immense concourse of spectators instinctively uncovered their heads. "Why do you take off your hat?" playfully remarked my friend to an acquaintance who stood by. "In honor, of course, of Henry Clay," he replied. "But Henry is not there in the flesh. You see nothing but *clay*." "But my intention, sir," he continued, "is to do honor to the original." He answered correctly. And yet how many of the same people would be shocked if they saw a man take off his hat in the presence of a statue of St. Peter! It is not, therefore, the making of the image, but its worship, that is condemned by the Decalogue.

Having seen the lawfulness of sacred images, let us now consider the advantages to be derived from their use.

First—*Religious paintings embellish the house of God.* What is more becoming than to adorn the church, which is the shadow of the heavenly Jerusalem, so beautifully described by St. John? [3] Solomon decorated the temple of God with images of cherubim and other representations. "And he overlaid the cherubim with gold. And all the walls of the temple round about he carved with divers figures and carvings." [4] If it was meet and proper to adorn Solomon's temple, which contained only the Ark of the Lord, how much more fitting is it to decorate our churches, which contain the Lord of the Ark? When I see a church tastefully ornamented it is a sure sign that the Master is at home, and that His devoted subjects pay homage to Him in His court.

What beauty, what variety, what charming pictures are presented to our view in this temple of nature which we inhabit! Look at the canopy of heaven. Look at the exquisite pictures painted by the Hand of the Divine Artist on this earth. "Consider the lilies of the field. . . . I say to you that not even Solomon in all his glory was arrayed as one of these." If the temple of nature is so richly adorned, should not our temples made with hands bear some resemblance to it?

How many professing Christians must, like David, reproach themselves for "dwelling in a house of cedar, while the ark of

[3] Apoc. xxi.   [4] III. Kings vi.

God is lodged with skins." [5] How many are there whose private apartments are adorned with exquisite paintings, who affect to be scandalized at the sight of a single pious emblem in their house of worship? On the occasion of the celebration of Henry W. Beecher's silver wedding several wealthy members of his congregation adorned the walls of Plymouth church with their private paintings. Their object, of course, in doing so was not to honor God, but their pastor. But if the portraits of men were no desecration to that church, how can the portraits of Saints desecrate ours? [6] And what can be more appropriate than to surround the Sanctuary of Jesus Christ with the portraits of the Saints, especially of Mary and of the Apostles, who, in their life, ministered to His sacred person? And is it not natural for children to adorn their homes with the likenesses of their Fathers in the faith?

Second—*Religious paintings are the catechism of the ignorant.* In spite of all the efforts of Church and State in the cause of education a great proportion of the human race will be found illiterate. Descriptive pictures will teach those what books make known to the learned.

How many thousands would have died ignorant of the Christian faith if they had not been enlightened by paintings! When Augustine, the Apostle of England, first appeared before King Ethelbert to announce to him the Gospel, a silver crucifix and a painting of our Savior were borne before the preacher, and these images spoke more tenderly to the eyes than his words to the ears of his audience.

By means of religious emblems St. Francis Xavier effected many conversions in India; and by the same means Father De Smet made known the Gospel to the savages of the Rocky Mountains.

Third—By exhibiting religious paintings in our rooms *we make a silent, though eloquent, profession of our faith.* I once

[5] II. Kings vii. 2.

[6] At the Washington and Lee University, Lexington, Va., in the *sanctuary of the chapel*, the portrait of an opulent benefactor holds a conspicuous place.

called on a gentleman in a distant city, some time during our late war, and, on entering his library, I noticed two portraits, one of a distinguished General, the other of an Archbishop. These portraits at once proclaimed to me the religious and patriotic sentiments of the proprietor of the house. "Behold!" he said to me, pointing to the pictures, "my religious creed and my political creed." If I see a crucifix in a man's room I am convinced at once that he is not an infidel.

Fourth—By the aid of sacred pictures *our devotion and love for the original are intensified, because we can concentrate our thoughts more intently on the object of our affections.* Mark how the eye of a tender child glistens on confronting the painting of an affectionate mother. What Christian can stand unmoved when contemplating a picture of the Mother of Sorrows? How much devotion has been fostered by the Stations of the Cross? Observe the intense sympathy depicted on the face of the humble Christian woman as she silently passes from one station to another. She follows her Savior step by step from the Garden to Mount Calvary. The whole scene, like a panoramic view, is imprinted on her mind, her memory and her affections. Never did the most pathetic sermon on the Passion enkindle such heartfelt love, or evoke such salutary resolutions, as have been produced by the silent spectacle of our Savior hanging on the cross.

Fifth—The portraits of the Saints stimulate us to the *imitation of their virtues;* and this is the principal aim which the Church has in view in encouraging the use of pious representations. One object, it is true, is to honor the Saints; another is to invoke them; but the principal end is to incite us to an imitation of their holy lives. We are exhorted to "look and do according to the pattern shown us on the mount." [7] Nor do I know a better means for promoting piety than by example.

If you keep at home the likenesses of George Washington, of Patrick Henry, of Chief Justice Taney, or of other distinguished men, the copies of such eminent originals cannot fail to exercise a salutary though silent influence on the mind and heart of your

[7] Exod. xxv. 40.

child. Your son will ask you: "Who are those men?" And when you tell him: "This is Washington, the Father of his Country; this is Patrick Henry, the ardent lover of civil liberty; and this is Taney, the incorruptible Judge," your boy will imperceptibly imbibe not only a veneration for those men, but a relish for the civic virtues for which they were conspicuous. And in like manner, when our children have constantly before their eyes the purest and most exalted models of sanctity, they cannot fail to draw from such contemplation a taste for the virtues that marked the lives of the originals.

Is not our country flooded with obscene pictures and immodest representations which corrupt our youth? If the agents of Satan employ means so vile for a bad end; if they are cunning enough to pour through the senses into the hearts of the unwary the insidious poison of sin, by placing before them lascivious portraits, in God's name, why should not we sanctify the souls of our children by means of pious emblems? Why should not we make the eye the instrument of edification as the enemy makes it the organ of destruction? Shall the pen of the artist, the pencil of the painter and the chisel of the sculptor be prostituted to the basest purposes? God forbid! The arts were intended to be the handmaids of religion.

Almost every moment of the day the eye is receiving impressions from outward objects and instantly communicating these impressions to the soul. Thus the soul receives every day thousands of impressions, good or bad, according to the character of the objects presented to its gaze.

We cannot, therefore, over-estimate the salutary effect produced upon us in a church or room adorned with sacred paintings. We feel, while in their presence, that we are in the company of the just. The contemplation of these pious portraits chastens our affections, elevates our thoughts, checks our levity and diffuses around us a healthy atmosphere.

I am happy to acknowledge that the outcry formerly raised against images has almost subsided of late. The epithet of *idolaters* is seldom applied to us now. Even some of our dissenting brethren are beginning to recognize the utility of religious symbols and to regret that we have been permitted, by the intemperate zeal of the Reformers, to have so long the monopoly of them. Crosses already surmount some of our Protestant churches and replace the weather-cock.

A gentleman of Richmond recently informed me that during the preceding Holy Week he adorned with twelve crosses an Episcopal church in which, eleven years before, the sight of a single one was viewed with horror by the minister.

May the day soon come when all Christians will join with us not only in venerating the sacred symbol of salvation, but in worshiping at the same altar.

CHAPTER XVI

PURGATORY AND PRAYERS FOR THE DEAD

THE Catholic Church teaches that, besides a place of eternal torments for the wicked and of everlasting rest for the righteous, there exists in the next life a middle state of temporary punishment, allotted for those who have died in venial sin, or who have not satisfied the justice of God for sins already forgiven. She also teaches us that, although the souls consigned to this intermediate state, commonly called purgatory, cannot help themselves, they may be aided by the suffrages of the faithful on earth. The existence of purgatory naturally implies the correlative dogma—the utility of praying for the dead—for the souls consigned to this middle state have not reached the term of their journey. They are still exiles from heaven and fit subjects for Divine clemency.

The doctrine of an intermediate state is thus succinctly asserted by the Council of Trent: "There is a Purgatory, and souls there detained, are helped by the prayers of the faithful, and especially by the acceptable Sacrifice of the Altar." [1]

It is to be noted that the Council studiously abstains from specifying the nature of the expiating sufferings endured therein.

Is it not strange that this cherished doctrine should also be called in question by the leveling innovators of the sixteenth century, when we consider that it is clearly taught in the Old Testament; that it is, at least, insinuated in the New Testament; that it is unanimously proclaimed by the Fathers of the Church; that

[1] Sess. xxv.

it is embodied in all the ancient liturgies of the Oriental and the
Western church, and that it is a doctrine alike consonant with
our reason and eminently consoling to the human heart?

First—It is a doctrine plainly contained in the Old Testament
and piously practiced by the Hebrew people. At the close of an
engagement which Judas Machabeus had with the enemy he ordered prayers and sacrifices to be offered up for his slain com-
rades. "And making a gathering, he sent twelve thousand
drachms of silver to Jerusalem for sacrifice to be offered for the
sins of the dead, thinking well and religiously concerning the
resurrection. For, if he had not hoped that they that were slain
should rise again, it would have seemed superfluous and vain to
pray for the dead. . . . It is, therefore, a holy and wholesome
thought to pray for the dead, that they may be loosed from sins." [2]

These words are so forcible that no comment of mine could
render them clearer. The passage proved a great stumbling-block
to the Reformers. Finding that they could not by any evasion
weaken the force of the text, they impiously threw overboard the
Books of Machabees, like a man who assassinates a hostile witness, or like the Jews who sought to kill Lazarus, lest his resurrection should be a testimony in favor of Christ, and pretended
that the two books of Machabees were apocryphal. And yet they
have precisely the same authority as the Gospel of St. Matthew or
any other portion of the Bible, for the canonicity of the Holy
Scriptures rests solely on the authority of the Catholic Church,
which proclaimed them inspired.

But even admitting, for the sake of argument, that the Books
of Machabees were not entitled to be ranked among the canonical
Books of Holy Scripture, no one, at least, has ever denied that
they are truthful historical monuments, and as such that they
serve to demonstrate that it was a prevailing practice among the
Hebrew people, as it is with us, to offer up prayers and sacrifices
for the dead.

Second—When our Savior, the Founder of the New Law, appeared on earth, He came to lop off those excrescences which had

[2] II. Mach. xii. 43-46.

grown on the body of the Jewish ecclesiastical code, and to purify the Jewish Church from those human traditions which, in the course of time, became like tares mixed with the wheat of sound doctrine. For instance, He condemns the Pharisees for prohibiting the performance of works of charity on the Sabbath day, and in the twenty-third chapter of St. Matthew He cites against them a long catalogue of innovations in doctrine and discipline.

But did our Lord, at any time, reprove the Jews for their belief in a middle state, or for praying for the dead, a practice which, to His knowledge, prevailed among the people? Never. On the contrary, more than once both He and the Apostle of the Gentiles insinuate the doctrine of purgatory.

Our Savior says: "Whosoever shall speak a word against the Son of man it shall be forgiven him. But he that shall speak against the Holy Ghost it shall not be forgiven him, neither in this world nor in the world to come." [3] When our Savior declares that a sin against the Holy Ghost shall not be forgiven in the next life, He evidently leaves us to infer that there are some sins which will be pardoned in the life to come. Now in the next life, sins cannot be forgiven in heaven, for, nothing defiled can enter there; nor can they be forgiven in hell, for, out of hell there is no redemption. They must, therefore, be pardoned in the intermediate state of Purgatory.

St. Paul tells us that "every man's work shall be manifest" on the Lord's day. "The fire shall try every man's work of what sort it is. If any man's work abide," that is, if his works are holy, "he shall receive a reward. If any man's work burn," that is, if his works are faulty and imperfect, "he shall suffer loss; but he himself shall be saved, yet so as by fire." [4] His soul will be ultimately saved, but he shall suffer, for a temporary duration, in the purifying flames of Purgatory.

This interpretation is not mine. It is the unanimous voice of the Fathers of Christendom. And who are they that have removed the time-honored landmarks of Christian faith by rejecting the doctrine of purgatory? They are discontented churchmen impatient

[3] Matt. xii. 32.   [4] I. Cor. iii. 13-15.

of the religious yoke, men who appeared on the stage sixteen hundred years after the foundation of Christianity. Judge you, reader, whom you ought to follow. If you want to know the true import of a vital question in the Constitution, would you not follow the decision of a Story, a Jefferson, a Marshall, a Taney, jurists and statesmen, who were the recognized expounders of the Constitution? Would you not prefer their opinion to that of political demagogues, who have neither learning, nor authority, nor history to support them, but some selfish end to further? Now, the same motive which you have for rejecting the opinion of an ignorant politician and embracing that of eminent jurists, on a constitutional question, impels you to cast aside the novelties of religious innovators and to follow the unanimous sentiments of the Fathers in reference to the subject of purgatory.

Third—I would wish to place before you extended extracts from the writings of the early Fathers of the Church bearing upon this subject; but I must content myself with quoting a few of the most prominent lights of primitive Christianity.

Tertullian, who lived in the second century, says that "the faithful wife will pray for the soul of her deceased husband, particularly on the anniversary day of his falling asleep (death). And if she fail to do so she hath repudiated her husband as far as in her lies." [5]

Eusebius, the historian (fourth century), describing the funeral of Constantine the Great, says that the body of the blessed prince was placed on a lofty bier, and the ministers of God and the multitude of the people, with tears and much lamentation, offered up prayers and sacrifice for the repose of his soul. He adds that this was done in accordance with the desires of that religious monarch, who had erected in Constantinople the great church in honor of the Apostles, so that after his death the faithful might there remember him. [6]

St. Cyril of Jerusalem, fourth century, writes: "We commemorate the Holy Fathers, and Bishops, and all who have fallen asleep from amongst us, believing that the supplications which we pre-

[5] De Monogam., n. x.   [6] Euseb., B. iv., c. 71.

sent will be of great assistance to their souls, while the holy and tremendous Sacrifice is offered up." He answers by an illustration those that might be disposed to doubt the efficacy of prayers for the dead: "If a king had banished certain persons who had offended him, and their relations, having woven a crown, should offer it to him in behalf of those under his vengeance, would he not grant a respite to their punishments? So we, in offering up a crown of prayers in behalf of those who have fallen asleep, will obtain for them forgiveness through the merits of Christ." [7]

St. Ephrem, in the same century, says: "I conjure you, my brethren and friends, in the name of that God who commands me to leave you, to remember me when you assemble to pray. Do not bury me with perfumes. Give them not to me, but to God. Me, conceived in sorrows, bury with lamentations, and instead of perfumes assist me with your prayers; for the dead are benefited by the prayers of living Saints." [8]

St. Ambrose (same century), on the death of the Emperors Gratian and Valentinian, says: "Blessed shall both of you be (Gratian and Valentinian), if my prayers can avail anything. No day shall pass you over in silence. No prayer of mine shall omit to honor you. No night shall hurry by without bestowing on you a mention in my prayers. In every one of the oblations will I remember you." On the death of the Emperor Theodosius he offers the following prayer: "Give perfect rest to Thy servant Theodosius, that rest which Thou hast prepared for Thy Saints. May his soul return thither whence it descended, where it cannot feel the sting of death. . . . I loved him and therefore will I follow him, even unto the land of the living. Nor will I leave him until, by tears and prayers, I shall lead him . . . unto the holy mountain of the Lord, where is life undying, where corruption is not, nor sighing nor mourning." [9]

St. Jerome, in the same century, in a letter of condolence to Pammachius, on the death of his wife Paulina, writes: "Other

[7] Catech., n. 9, 10, p. 328.
[8] Apud Faith of Catholics. Vol. III., p. 162 and seq.
[9] See Faith of Catholics, Vol. III., p. 176.

husbands strew violets and roses on the graves of their wives. Our Pammachius bedews the hallowed dust of Paulina with balsams of alms." [10]

St. Chrysostom writes: "It was not without good reason *ordained by the Apostles* that mention should be made of the dead in the tremendous mysteries, because they knew well that they would receive great benefit from it." [11]

St. Augustine, who lived in the beginning of the fifth century, relates that when his mother was at the point of death she made this last request of him: "Lay this body anywhere; let not the care of it in anyway disturb you. This only I request of you, that you would remember me at the altar of the Lord, wherever you be."

And that pious son prays for his mother's soul in the most impassioned language: "I therefore," he says, "O God of my heart, do now beseech Thee for the sins of my mother. Hear me through the medicine of the wounds that hung upon the wood. . . . May she, then, be in peace with her husband. . . . And inspire, my Lord, . . . Thy servants, my brethren, whom with voice and heart and pen I serve, that as many as shall read these words may remember at Thy altar, Monica, Thy servant. . . ." [12]

These are but a few specimens of the unanimous voice of the Fathers regarding the salutary practice of praying for the dead.

You now perceive that this devotion is not an invention of modern times, but a doctrine universally enforced in the first and purest ages of the Church.

You see that praying for the dead was not a devotion cautiously recommended by some obscure or visionary writer, but an act of religion preached and inculcated by all the great Doctors and Fathers of the Church, who are the recognized expounders of the Christian religion.

You see them, too, inculcating this doctrine not as a cold and abstract principle, but as an imperative act of daily piety, and embodying it in their ordinary exercises of devotion.

[10] Ibid., p. 177.   [11] Ibid., Vol. II.   [12] Confessions, Book ix.

They prayed for the dead in their morning and evening devotions. They prayed for them in their daily office, and in the Sacrifice of the Mass. They asked the prayers of the congregation for the souls of the deceased in the public services of Sunday. On the monuments which were erected to the dead, some of which are preserved even to this day, epitaphs were inscribed, earnestly invoking for their souls the prayers of the living. How gratifying it is to our Catholic hearts that a devotion so soothing to afflicted spirits is at the same time so firmly grounded on the tradition of ages!

Fourth—That the practice of praying for the dead has descended from Apostolic times is evident also from the *Liturgies* of the Church. A Liturgy is the established formulary of public worship, containing the authorized prayers of the Church. The Missal, or Mass-book, for instance, which you see on our altars, contains a portion of the Liturgy of the Catholic Church. The principal Liturgies are the Liturgy of St. James the Apostle, who founded the Church of Jerusalem; the Liturgy of St. Mark the Evangelist, founder of the Church of Alexandria, and the Liturgy of St. Peter, who established the Church in Rome. These Liturgies are called after the Apostles who compiled them. There are, besides, the Liturgies of St. Chrysostom and St. Basil, which are chiefly based on the model of that of St. James.

Now, all these Liturgies, without exception, have prayers for the dead, and their providential preservation serves as another triumphant vindication of the venerable antiquity of this Catholic doctrine.

The Eastern and the Western churches were happily united until the fourth and fifth centuries, when the heresiarchs Arius, Nestorius and Eutyches withdrew millions of souls from the centre of unity. The followers of these sects were called, after their founders, Arians, Nestorians and Eutychians, and from that day to the present the two latter bodies have formed distinct communions, being separated from the Catholic Church in the East, just as the Protestant churches are separated from her in the West.

The Greek schismatic church, of which the present Russo-

Greek church is the offspring, severed her connection with the See of Rome in the ninth century.

But in leaving the Catholic Church these Eastern sects retained the old Liturgies, which they use to this day, as I shall presently demonstrate.

During my sojourn in Rome at the Ecumenical Council I devoted a great deal of my leisure time to the examination of the various Liturgies of the schismatic churches of the East. I found in all of them formulas of prayers for the dead almost identical with that of the Roman Missal: "Remember, O Lord, Thy servants who are gone before us with the sign of faith, and sleep in peace. To these, O Lord, and to all who rest in Christ grant, we beseech Thee, a place of refreshment, light and peace, through the same Jesus Christ our Lord."

Not content with studying their books, I called upon the Oriental Patriarchs and Bishops in communion with the See of Rome, who belong to the Armenian, the Chaldean, the Coptic, the Maronite and Syriac rites. They all assured me that the schismatic Christians of the East among whom they live have, without exception, prayers and sacrifices for the dead.

Now, I ask, when could those Eastern sects have commenced to adopt the Catholic practice of praying for the dead? They could not have received it from us since the ninth century, because the Greek church separated from us then and has had no communion with us since that time, except at intervals, up to the twelfth century. Nor could they have adopted the practice since the fourth or fifth century, inasmuch as the Arians, Nestorians and Eutychians have had no religious communication with us since that period. Therefore, in common with us, they received this doctrine from the Apostles. If men living in different countries drink wine having the same flavor and taste and color, the inference is that the wine was made from the same species of grape. So must we conclude that this refreshing doctrine of intercession for the dead has its root in the Apostolic tree of knowledge planted by our Savior.

Fifth—I have already spoken of the devotion of the ancient

Jewish church to the souls of the departed. But perhaps you are not aware that the Jews retain to this day, in their Liturgy, the pious practice of praying for the dead. Yet such in reality is the case.

Amid all the wanderings and vicissitudes of life, though dismembered and dispersed like sheep without a shepherd over the face of the globe, the children of Israel have never forgotten or neglected the sacred duty of praying for their deceased brethren.

Unwilling to make this assertion without the strongest evidence, I procured from a Jewish convert an authorized Prayer-Book of the Hebrew church, from which I extract the following formula of prayers which are prescribed for funerals: "Departed brother! mayest thou find open the gates of heaven, and see the city of peace and the dwellings of safety, and meet the ministering angels hastening joyfully toward thee. And may the High Priest stand to receive thee, and go thou to the end, rest in peace, and rise again into life. May the repose established in the celestial abode . . . be the lot, dwelling and the resting-place of the soul of our deceased brother (whom the Spirit of the Lord may guide into Paradise), who departed from this world, according to the will of God, the Lord of heaven and earth. May the supreme King of kings, through His infinite mercy, hide him under the shadow of His wing. May He raise him at the end of his days and cause him to drink of the stream of His delights." [13]

Among the many-sided merits of Shakespeare may be mentioned his happy faculty of portraying to life the manners and customs and traditional faith of the times which he describes. How deep-rooted in the Christian heart in pre-Reformation times, was the belief in Purgatory, may be inferred from a passage in Hamlet who probably lived in the early part of the eighth century. Thus speaks to Hamlet the spirit of his murdered father:

> "I am thy father's spirit,
> Doom'd for a certain time to walk the night;
> And for the day confin'd too fast in fires,
> Till the foul crimes done in my days of nature
> Are burnt and purg'd away." [14]

[13] Jewish Prayer Book. Edited by Isaac Leeser, published by Slote & Mooney, Philadelphia.   [14] Act I.

I am happy to say that the more advanced and enlightened members of the Episcopalian church are steadily returning to the faith of their forefathers regarding prayers for the dead. An acquaintance of mine, once a distinguished clergyman of the Episcopal communion, but now a convert, informed me that hundreds of Protestant clergymen in this country, and particularly in England, have a firm belief in the efficacy of prayers for the dead, but for well-known reasons they are reserved in the expression of their faith. He easily convinced me of the truth of his assertion, particularly as far as the Church of England is concerned, by sending me six different works published in London, all bearing on the subject of Purgatory. These books are printed under the auspices of the Protestant Episcopal church; they all contain prayers for the dead and prove, from Catholic grounds, the existence of a middle state after death and the duty of praying for our deceased brethren.[15]

To sum up, we see the practice of praying for the dead enforced in the ancient Hebrew church and in the Jewish synagogue of today. We see it proclaimed age after age by all the Fathers of Christendom. We see it incorporated in every one of the ancient Liturgies of the East and of the West. We see it zealously taught by the Russian church of today, and by that immense family of schismatic Christians scattered over the East. We behold it, in fine, a cherished devotion of three hundred millions of Catholics, as well as of a respectable portion of the Episcopal church.

Would it not, my friend, be the height of rashness and presumption in you to prefer your private opinion to this immense weight of learning, sanctity and authority? Would it not be impiety in you to stand aside with sealed lips while the Christian world is sending up an unceasing *De profundis* for departed brethren? Would it not be cold and heartless in you not to pray for your deceased friends, on account of prejudices which have no grounds in Scripture, tradition or reason itself?

If a brother leaves you to cross the broad Atlantic, religion and

[15] See Path of Holiness, Rivington's, London. Treasury of Devotion, Ibid. Catechism of Theology, Masten, London.

affection prompt you to pray for him during his absence. And if the same brother crosses the narrow sea of death to pass to the shores of eternity, why not pray for him then also? When he crosses the Atlantic his soul, imprisoned in the flesh, is absent from you; when he passes the sea of death his soul, released from the flesh, has gone from you. What difference does this make with regard to the duty of your intercession? For what is death? A mere separation of body and soul. The body, indeed, dies, but the soul "lives and moves and has its being." It continues after death, as before, to think, to remember, to love. And do not God's dominion and mercy extend over that soul beyond the grave as well as this side of it? Who shall place the limits to God's empire and say to Him: "Thus far Thou shalt go and no farther?" Two thousand years after Abraham's death our Lord said: "I *am* the God of Abraham, of Isaac, and of Jacob. He *is* not the God of the dead, but of the living." [16]

If, then, it is profitable for you to pray for your brother in the flesh, why should it be useless for you to pray for him out of the flesh? For while he was living you prayed not for his body, but for his soul.

If this brother of yours dies with some slight stains upon his soul, a sin of impatience, for instance, or an idle word, is he fit to enter heaven with these blemishes upon his soul? No; the sanctity of God forbids it, for "nothing defiled shall enter the Kingdom of Heaven." [17] Will you consign him, for these minor transgressions, to eternal torments with adulterers and murderers? No; the justice and mercy of God forbid it. Therefore, your common sense demands a middle place of expiation for the purgation of the soul before it is worthy of enjoying the companionship of God and His Saints.

God "will render to every man according to his works,"—to the pure and unsullied everlasting bliss; to the reprobate eternal damnation; to souls stained with minor faults a place of temporary purgation. I cannot recall any doctrine of the Christian

[16] Mark xii. 26, 27.
[17] Apoc. xxi. 27.

religion more consoling to the human heart than the article of faith which teaches the efficacy of prayers for the faithful departed. It robs death of its sting. It encircles the chamber of mourning with a rainbow of hope. It assuages the bitterness of our sorrow, and reconciles us to our loss. It keeps us in touch with the departed dead as correspondence keeps us in touch with the absent living. It preserves their memory fresh and green in our hearts.

It gives us that keen satisfaction which springs from the consciousness that we can aid those loved ones who are gone before us by alleviating their pains, shortening their exile, and hastening their entrance into their true country.

It familiarizes us with the existence of a life beyond the grave, and with the hope of being reunited with those whom we cherished on earth, and of dwelling with them in that home where there is no separation, or sorrow, or death, but eternal joy and peace and rest.

I have seen a devoted daughter minister with tender solicitude at the sick-bed of a fond parent. Many an anxious day and sleepless night did she watch at his bedside. She moistened the parched lips, and cooled the fevered brow, and raised the drooping head on its pillow. Every change in her patient for better or worse brought a corresponding sunshine or gloom to her heart. It was filial love that prompted all this. Her father died and she followed his remains to the grave. Though not a Catholic, standing by the bier she burst those chains which a cruel religious prejudice had wrought around her heart, and, rising superior to her sect, she cried out: *Lord, have mercy on his soul.* It was the voice of nature and of religion.

Oh, far from us a religion which would decree an eternal divorce between the living and the dead. How consoling is it to the Catholic to think that, in praying thus for his departed friend, his prayers are not in violation of, but in accordance with, the voice of the Church; and that as, like Augustine, he watches at the pillow of a dying mother, so like Augustine, he can continue the same office of piety for her soul after she is dead by praying for her! How cheering the reflection that the golden link of prayer unites you still to those who "fell asleep in the Lord," that you can still speak to them and pray for them!

Tennyson grasps the Catholic feeling when he makes his hero, whose course is run, thus address his surviving comrade, Sir Bedivere:

> "I have lived my life, and that which I have done
> May He within Himself make pure; but thou,
> If thou shouldst never see my face again,
> Pray for my soul. More things are wrought by prayer
> Than this world dreams of. Wherefore, let thy voice
> Rise like a fountain for me night and day.
> For what are men better than sheep or goats
> That nourish a blind life within the brain,
> If knowing God they lift not hands of prayer
> Both for themselves and those who call them friend?
> For so the whole round earth is every way
> Bound by gold chains about the feet of God." [18]

Oh! it is this thought that robs death of its sting and makes the separation of friends endurable. If your departed friend needs not your prayers, they are not lost, but, like the rain absorbed by the sun, and descending again in fruitful showers on our fields, they will be gathered by the Sun of justice, and will fall in refreshing showers of grace upon your head: "Cast thy bread upon the running waters; for, after a long time, thou shalt find it again." [19]

[18] Morte D'Arthur.
[19] Eccles. xi. 1.

CHAPTER XVII

CIVIL AND RELIGIOUS LIBERTY

A MAN enjoys *religious* liberty when he possesses the free right of worshiping God according to the dictates of a right conscience, and of practicing a form of religion most in accordance with his duties to God. Every act infringing on his freedom of conscience is justly styled religious intolerance. This religious liberty is the true right of every man because it corresponds with a most certain duty which God has put upon him.

A man enjoys *civil* liberty when he is exempt from the arbitrary will of others, and when he is governed by equitable laws established for the general welfare of society. So long as, in common with his fellow-citizens, he observes the laws of the state, any exceptional restraint imposed upon him, in the exercise of his rights as a citizen, is so far an infringement on his civil liberty.

I here assert the proposition, which I hope to confirm by historical evidence, that the Catholic Church has always been the zealous promoter of religious and civil liberty; and that whenever any encroachments on these sacred privileges of man were perpetrated by professing members of the Catholic faith, these wrongs, far from being sanctioned by the Church, were committed in palpable violation of her authority.

Her doctrine is, that as man by his *own free will* fell from grace, so of his *own free will* must he return to grace. Conversion and coercion are two terms that can never be reconciled. It has ever been a cardinal maxim, inculcated by sovereign Pontiffs and other Prelates, that no violence or undue influence should be

186

exercised by Christian princes or missionaries in their efforts to convert souls to the faith of Jesus Christ.

Pope Gregory I. in the latter part of the Sixth Century, compelled the Bishop of Terracina to restore to the Jews, the synagogue which he had seized, declaring that they should not be coerced into the Church, but should be treated with meekness and charity. The great Pontiff issued the same orders to the Prelates of Sardinia and Sicily in behalf of the persecuted Jews.

St. Augustine and his companions, who were sent by Pope Gregory I. to England for the conversion of that nation, had the happiness of baptizing in the true faith King Ethelbert and many of his subjects. That monarch, in the fervor of his zeal, was most anxious that all his subjects should immediately follow his example; but the missionaries admonished him that he should scrupulously abstain from violence in the conversion of his people, for the Christian religion should be voluntarily embraced.

Pope Nicholas I. also warned Michael, king of the Bulgarians, against employing force or constraint in the conversion of idolaters.

The fourth Council of Toledo, held in 633, a synod of great authority in the Church, ordained that no one should be compelled against his will to make a profession of the Christian faith. Be it remembered that this Council was composed of all the Bishops of Spain, that it was assembled in a country and at a time in which the Church held almost unlimited sway, and among a people who have been represented as the most fanatical and intolerant of all Europe.

Perhaps no man can be considered a fairer representative of the age in which he lived than St. Bernard, the illustrious Abbot of Clairvaux. He was the embodiment of the spirit of the Middle Ages. His life is the key that discloses to us what degree of toleration prevailed in those days. Having heard that a fanatical preacher was stimulating the people to deeds of violence against the Jews as the enemies of Christianity, St. Bernard raised his eloquent voice against him, and rescued those persecuted people from the danger to which they were exposed.

Pope Innocent III. in the Thirteenth Century promulgated the following Decree in behalf of the Hebrews: "Let no Jew be *constrained* to receive baptism, and he that will not consent to be baptized, let him not be molested. Let no one unjustly seize their property, disturb their feasts, or lay waste their cemeteries."

Other succeeding Pontiffs, notably Gregory IX. and Innocent IV., issued similar instructions.

Not to cite too many examples, let me quote for you only the beautiful letter addressed by Fenelon, Archbishop of Cambray, to the son of King James II. of England. This letter not only reflects the sentiments of his own heart, but formularizes in this particular the decrees of the Church, of which he was a distinguished ornament. "Above all," he writes, "never force your subjects to change their religion. No human power can reach the impenetrable recess of the free will of the heart. Violence can never persuade men; it serves only to make hypocrites. Grant civil liberty to all, not in approving everything as indifferent, but in tolerating with patience whatever Almighty God tolerates, and endeavoring to convert men by mild persuasion." [1]

It is true, indeed, that the Catholic Church spares no pains and stops at no sacrifice in order to induce mankind to embrace her faith. Otherwise she would be recreant to her sacred mission. But she scorns to exercise any undue influence in her efforts to convert souls.

The only argument she would use, is the argument of reason and persuasion; the only tribunal to which she would summon you, is the tribunal of conscience; the only weapon she would wield, is "the Sword of the Spirit, which is the Word of God." It is well known that the superior advantages of our female academies throughout the country lead many of our dissenting brethren to send their daughters to these institutions. It is also well known that so warm is the affection which these young ladies entertain for their religious teachers, so hallowed is the atmosphere they breathe within these seats of learning, that they often beg to embrace a religion which fosters so much piety and

[1] Vie de Fenelon.

which produces lilies so fragrant and so pure. Do the sisters take advantage of this influence in the cause of proselytism? By no means. So delicate is their regard for the religious conscience of their pupils, that they rarely consent to have these young ladies baptized till, after being thoroughly instructed in all the doctrines of the Church, they have obtained the free permission of their parents or guardians.

The Church is, indeed, intolerant in this sense, that she can never confound truth with error; nor can she admit that any man is conscientiously free to reject the truth when its claims are convincingly brought home to the mind. Many Protestants seem to be very much disturbed by some such argument as this: Catholics are very ready now to proclaim freedom of conscience, because they are in the minority. When they once succeed in getting the upper hand in numbers and power they will destroy this freedom, because their faith teaches them to tolerate no doctrine other than the Catholic. It is, then, a matter of absolute necessity for us that they should never be allowed to get this advantage.

Now, in all this, there is a great mistake, which comes from not knowing the Catholic doctrine in its fulness. I shall not lay it down myself, lest it seem to have been gotten up for the occasion. I shall quote the great theologian Becanus, who taught the doctrine of the schools of Catholic Theology at the time when the struggle was hottest between Catholicity and Protestantism. He says that religious liberty may be tolerated by a ruler when it would do more harm to the state or to the community to repress it. The ruler may even enter into a compact in order to secure to his subjects this freedom in religious matters; and when once a compact is made it must be observed absolutely in every point, just as every other lawful and honest contract.[2] This is the true Catholic teaching on this point, according to Becanus and all Catholic theologians. So that if Catholics should gain the majority in a community where freedom of conscience is already secured to all by law, their very religion obliges them to respect the rights thus acquired by their fellow-citizens. What danger

[2] Becanus, de Virtutibus Theologicis, c. 16, quæst. 4, No. 2.

can their be, then, for Protestants, if Catholics should be in the majority here? Their apprehensions are the result of vain fears, which no honest mind ought any longer to harbor.

The Church has not only respected the conscience of the people in embracing the religion of their choice, but she has also defended their *civil* rights and liberties against the encroachments of temporal sovereigns. One of the popular errors that have taken possession of some minds in our times is that in former days the Church was leagued with princes for the oppression of the people. This is a base calumny, which a slight acquaintance with ecclesiastical history would soon dispel.

The truth is, the most unrelenting enemies of the Church have been the princes of this world, and so-called Christians princes, too.

The conflict between Church and State has never died out, because the Church has felt it to be her duty, in every age, to raise her voice against the despotic and arbitrary measures of princes. Many of them chafed under the salutary discipline of the Church. They wished to be rid of her yoke. They desired to be governed by no law except the law of their licentious passions and boundless ambitions. And as a Protestant American reviewer[3] well said about forty years ago, it was a blessing of Providence that there was a spiritual Power on earth that could stand like a wall of brass against the tyranny of earthly sovereigns and say to them: "Thus far you shall go, and no farther, and here you shall break your swelling waves" of passion; a Power that could say to them what John said to Herod: "This thing is not lawful for thee;" a Power that pointed the finger of reproof to them, even when the sword was pointed to her own neck, and that said to them what Nathan said to David: "Thou art the man." She told princes that if the people have their obligations they have their rights, too; that if the subject must render to Cæsar the things that are Cæsar's, Cæsar must render to God the things that art God's.

Yes; the Church, while pursuing her Divine mission of leading

[3] Dr. Brownson, who was then a Protestant.

souls to God, has ever been the defender of the people's rights.

St. Ambrose, Archbishop of Milan, affords us a striking instance of the strenuous efforts made by the Catholic Church in vindicating the interests of the citizen against the oppression of rulers.

A portion of the people of Thessalonica had committed an outrage against the just authority of the Emperor Theodosius. The offence of those citizens was indeed most reprehensible; but the Emperor requited the insult offered to him by a shocking and disproportioned act of retribution, which has left an indelible stain upon his otherwise excellent character. The inhabitants were assembled together for the ostensible purpose of witnessing a chariot race, and at a given signal the soldiery fell upon the people and involved men, women and children in an indiscriminate massacre, to the number of about seven thousand. Some time after the Emperor presented himself at the Cathedral of Milan; but the intrepid Prelate told him that his hands were dripping with the blood of his subjects, and forbade him entrance to the church till he had made all the reparation in his power to the afflicted people of Thessalonica.

People affect to be shocked at the sentence of ex-communication occasionally inflicted by the Church on evil-doers. Here is an instance of this penalty. Who can complain of it as being too severe? It was a salutary punishment and the only one that could bring rulers to a sense of duty.

The greatest bulwark of civil liberty is the famous *Magna Charta*. It is the foundation not only of British, but also of American constitutional freedom. Among other blessings contained in this instrument it establishes trial by jury and the right of *Habeas Corpus,* and provides that there shall be no taxation without representation.

Who were the framers of this memorable charter? Archbishop Langton, of Canterbury, and the Catholic Barons of England. On the plains of Runnymede, in 1215, they compelled King John to sign that paper which was the death-blow to his arbitrary power and the cornerstone of constitutional government.

Turning to our own country, it is with no small degree of satisfaction that I point to the State of Maryland as the cradle of civil and religious liberty and the "land of the sanctuary." Of the thirteen original American Colonies, Maryland was the only one settled by Catholics. She was, also, the only one that raised aloft over her fair lands the banner of liberty of conscience, and that invited the oppressed of other colonies to seek an asylum beneath its shadow.

Lest I should be suspected of being too partial in my praise of Maryland toleration, I shall take most of my historical facts from Bancroft, a New England Protestant clergyman.

Leonard Calvert, the brother of Lord Baltimore and the leader of the Catholic colony, having sailed from England in the *Ark* and the *Dove,* reached his destination on the Potomac in March, 1634.

"The Catholics took quiet possession of the little place, and religious liberty obtained a home, *its only home* in the wide world, at the humble village which bore the name of St. Mary." [4]

"The foundation of the colony of Maryland was peacefully and happily laid. Within six months it had advanced more than Virginia had done in as many years. . . . But far more memorable was the character of the Maryland institutions. Every other country in the world had persecuting laws; but through the benign administration of the government of that province, no person professing to believe in Jesus Christ was permitted to be molested on account of religion. Under the munificence and superintending mildness of Lord Baltimore, a dreary wilderness was soon quickened with the swarming life and activity of prosperous settlements; the Roman Catholics who were oppressed

NOTE—The first edition of Bancroft's History was published in 1834. From that date till nearly half a century afterward upwards of twenty editions were issued, all of which retain the passages I have cited on Maryland toleration. Early in the 80s a new edition was given out, which omits or abridges some of the passages quoted in this chapter. I may add that all of Bancroft's eulogies of Lord Baltimore's benevolent administration are borne out by the original documents, and by McMahon, Bozman and McSherry, and other historians of Maryland.

[4] Bancroft's "History of the United States," Vol. I., ch. vii. 20th Edition, 1864.

by the laws of England were sure to find a peaceful asylum in the quiet harbors of the Chesapeake; and there *too, Protestants were sheltered against Protestant intolerance.* Such were the beautiful auspices under which Maryland started into being. . . . Its history is the history of benevolence, gratitude and toleration."

"Maryland was the abode of happiness and liberty. Conscience was without restraint. A mild and liberal proprietary conceded every measure which the welfare of the colony required; domestic union, a happy concert between all the branches of government, an increasing emigration, a productive commerce, a fertile soil, which heaven had richly favored with rivers and deep bays, united to perfect the scene of colonial felicity. Ever intent on advancing the interests of his colony, Lord Baltimore invited the Puritans of Massachusetts to emigrate to Maryland, offering them lands and privileges and free liberty of religion; but Gibbons, to whom he had forwarded the commission, was so wholly tutored in the New England discipline, that he would not advance the wishes of the Irish Peer, and so the invitation was declined." [5]

On the 2d of April, 1649, the General Assembly of Maryland passed the following Act, which will reflect unfading glory on that State as long as liberty is cherished in the hearts of men.

"Whereas, the enforcing of conscience in matters of religion hath frequently fallen out to be of dangerous consequence in those commonwealths where it has been practiced, and for the more quiet and peaceable government of this province, and the better to preserve mutual love and unity amongst the inhabitants, no person whatsoever within this province professing to believe in Jesus Christ shall from henceforth be anyways troubled or molested for his or her religion, nor in the free exercise thereof, nor anyway compelled to the belief or exercise of any other religion against his or her consent." [6]

Upon this noble statute Bancroft makes the following candid and judicious comment: "The design of the law of Maryland

[5] Bancroft's "History of the United States," Vol. I., ch. vii.
[6] Bancroft's "History of the United States," Vol. I., ch. vii. Vide Bacon's Laws

was to protect freedom of conscience; and some years after it had been confirmed the apologist of Lord Baltimore could assert that his government had never given disturbance to any person in Maryland for matter of religion; that the colonists enjoyed freedom of conscience, not less than freedom of person and estate, as amply as ever any people in any place of the world. The disfranchised friends of Prelacy from Massachusetts and the Puritans from Virginia were welcomed to equal liberty of conscience and political rights in the Roman Catholic province of Maryland." [7]

Five years later, when the Puritans gained the ascendency in Maryland, they were guilty of the infamous ingratitude of disfranchising the very Catholic settlers by whom they had been so hospitably entertained. They "had neither the gratitude to respect the rights of the government by which they had been received and fostered, nor magnanimity to continue the toleration to which alone they were indebted for their residence in the colony. An act concerning religion forbade liberty of conscience to be extended to 'Popery,' 'Prelacy,' or 'licentiousness of opinion.'" [8]

I shall also quote from "Maryland, the History of a Palatinate," by William Hand Browne.[9] Mr. Browne was a graduate of the University of Maryland. For several years he was editor of the Maryland Archives, and of the Maryland Historical Society. He became afterward Professor of English Literature in the Johns Hopkins University. He devoted his long life to the Colonial history of Maryland, and is justly recognized as a standard authority on that subject. I may add that he cannot be suspected of undue partiality, as he was not a member of the Catholic Church.

Speaking of Calvert, the Proprietary of the Maryland Colony, the author remarks that "while as yet there was no spot in Christendom where religious belief was free, and when even the Commons of England had openly declared against toleration,

---

[7] Ibid.
[8] Bancroft's "History of the United States," Vol. I., ch. vii. Vide Bacon's Laws.
[9] Boston, Houghton, Mifflin & Co., 1884.

Calvert founded a community wherein no man was to be molested for his faith. At a time when absolutism had struck down representative government in England and it was doubtful if a Parliament of freemen would ever meet again, he founded a community in which no laws were to be made without the consent of the freemen.

The *Ark* and the *Dove* were names of happy omen. The one saved from the general wreck the germs of political liberty; and the other bore the olive branch of religious peace." [10]

When the rule of the Catholic Proprietary was overthrown and the Puritans had gained the ascendency in the Province, "the new Commissioners issued writs of election to a general assembly —writs of a tenor hitherto unknown in Maryland. No man of the Roman Catholic faith could be elected as a burgess, or even cast a vote. The Assembly obtained by this process of selection, justified its choice. It at once repealed the Toleration Act of 1649 and created a new one, more to its mind, which also bore the title: "An Act concerning Religion," but it was toleration with a difference. It provided that none who professed the Popish religion should be protected in the Province, but were to be restrained from the exercise thereof.

For Protestants it provided that no one professing faith in Christ was to be restrained from the exercise of his religion, "provided that this liberty be not extended to Popery, or Prelacy, nor to such as under the profession of Christ, hold forth and practice licentiousness. That is, with the exception of the Roman Catholics and churchmen, together with the Brownists, Quakers, Anabaptists, and other miscellaneous Protestant sects, all others might profess their faith without molestation." [11]

After the overthrow of the Puritan authority, and the advent to power of the members of the Church of England, the second act of the Assembly was to make the Protestant Episcopal Church the established church of the Province.

The Act imposed an annual tax of forty pounds of tobacco per poll on all taxables for the purpose of building churches, and

[10] Ibid., Chapter iii.   [11] Ibid., Chap. v.

maintaining the clergy. In 1702 it was re-enacted with a toleration
clause: "Protestant Dissenters and Quakers were exempted from
the penalties and disabilities, and might have separate meeting-
houses, provided that they paid their forty pounds per poll to
support the Established Church. As for the 'Papists,' it is need-
less to say that there was no exemption nor license for them."[12]

The author then sets before us the three kinds of toleration,
like three portraits, so that their distinctive features appear in
bold relief.

"We may now," he says, "place side by side the three tolera-
tions of Maryland."

The toleration of the (Catholic) Proprietaries lasted fifty years,
and under it all believers in Christ were equal before the law,
and all support to churches or ministers was voluntary.

The Puritan toleration lasted six years, and included all but
Papists, Prelatists and those who held objectional doctrines.

The Anglican toleration lasted eighty years, and had glebes
and churches for the Establishment, connivance for Dissenters,
the penal laws for Catholics, and for all, the forty per poll.

In fact, an additional turn was given to the screw in this year;
the oath of "abhorrency," a more offensive form of the oath of
supremacy, being required, beside the oath of allegiance, and for
one thing, no Catholic attorney was allowed to practise in the
Province."[13]

When the members of the Constitutional Convention declared
in 1787, that "Congress shall make no law respecting an establishment of religion, or prohibiting the free exercise thereof," it
is worthy of note that they were echoing the sentiments, and even
repeating the language of the Maryland Assembly of 1649, which
declared that "No person whatsoever within this Province, professing to believe in Jesus Christ, shall from henceforth be any
ways molested for his or her religion, nor in the free exercise
thereof."

We may therefore affirm that Lord Baltimore's Toleration Act

[12] Ibid., Chap. xi.
[13] Ibid., Chap. xi.

of 1649 was the bright dawn that ushered in the noon-day sun of freedom in 1787. And we have every reason to believe that the Proprietary's charter of liberty with its attendant blessings, served as an example, an incentive, and an inspiration to some at least of the framers of the Constitution, to extend over the new Republic, the precious boon of civil and religious liberty.

It is proper to also observe that the Act of 1649 was not a new declaration of religious freedom on the part of Lord Baltimore's administration, but was a solemn affirmation of the toleration granted by the Catholic Proprietary from the beginning of the Settlement in 1634.

I will close this subject in the words of a distinguished member of the Maryland Historical Society: "Higher than all titles and badges of honor, and more exalted than royal nobility is the imperishable distinction which the passage of this broad and liberal Act won for Maryland, and for the members of that never-to-be-forgotten session, and sacred forever be the hallowed spot which gave it birth." [14]

What shall I say of the prominent part that was taken by distinguished representatives of the Catholic Church in the cause of our American Independence? What shall I say of Charles Carroll of Carrollton, who, at the risk of sacrificing his rich estates, signed the Declaration of Independence; of Rev. John Carroll, afterward the first Archbishop of Baltimore, who, with his cousin Charles Carroll and Benjamin Franklin, was sent by Congress to Canada to secure the co-operation of the people of that province in the struggle for liberty; of Kosciusko, Lafayette, Pulaski, Barry and a host of other Catholic heroes who labored so effectually in the same glorious cause? American patriots without number the Church has nursed in her bosom; a traitor, never.

The Father of his Country was not unmindful of these services. Shortly after his election to the Presidency, replying[15] to an address of his Catholic fellow-citizens, he uses the following

[14] James Walter Thomas.
[15] The original of Washington's reply is still preserved in the Archives of the Baltimore Cathedral.

language: "I presume that your fellow-citizens will not forget the patriotic part which you took in the accomplishment of their revolution, and the establishment of their government; or the important assistance they received from a nation in which the Roman Catholic faith is professed."

And the Catholics of our generation have nobly emulated the patriotism and the spirit of toleration exhibited by their ancestors. They can neither be accused of disloyalty nor of intolerance to their dissenting brethren. In more than one instance of our nation's history our churches have been desecrated and burned to the ground; our convents have been invaded and destroyed; our clergy have been exposed to insult and violence. These injuries have been inflicted on us by incendiary mobs animated by hatred of Catholicism. Yet, in spite of these provocations, our Catholic citizens, though wielding an immense numerical influence in the localities where they suffered, have never retaliated. It is in a spirit of just pride that we can affirm that hitherto in the United States no Protestant house of worship or educational institution has been destroyed, nor violence offered to a Protestant minister by those who profess the Catholic faith. God grant that such may always be our record!

It is just because the Church has ever resisted the tyranny of kings, in their encroachments on the sacred rights of conscience, that she has always been the victim of royal persecution. In every age, in the language of the Psalmist, "the kings of the earth rose up, and the princes assembled together against the Lord and against His Christ." [16] The brightest and most thrilling pages of ecclesiastical history are those which record the sufferings of Popes and Prelates at the hands of temporal sovereigns for conscience' and for justice' sake.

Take, for instance, St. John Chrysostom, the great Archbishop of Constantinople in the fifth century, and the idol of the people. He had the courage, like John the Baptist, to raise his eloquent voice against the lasciviousness of the court, and particularly against the Empress Eudoxia, who ruled like another Jezabel.

[16] Ps. ii.

He was banished from his See, treated with the utmost indignity by the soldiers, and died in exile from sheer exhaustion and ill-treatment.

Witness Pope Gregory VII., the fearless Hildebrand, in his life-long struggle with the German Emperor, Henry IV. Gregory directed all the energies of his great mind towards reforming the abuses which had crept into the church of France and Germany in the eleventh century. In those days the Emperor of Germany assumed the right of naming or appointing Bishops throughout his Empire. This sacred office was commonly bestowed on very unworthy candidates, and very often put up at auction, to be sold to the highest bidder, as is now the case with the schismatic Greek church in Turkey.

These Bishops too often repaid their imperial benefactor by pandering to his passions and by the most servile flattery. The intrepid Pope partially succeeded in uprooting the evil, though the effort cost him his life. The Emperor invaded Rome and drove Gregory from his See, who died uttering these words with his last breath: "I have loved justice and hated iniquity, and therefore I die in exile."

For the same cause Thomas à Becket, Archbishop of Canterbury, was slain at the altar by the hired assassins of Henry II., of England.

Observe how Pius VII. was treated by the first Napoleon in the beginning of the present century. The day-dream of Napoleon was to be master of Europe, and to place his brothers and friends on the thrones of the continent, that they might revolve, like so many satellites, around his throne in France. Napoleon makes two demands on the venerable Pontiff: First—That he dissolve the marriage which had been contracted between the Emperor's brother, Jerome, and Miss Patterson, of Baltimore. His ostensible reason for having the marriage dissolved was because Miss Patterson was a Protestant, but his real motive was to secure a royal bride for his brother instead of an American lady. Second—That he close his ports against the commerce of England, with which nation Napoleon was then at war, and make common cause with the Emperor against his enemies. The Pope rejected both demands. He told the Emperor that the Church held all marriages performed by her as indissoluble, even when one of the parties was not a Catholic; and that, as the common father of Christendom, he could close his port against no Christian power. For refusing to comply with this second demand the Pope was arrested and sent into exile, where he lingered for years.

At this very moment the old conflict between the Church and despotic governments is raging fiercely throughout Europe. The scene enacted by John and Herod is today reproduced in almost every kingdom of the old world. It is the old fight between brute force and the God-given rights of conscience.

In Russia we see the Bishop of Plock exiled for life from his See to Siberia. His only offence is his refusal to acknowledge that the Emperor Alexander is the head of the Christian Church.

If we pass over into Italy we see religious men and women driven from their homes; their houses and libraries confiscated— libraries which pious and learned men had been collecting and consulting for ages. The only crime of those religious is that they have not the power to resist brute force.

Cross the Alps into France and there you will see that many-headed monster, the Commune, assassinating the Archbishop of Paris and his clergy, solely because he and they were the representatives of law and order.

In the Republic of Switzerland Bishop Mermillod is expelled from Geneva without the slightest charge adduced against his character as a citizen and a Christian Prelate. Faithful clergymen are deprived by the government of their parochial rights and renegade Priests are intruded in their place. The shepherd is driven away and wolves lay waste the fold.

Go to Prussia; what do you behold there? A Prime Minister flushed with his recent victories over France. He is not content with seeing his master wear the imperial crown of Germany; he wants him to wear also the tiara of the Pope. Bismarck, like Aman, the minister of King Assuerus, is not satisfied with being second in the kingdom so long as Mardochai, that is the Church, refuses to bow down and worship him.

He fines the venerable Archbishop of Gnesen-Posen and other Prussian Prelates again and again, sells their furniture and finally sends them to prison for a protracted period. St. John Chrysostom beautifully remarks that St. Paul, elevated to the third heaven, was glorious to contemplate; but that far more glorious is Paul buried in the dungeons of Rome. I can say in like manner, of Archbishop Ledochowski of Posen, that he was conspicuous in the Vatican Council among his peers; but he was still more conspicuous sitting solitary in his Prussian prison.

The loyalty of the Prussian clergy is above reproach. The Bishops are imprisoned because they insist on the right of educating students for the ministry, ordaining and appointing clergy, without consulting the government. They are denied a right which in this country is possessed by Free Masons and every other human organization in the land.

Perhaps a simple illustration will present to you in a clearer light the odious character of the penal laws to which I have alluded. Suppose the government of the United States were to issue a general order requiring the clergy of the various Christian denominations to be educated in government establishments, forcing them to take an oath before entering on the duties of the ministry, and forbidding the ecclesiastical authorities to appoint or remove any clergyman without permission of the civil power at Washington. Would not the American people rise up in their might before they would submit to have fetters so galling forged on their conscience? And yet this is precisely the odious legislation which the Prussian government is enacting against the Church. And the Catholic Church, in resisting these laws, is not only fighting her own battles, but she is contending for the principle of freedom of conscience everywhere.

But, thank God, we live in a country where liberty of conscience is respected, and where the civil constitution holds over us the ægis of her protection, without intermeddling with ecclesiastical affairs. From my heart, I say: America, with all thy faults, I love thee still. Perhaps at this moment there is no nation on the face of the earth where the Church is less trammelled, and where she has more liberty to carry out her sublime destiny than in these United States.

For my part, I much prefer the system which prevails in this country, where the temporal needs of the Church are supplied by voluntary contributions of the faithful, to the system which obtains in some Catholic countries of Europe, where the Church is supported by the government, thereby making feeble reparation for the gross injustice it has done to the Church by its former wholesale confiscation of ecclesiastical property. And the Church pays dearly for this indemnity, for she has to bear the perpetual attempts at interference and the vexatious enactments of the civil power, which aims at making her wholly dependent upon itself.

Some years ago, on my return from Rome, in company with the late Archbishop Spalding I paid a visit to the Bishop of Annecy, in Savoy. I was struck by the splendor of his palace and saw a sentinel at the door, placed there by the French government as a guard of honor. But the venerable Bishop soon disabused me of my favorable impressions. He told me that he was in a state of gilded slavery. I cannot, said he, build as much as a sacristy without obtaining permission of the government.

I do not wish to see the day when the Church will invoke or receive any government aid to build our churches, or to pay the salary of our clergy, for the government may then begin to dictate to us what doctrines we ought to preach. If it is a great wrong to muzzle the press, it is a greater wrong to muzzle the pulpit. No amount of State subsidy would compensate for the evils resulting from the Government censorship of the Gospel, and the suppression of Apostolic freedom in proclaiming it. St. Paul exults in the declaration that, though he is personally in chains, the word of God is not enchained.[17]

And moreover, in proportion as State patronage would increase, the sympathy and aid of the faithful would diminish.

[17] II. Tim. ii. 9.

May the happy condition of things now existing among us always continue, in which the relations between the clergy and the people will be direct and immediate, in which Bishops and Priests will bestow upon their spiritual children their voluntary labors, their tender solicitude, their paternal affection, and pour out like water their hearts' blood, if necessary; and in which they will receive in return the free-will offerings—the devotion and gratitude of a filial people.

CHAPTER XVIII

CHARGES OF RELIGIOUS PERSECUTION

THE SPANISH INQUISITION—THE MASSACRE OF ST. BARTHOLOMEW—
QUEEN MARY OF ENGLAND

I

THE SPANISH INQUISITION

BUT did not the Spanish Inquisition exercise enormous cruelties against heretics and Jews? I am not the apologist of the Spanish Inquisition, and I have no desire to palliate or excuse the excesses into which that tribunal may at times have fallen. From my heart I abhor and denounce every species of violence, and injustice, and persecution of which the Spanish Inquisition may have been guilty. And, in raising my voice against coercion for conscience' sake I am expressing not only my own sentiments, but those of every Catholic Priest and layman in the land.

Our Catholic ancestors, for the last three hundred years, have suffered so much for freedom of conscience that they would rise up in judgment against us were we to become the advocates and defenders of religious persecution. We would be a disgrace to our sires were we to trample on the principle of liberty which they held dearer than life.

When I denounce the cruelties of the Inquisition I am not standing aloof from the Church, but I am treading in her footprints. Bloodshed and persecution form no part of the creed of the Catholic Church. So much does she abhor the shedding of blood that a man becomes disqualified to serve as a minister at her altars who, by act or counsel, voluntarily sheds the blood of another. Before you can convict the Church of intolerance you must first bring forward some authentic act of her Popes or Councils sanctioning the policy of vengeance. In all my readings I have yet to find one decree of hers advocating torture or death for conscience' sake. She is indeed intolerant of error; but her only weapons against error are those pointed out by St. Paul to Timothy: "Preach the word; be instant in season, out of season; reprove, entreat; rebuke with all patience and doctrine." [1]

But you will tell me: Were not the authors of the Inquisition children of the Church, and did they not exercise their enormities in her name? Granted. But I ask you: Is it just or fair to hold the Church responsible for those acts of her children which she disowns? You do not denounce liberty as mockery because many crimes are committed in her name; neither do you hold a father accountable for the sins of his disobedient children.

We should also bear in mind that the Spaniards were not the only people who have proscribed men for the exercise of their religious belief. If we calmly study the history of other nations our enmity towards Spain will considerably relax, and we shall have to reserve for her neighbors a portion of our indignation. No impartial student of history will deny that the leaders of the reformed religions, whenever they gained the ascendency, exercised violence toward those who differed from them in faith. I mention this not by way of recrimination, nor in palliation of the proscriptions of the Spanish government; for one offence is not justified by another. My object is merely to show that "they who live in glass houses should not throw stones;" and that it is not honest to make Spain the scapegoat, bearing alone on her shoulders the odium of religious intolerance.

It should not be forgotten that John Calvin burned Michael Servetus at the stake for heresy; that the arch-reformer not only avowed but also justified the deed in his writings; and that he established in Geneva an Inquisition for the punishment of refractory Christians.

[1] II. Tim. iv. 2.

It should also be remembered that Luther advocated the most merciless doctrine towards the Jews. According to his apologist, Seckendorf, the German Reformer said that their synagogues ought to be destroyed, their houses pulled down, their prayer-books, and even the books of the Old Testament, to be taken from them. Their rabbis ought to be forbidden to teach and be compelled to gain their livelihood by hard labor.

It should also be borne in mind that Henry VIII. and his successors for many generations inflicted fines, imprisonment and death on thousands of their subjects for denying the spiritual supremacy of the temporal sovereign. This galling Inquisition lasted for nearly three hundred years, and the severity of its decrees scarcely finds a parallel in the Spanish Inquisition. Prescott avows that the administration of Elizabeth was "not a whit less despotic and scarcely less sanguinary than" [2] that of Isabella. The clergy of Ireland, under Cromwell, were ordered, under pain of death, to quit their country, and theological students were obliged to pursue their studies in foreign seminaries. Any Priest who dared to return to his native country forfeited his life. Whoever harbored a Priest suffered death, and they who knew his hiding-place and did not reveal it to the Inquisitors had both their ears cut off.

At this very moment not only in England, but in Ireland, Scotland and Holland, Protestants are worshiping in some of the churches erected by the piety of our Catholic forefathers and wrested from them by violence.

Observe, also, that in all these instances the persecutions were inflicted by the express authority of the *founders* and *heads* of Protestant churches.

The Puritans of New England inflicted summary vengeance on those who were rash enough to differ from them in religion. In Massachusetts "the Quakers were whipped, branded, had their ears cut off, their tongues bored with hot irons, and were banished upon pain of death in case of their return and actually executed upon the gallows." [3]

[2] "Ferdinand and Isabella," Vol. III., p. 202.　　　　[3] Blue Laws.

Who is ignorant of the number of innocent creatures that suffered death in the same State on the ridiculous charge of witchcraft toward the end of the seventeenth century? Well does it become their descendants to taunt Catholics with the horrors of the Spanish Inquisition!

In the religious riots of Philadephia in 1844 Catholic churches were burned down in the name of Protestantism and private houses were sacked. I was informed by an eye-witness that owners of houses were obliged to mark on their doors these words, *This house belongs to Protestants,* in order to save their property from the infuriated incendiaries. For these acts I never heard of any retaliation on the part of Catholics, and I hope I never shall, no matter how formidable may be their numbers and tempting the provocation.

In spite of the boasted toleration of our times, in cannot be denied that there still lurks a spirit of inquisition, which does not, indeed, vent itself in physical violence, but is, nevertheless, most galling to its victims. How many persons have I met in the course of my ministry who were ostracized by their kindred and friends, driven from home, nay, disinherited by their parents, for the sole crime of carrying out the very shibboleth of Protestantism —the exercise of private judgment, and of obeying the dictates of their conscience, by embracing the Catholic faith! Is not this the most exquisite torture that can be inflicted on refined natures?

Ah! there is an imprisonment more lonely than the dungeon; it is the imprisonment of our most cherished thoughts in our own hearts, without a member of the family with whom to communicate.

There is a sword more keen than the executioner's knife; it is the envenomed tongue of obloquy and abuse. There is a banishment less tolerable than exile from one's country; it is the excommunication from the parental roof and from the affections of those we love.

Have I a right to hold the members of the Episcopal, Lutheran, Presbyterian and Congregationalist churches responsible for these proscriptive measures to which I have referred, most of which have been authorized by their respective founders and leaders? God forbid! I know full well that these acts of cruelty form no part of the creed of the Protestant churches. I have been acquainted with Protestants from my youth. They have been among my most intimate and cherished friends, and, from my knowledge of them, I am convinced that they would discountenance any physical violence which would be inflicted on their fellow-citizens on account of their religious convictions. They would justly tell me that the persecutions of former years of which I have spoken should be ascribed to the peculiar and unhappy state of society in which their ancestors lived, rather than to the inherent principles of their religion.

For precisely the same reasons, and for reasons still more forcible, Protestants should not reproach the Catholic Church for the atrocities of the Spanish Inquisition. The persecutions to which I have alluded were for the most part perpetrated by the founders and heads of the Protestant churches, while the rigors of the Spanish tribual were inflicted by laymen and subordinate ecclesiastics, either without the knowledge or in spite of the protests of the Bishops of Rome.

Let us now present the Inquisition in its true light. In the first place, the number of its victims has been wildly exaggerated, as even Prescott is forced to admit. The popular historian of the Inquisition is Llorente, from whom our American authors generally derive their information on this subject. Now who was Llorente? He was a degraded Priest, who was dismissed from the Board of Inquisitors, of which he had been Secretary. Actuated by interest and revenge, he wrote his history at the instance of Joseph Bonaparte, the new King of Spain, and, to please his royal master he did all he could to blacken the character of that institution. His testimony, therefore, should be received with great reserve. To give you one instance of his unreliability, he quotes the historian Mariana as his authority for saying that two thousand persons were put to death in one year in the dioceses of Seville and Cadiz alone. By referring to the pages of Mariana we find that author saying that two thousand were put to death *in all*

Spain during the entire administration of Torquemada, which embraced a period of fifteen years.

Before beginning to examine the character of this tribunal it must be clearly understood that the Spanish Inquisition was not a purely ecclesiastical institution, but a mixed tribunal. It was conceived, systematized, regulated in all its procedures and judgments, equipped with officers and powers, and its executions, fines and confiscations were carried out by the royal authority alone, and not by the Church.[4]

To understand the true character of the Spanish Inquisition, and the motives which prompted King Ferdinand in establishing that tribunal, we must take a glance at the internal condition of Spain at the close of the fifteenth century. After a struggle of eight centuries the Spanish nation succeeded in overthrowing the Moors, and in planting the national flag over the entire country. At last the Cross conquered the Crescent, and Christianity triumphed over Mahometanism. The empire was consolidated under the joint reign of Ferdinand and Isabella.

But there still remained elements of discord in the nation. The population was composed of three conflicting races—the Spaniards, Moors and Jews. Perhaps the difficulties which beset our own Government in its efforts to harmonize the white, the Indian and the colored population, will give us some idea of the formidable obstacles with which the Spanish court had to contend in its efforts to cement into one compact nation a conquering and a conquered people of different race and religion.

The Jews and the Moors were disaffected toward the Spanish government not only on political, but also on religious grounds. They were suspected, and not unjustly, of desiring to transfer their allegiance from the King of Spain to the King of Barbary or to the Grand Turk.

The Spanish Inquisition was accordingly erected by King Ferdinand, less from motives of religious zeal than from those of human policy. It was established, not so much with the view of

---

[4] For an impartial account of the Inquisition, the reader is referred to the "Letters on the Spanish Inquisition," by the Count de Maistre.

preserving the Catholic faith, as of perpetuating the integrity of his kingdom. The Moors and Jews were looked upon not only as enemies of the altar, but chiefly as enemies of the throne. Catholics were upheld not for their faith alone, but because they united faith to loyalty. The baptized Moors and Israelites were oppressed for their heresy because their heresy was allied to sedition.

It must be remembered that in those days heresy, especially if outspoken, was regarded not only as an offence against religion, but also as a crime against the state, and was punished accordingly. This condition of things was not confined to Catholic Spain, but prevailed across the sea in Protestant England. We find Henry VIII. and his successors pursuing the same policy in Great Britain toward their Catholic subjects and punishing Catholicism as a crime against the state, just as Islamism and Judaism were proscribed in Spain.

It was, therefore, rather a royal and political than an ecclesiastical institution. The King nominated the Inquisitors, who were equally composed of lay and clerical officials. He dismissed them at will. From the King, and not from the Pope, they derived their jurisdiction, and into the King's coffers, and not into the Pope's, went all the emoluments accruing from fines and confiscations. In a word, the authority of the Inquisition began and ended with the crown.

In confirmation of these assertions I shall quote from Ranke, a German Protestant historian, who cannot be suspected of partiality to the Catholic Church. "In the first place," says this author, "the Inquisitors were royal officers. The Kings had the right of appointing and dismissing them. . . . The courts of the Inquisition were subject, like other magistracies, to royal visitors. 'Do you not know,' said the King (to Ximenes), 'that if this tribunal possesses jurisdiction, it is from the King it derives it?'

"In the second place, all the profit of the confiscations by this court accrued to the King. These were carried out in a very unsparing manner. Though the *fueros* (privileges) of Aragon forbade the King to confiscate the property of his convicted subjects, he deemed himself exalted above the law in matters pertaining to this court. . . . The proceeds of these confiscations formed a sort of regular income for the royal exchequer. It was even believed, and asserted from the beginning, that the Kings had been moved to establish and countenance this tribunal more by their hankering after the wealth it confiscated than by motives of piety.

"In the third place, it was the Inquisition, and the Inquisition alone, that completely shut out all extraneous interference with the state. The sovereign had now at his disposal a tribunal from which no grandee, no Archbishop, could withdraw himself. As Charles knew no other means of bringing certain punishment on the Bishops who had taken part in the insurrection of the *Communidades* (or communes who were struggling for their rights and liberties), he chose to have them judged by the Inquisition. . . .

"It was in spirit and tendency a political institution. *The Pope had an interest in thwarting it, and he did so;* but the King had an interest in constantly upholding it." [5]

That the Inquisition acted independently of the Holy See, and that even the Catholic hierarchy fell under the ban of this royal tribunal, is also apparent from the following fact: After the convening of the Council of Trent, Bartholomew Caranza, Archbishop of Toledo, was arrested by the Inquisition on a charge of heresy, and his release from prison could not be obtained either by the interposition of Pius IV. or the remonstrance of the Council.

It is true that Sixtus IV., yielding to the importunities of Queen Isabella, consented to its establishment, being advised that it was necessary for the preservation of order in the kingdom; but in 1481, the year following its introduction, when the Jews complained to him of its severity, the same Pontiff issued a Bull against the Inquisitors, as Prescott informs us, in which "he rebuked their intemperate zeal and even threatened them with deprivation." He wrote to Ferdinand and Isabella that "mercy to-

[5] "The Ottoman and Spanish Empires," by Leopold Ranke.

wards the guilty was more pleasing to God than the severity which they were using."

When the Pope could not eradicate the evil he encouraged the sufferers to flee to Rome, where they found an asylum, and where he took the fugitives under his protection. In two years he received four hundred and fifty refugees from Spain. Did the Pontiff send them back, or did he inflict vengeance on them at home? Far from it; they were restored to all the rights of citizens. How can we imagine that the Pope would encourage in Spain the legalized murder of men whom he protected from violence in his own city, where he might have crushed them with impunity? I can find no authenticated instance of any Pope putting to death, in his own dominions, a single individual for his religious belief.

Moreover, sometimes the Pope, when he could not reach the victims, censured and excommunicated the Inquisitor, and protected the children of those whose property was confiscated to the crown.

After a struggle he succeeded in preventing the Spanish government from establishing its Inquisition in Naples or Milan, which then belonged to Spain, so great was his abhorrence of its cruelties.

To sum up: I have endeavored to show that the Church disavows all responsibility for the excesses of the Spanish Inquisition, because oppression forms no part of her creed; that these atrocities have been grossly exaggerated; that the Inquisition was a political tribunal; that Catholic Prelates were amenable to its sentence as well as Moors and Jews, and that the Popes denounced and labored hard to abolish its sanguinary features.

And yet Rome has to bear all the odium of the Inquisition!

I heartily pray that religious intolerance may never take root in our favored land. May the only king to force our conscience be the King of kings; may the only prison erected among us for the sin of unbelief or misbelief be the prison of a troubled conscience; and may our only motive for embracing truth be not the fear of man, but the love of truth and of God.

II

WHAT ABOUT THE MASSACRE OF ST. BARTHOLOMEW?

I have no words strong enough to express my detestation of that inhuman slaughter. It is true that the number of its victims has been grossly exaggerated by partisan writers, but that is no extenuation of the crime itself. I most emphatically assert that the Church had no act or part in this atrocious butchery, except to deplore the event and weep over its unhappy victims. Here are the facts briefly presented:

First—In the reign of Charles IX. of France the Huguenots were a formidable power and a seditious element in that country. They were under the leadership of Admiral Coligny, who was plotting the overthrow of the ruling monarch. The French King, instigated by his mother, Catherine de Medicis, and fearing the influence of Coligny, whom he regarded as an aspirant to the throne, compassed his assassination, as well as that of his followers in Paris, August 24th, 1572. This deed of violence was followed by an indiscriminate massacre in the French capital and other cities of France by an incendiary populace, who are easily aroused but not easily appeased.

Second—Religion had nothing to do with the massacre. Coligny and his fellow Huguenots were slain not on account of their creed, but exclusively on account of their alleged treasonable designs. If they had nothing but their Protestant faith to render them odious to King Charles, they would never have been molested; for, neither did Charles nor his mother ever manifest any special zeal for the Catholic Church nor any special aversion to Protestantism, unless when it threatened the throne.

Third—Immediately after the massacre Charles despatched an envoy extraordinary to each of the courts of Europe, conveying the startling intelligence that the King and royal family had narrowly escaped from a horrible conspiracy, and that its authors had been detected and summarily punished. The envoys, in their narration, carefully suppressed any allusion to the indiscriminate massacre which had taken place, but announced the event in the following words: On that "memorable night, by the destruction of a few seditious men, the king had been delivered from immediate danger of death, and the realm from the perpetual terror of civil war."

Pope Gregory XIII., to whom also an envoy was sent, acting on this garbled information, ordered a "Te Deum" to be sung, and a commemorative medal to be struck in thanksgiving to God, not for the massacre, of which he was utterly ignorant, but for the preservation of the French King from an untimely and violent death, and of the French nation from the horrors of a civil war.

Sismondi, a Protestant historian, tells us that the Pope's nuncio in Paris was purposely kept in ignorance of the designs of Charles; and Ranke, in his *History of the Civil Wars,* informs us that Charles and his mother suddenly left Paris in order to avoid an interview with the Pope's legate, who arrived soon after the massacre; their guilty conscience fearing, no doubt, a rebuke from the messenger of the Vicar of Christ, from whom the real facts were not long concealed.

Fourth—It is scarcely necessary to vindicate the innocence of the Bishops and clergy of France in this transaction, as no author, how hostile soever to the Church, has ever, to my knowledge, accused them of any complicity in the heinous massacre.

On the contrary, they used their best efforts to arrest the progress of the assailants, to prevent further bloodshed and to protect the lives of the fugitives. More than three hundred Calvinists were sheltered from the assassins by taking refuge in the house of the Archbishop of Lyons. The Bishops of Lisieux, Bordeaux, Toulouse and of other cities offered similar protection to those who sought safety in their homes.

Thus we see that the Church slept in tranquil ignorance of the stormy scene until she was aroused to a knowledge of the tempest by the sudden uproar it created. Like her Divine Spouse on the troubled waters, she presents herself only to say to them: "Peace be still."

III

I am asked: *Must you not admit that Mary, Queen of England, persecuted the Protestants of the British realm?* I ask this question in reply: *How is it that Catholics are persistently reproached for the persecutions under Mary's reign, while scarcely a voice is raised in condemnation of the legalized fines, confiscations and deaths inflicted on the Catholics of Great Britain and Ireland for three hundred years—from the establishment of the church of England, in 1534, to the time of the Catholic emancipation?* Elizabeth's hands were steeped in the blood of Catholics, Puritans and Anabaptists. Why are these cruelties suppressed or glossed over, while those of Mary form the burden of every nursery tale? Is it because persecution becomes justice when Catholics happen to be the victims, or is it because they are expected, from long usage, to be insensible to torture?

If we weigh in the scales of impartial justice the reigns of both sisters, we shall be compelled to bring a far more severe verdict against Elizabeth.

First—Mary reigned only five years and four months. Elizabeth's reign lasted forty-four years and four months. The younger sister, therefore, swayed the sceptre of authority nearly nine times longer than the elder; and the number of Catholics who suffered for their faith during the long administration of Elizabeth may be safely said to exceed in the same proportion the victims of Mary's reign. Hallam asserts that "the rack seldom stood idle in the tower for all the latter part of Elizabeth's reign;"[6] and its very first month was stained by an intolerant statute.[7]

Second—The most unpardonable act of Mary's life, in the judgment of her critics, was the execution of Lady Jane Grey. But Lady Jane was guilty of high treason, having usurped the throne of England, which she occupied for nine days.

[6] Constitutional History; Elizabeth, Chap. III.
[7] See Lingard, Vol. VII., pp. 244-5.

Elizabeth put to death her cousin Mary, Queen of Scots, after a long imprisonment, on the unsustained charge of aspiring to the English throne.

Third—Mary's zeal was exercised in behalf of the religion of her forefathers, and of the faith established in England for nearly a thousand years.

Elizabeth's zeal was employed in extending the new creed introduced by her father in a moment of passion, and modified by herself. Surely, the coercive enforcement of a new creed is more odious than the rigorous maintenance of the time-honored faith of a nation.

Mary, therefore, insisted on perpetuating the established order of things; Elizabeth on subverting it.

Fourth—The elder sister was propagating what she believed to be the unchangeable and infallible doctrines of Jesus Christ; the younger sister was propagating her own and her father's novel and more or less uncertain opinions.

Fifth—While Mary had no private or personal motives in oppressing Protestants, Elizabeth's hostility to the Catholic Church was intensified, if not instigated, by her hatred of the Pope, who had declared her illegitimate. Her legitimacy before the world depended on the success of the new religion, which had legalized her father's divorce from Catherine.

Sixth—Hence as Macaulay says, Mary was sincere in her religion; Elizabeth was not. "Having no scruple about conforming to the Romish Church when conformity was necessary to her own safety, retaining to the last moment of her life a fondness for much of the doctrine and much of the ceremonial of that Church, she yet subjected that Church to a persecution even more odious than the persecution with which her sister had harassed the Protestants. Mary . . . did nothing for her religion which she was not prepared to suffer for it. She had held it firmly under persecution. She fully believed it to be essential to salvation. Elizabeth, in opinion, was little more than half a Protestant. She had professed, when it suited her, to be wholly a Catholic. . . . What can be said in defence of a ruler who is at once indifferent and intolerant?"[8]

An intelligent gentleman in North Carolina once said to me tauntingly, What do you think of bloody Mary? Did you ever hear, I replied, of her sister's cruelties to Catholics? He answered that he never read of that *mild* woman persecuting for conscience' sake. I was amazed at his words, until he acknowledged that his historical library was comprised in one work—*D' Aubigné's History of the Reformation*. That *veracious* author has prudently suppressed, or delicately touched, Elizabeth's peccadilloes as not coming within the scope of his plan. How many are found, like our North Carolina gentleman, who are familiar from their childhood with the name of *Smithfield,* but who never once heard of *Tyburn!*

[8] Macaulay's Essays, "Review of Nares' Memoirs of Lord Burleigh."

CHAPTER XIX

GRACE—THE SACRAMENTS—ORIGINAL SIN—BAP-
TISM—ITS NECESSITY—ITS EFFECTS—
MANNER OF BAPTISING

THE grace of God is that supernatural assistance which He imparts to us, through the merits of Jesus Christ, for our salvation. It is called *supernatural,* because no one by his own natural ability can acquire it.

Without Divine grace we can neither conceive nor accomplish anything for the sanctification of our souls. "Not that we are sufficient," says the Apostle, "to think anything of ourselves, as of ourselves; but our sufficiency is from God." [1] "For it is God who worketh in you, both to will and to accomplish" [2] anything conducive to your salvation. "Without Me," says our Lord, "you can do nothing." [3] But in order that Divine grace may effectually aid us we must co-operate with it, or at least we must not resist it.

The grace of God is obtained chiefly by prayer and the Sacraments.

A Sacrament is a visible sign instituted by Christ by which grace is conveyed to our souls. Three things are necessary to constitute a Sacrament, viz.—a visible sign, invisible grace and the institution by our Lord Jesus Christ.

Thus, in the Sacrament of Baptism, there is the outward sign, which consists in the pouring of water and in the formula of words which are then pronounced; the interior grace or sanctifi-

---

[1] II. Cor. iii. 5.   [2] Phil. ii. 13.   [3] John xv. 5.

cation which is imparted to the soul: "Be baptized, . . . and you shall receive the gift of the Holy Ghost;" [4] and the ordinance of Jesus Christ, who said: "Teach all nations, baptizing them in the name of the Father, and of the Son, and of the Holy Ghost." [5]

Our Savior instituted seven Sacraments, namely, Baptism, Confirmation, Eucharist, Penance, Extreme Unction, Orders and Matrimony, which I shall explain separately.

According to the teachings of Holy Writ, man was created in a state of innocence and holiness, and after having spent on this earth his allotted terms of years he was destined, without tasting death, to be translated to the perpetual society of God in heaven.[6] But in consequence of his disobedience he fell from his high estate of righteousness; his soul was defiled by sin; he became subject to death and to various ills of body and soul and forfeited his heavenly inheritance.

Adam's transgression was not confined to himself, but was transmitted, with its long train of dire consequences, to all his posterity. It is called *original* sin because it is derived from our original progenitor. "Wherefore," says St. Paul, "as by one man sin entered into this world, and by sin death, and so death passed unto all men, in whom all have sinned." [7] And elsewhere he tells us that "we were by nature children of wrath." [8]

"Who," says Job, "can make him clean that is conceived of unclean seed," or, as the Septuagint version expresses it: "There is no one free from stain, not even though his life be of one day." [9] As an infant one day old cannot commit an actual sin, the *stain* must come from the original offense of Adam. "Behold," says David, "I was conceived in iniquities, and in sins did my mother conceive me." [10] The Scripture also tells us that Jeremiah and John the Baptist were sanctified before their birth, or purified from sin, and, of course, at that period of their existence they were incapable of actual sin. They were cleansed, therefore, from the original taint.

These passages clearly show that we have all inherited the

[4] Acts ii. 38.   [5] Matt. xxviii. 19.   [6] See Wisdom ii. 23.
[7] Rom. v. 12.   [8] Eph. ii. 3.   [9] Job xiv. 4.   [10] Ps. l. 7.

transgression of our first parents, and that we are born enemies of God. And it is equally plain that these texts apply to every member of the human family—to the infant of a day old as well as to the adult.

Indeed, even without the light of Holy Scripture, we have only to look into ourselves to be convinced that our nature has undergone a rude shock. How else can we account for the miseries and infirmities of our bodies, the blindness of our understanding, the perversity of our will—inclined always to evil rather than to good —the violence of our passions, which are constantly waging war in our hearts? How well does the Catholic doctrine explain this abnormal state. Hence, Paschal truly says that man is a greater mystery to himself without original sin than is the mystery itself.

The Church, however, declares that the Blessed Virgin Mary was exempted from the stain of original sin by the merits of our Savior Jesus Christ; and that, consequently, she was never for an instant subject to the dominion of Satan. This is what is meant by the doctrine of the Immaculate Conception.

But God, in passing sentence of condemnation on Adam, consoled him by the promise of a Redeemer to come. "I will put enmities," saith the Lord, "between thee and the woman, and thy seed and her seed; she shall crush thy head." [11] Jesus, the seed of Mary, is the chosen one who was destined to crush the head of the infernal serpent. And "when the fulness of time was come God sent His Son, made of a woman, . . . that He might redeem them that were under the law, that we might receive the adoption of sons." [12]

Jesus Christ, our Redeemer, came to wash away the defilement from our souls and to restore us to that Divine friendship which we had lost by the sin of Adam. He is the second Adam, who came to repair the iniquity of the first. It was our Savior's privilege to prescribe the conditions on which our reconciliation with God was to be effected.

Now He tells us in His Gospel that Baptism is the essential

[11] Gen. iii. 15.   [12] Gal. iv. 4, 5.

means established for washing away the stain of original sin and the door by which we find admittance into His Church, which may be called the second Eden. We must all submit to a new birth, or regeneration, before we can enter the kingdom of heaven. Water is the appropriate instrument of this new birth, as it indicates the interior cleansing of the soul; and the Holy Ghost, the Giver of spiritual life, is its Author.

The Church teaches that Baptism is necessary for all, for infants as well as adults, and her doctrine rests on the following grounds:

Our Lord says to Nicodemus: "Amen, amen, I say to thee, unless a man be born again of water and the Holy Ghost he cannot enter into the kingdom of God." [13] These words embrace the whole human family, without regard to age or sex, as is evident from the original Greek text, for τις, which is rendered *man* in our English translation, means any one—mankind in its broadest acceptation.

The Acts of the Apostles and the Epistles of St. Paul, although containing only a fragmentary account of the ministry of the Apostles, plainly insinuate that the Apostles baptized children as well as grown persons. We are told, for instance, that Lydia "was baptized, and her household," [14] by St. Paul; and that the jailer "was baptized, and all his family." [15] The same Apostle baptized also "the household of Stephanas." [16] Although it is not expressly stated that there were children among these baptized families, the presumption is strongly in favor of the supposition that there were. But if any doubt exists regarding the Apostolic practice of baptizing infants it is easily removed by referring to the writings of the primitive Fathers of the Church, who, as they were the immediate successors of the Apostles, ought to be the best interpreters of their doctrines and practice.

St. Irenæus, a disciple of Polycarp, who was a disciple of St. John the Evangelist, says: "Christ came to save all through Himself; all, I say, *who are born anew* (or baptized) through Him—

---

[13] John iii. 5.
[14] Acts xvi. 15.
[15] Ibid. xvi. 33.
[16] I. Cor. i. 16.

infants and little ones, boys and youths, and aged persons." [17]
Origen, who lived a few years later, writes: "The Church received the tradition from the Apostles, to give baptism even to infants." [18]

The early church of Africa bears triumphant testimony in vindication of infant baptism. St. Cyprian and sixty-six suffragan Prelates held a council in the metropolitan city of Carthage, in the year 253. While the Council is in session a Prelate named Fidus writes to the Fathers, asking them whether infants ought to be baptized before the eighth day succeeding their birth, or on the eighth day, in accordance with the practice of circumcision. The Bishops unanimously subscribe to the following reply: "As to what regards the baptism of infants, . . . we all judged that the mercy and grace of God should be denied to no human being from the moment of his birth. If even to the greatest delinquents the remission of sins is granted, how much less should the infant be repelled, who, being recently born according to Adam, has contracted at his first birth the contagion of the ancient death." [19] The African Council asserts here two prominent facts—the universal contagion of the human race through Adam's fall, and the universal necessity of Baptism without distinction of age.

Upon this decision, I will make two observations: First—Fidus did not inquire about the necessity of infant baptism, which he already admitted, but about the propriety of conferring it on the eighth day, in imitation of the Jewish law of circumcision. Second—The Bishops assembled in that Council were as numerous as the whole Episcopate of the United States, which contains about five thousand Priests and upwards of six millions of Catholics. We may therefore reasonably conclude that the judgment of the African Council represented the faith of several thousand Priests and several millions of Catholics.

St. Augustine, commenting on this decision, justly observes that St. Cyprian and his colleagues made no new decree, but maintained most firmly the faith of the Church. And this is the

[17] Lib. II. adr. Hær.   [18] In Ep. ad Rom.   [19] Epis. ad Fidum.

unanimous sentiment of tradition from the days of the Apostles to our own times.

Is it not ludicrous as well as impious to see a few German fanatics, in the sixteenth century, raising their feeble voice against the thunder tones of all Christendom, by decrying a practice which was universally held as sacred and essential? In judging between the teachings of Apostolical antiquity on the one hand and of the Anabaptists on the other, it is not hard to determine on which side lies the truth; for, what becomes of the Christian Church, if it has erred on so vital a point as that of Baptism during the entire period of its existence?

Original sin, as St. Paul has told us, is universal. Every child is, therefore, defiled at its birth with the taint of Adam's disobedience. Now, the Scripture says that nothing defiled can enter the kingdom of heaven.[20] Hence Baptism, which washes away original sin, is as essential for the infant as for the full grown man, in order to attain the kingdom of heaven.

I said that regeneration is necessary for all. But it is important to observe that if a man is heartily sorry for his sins, if he loves God with his whole heart, if he desires to comply with all the Divine ordinances, including Baptism, but has no opportunity of receiving it, or is not sufficiently instructed as to its necessity, God, in this case, accepts the will for the deed. Should this man die in these dispositions, he is saved by the *baptism of desire,* as happened to the Emperor Valentinian who died a Catechuman: "I lost him whom I was about to regenerate," says St. Ambrose, "but he did not lose that grace he sought for." Or, if an unbaptized person lays down his life for Christ, his death is accepted as more than an equivalent for baptism; for he dies not only sanctified, but he will wear a martyr's crown. *He is baptized in his own blood.*

But is not that a cruel and heartless doctrine which excludes from heaven so many harmless babes that have never committed any actual fault? To this I reply: Has not God declared that Baptism is necessary for all? And is not God the supreme Wisdom

and Justice and Mercy? I am sure, then, that there can be nothing cruel or unjust in God's decrees. The province of reason consists in ascertaining that God has spoken. When we know that
He has spoken, then our investigation ceases, and faith and
obedience begin. Instead of impiously criticising the Divine
decree, we should exclaim with the Apostle: "O! the depth of the
riches of the wisdom and knowledge of God! how incomprehensible are His judgments, and how unsearchable His ways! For,
who hath known the mind of the Lord? or who hath been His
counsellor?" [21]

Let us remember that heaven is a place to which none of us has
any inherent right or natural claim, but that it is promised to us
by the pure favor of God. He can reject and adopt whom He
pleases, and can, without injustice, prescribe His own conditions
for accepting His proffered boon. If your child is deprived of
heaven by being deprived of Baptism, God does it no wrong because He infringes no right to which your child had any inalien-
able title. If your child obtains the grace of Baptism be thankful
for the gift.

It is proper here to state briefly what the Church actually
teaches regarding the future state of unbaptized infants. Though
the Church, in obedience to God's Word, declares that unbaptized infants are excluded from the kingdom of heaven, it should
not hence be concluded that they are consigned to the place of
the reprobate. None are condemned to the torments of the
damned but such as merit Divine vengeance by their personal sins.

All that the Church holds on this point is that unregenerate
children are deprived of the beatific vision, or the possession of
God, which constitutes the essential happiness of the blessed.

Now, between the supreme bliss of heaven and the torments
of the reprobate, there is a very wide margin.

All admit that the condition of unbaptized infants is better
than non-existence. There are some Catholic writers of distinction who even assert that unbaptized infants enjoy a certain de-

[17] Rom. xi. 33, 34.

gree of natural beatitude—that is, a happiness which is based on the natural knowledge and love of God.

From what has been said you may well judge how reprehensible is the conduct of Catholic parents who neglect to have their children baptized at the earliest possible moment, thereby risking their own souls, as well as the souls of their innocent offspring. How different was the practice of the early Christians, who, as St. Augustine testifies, hastened with their new-born babes to the baptismal font that they might not be deprived of the grace of regeneration.

If an infant is sick, no expense is spared that its life may be preserved. The physician is called in, medicine is given to it, and the mother will spend sleepless nights watching every movement of the infant; she will sacrifice her repose, her health; nay, she will expose even her own life that the life of her offspring may be saved. And yet the supernatural happiness of the child is too often imperiled without remorse by the criminal postponement of Baptism.

But if they are to be censured who are slow in having their children baptized, what are we to think of that large body of professing Christians who, on principle, deny Baptism to little ones till they come to the age of discretion? What are we to think of those who set their private opinions above Scripture, the early Fathers of the Church and the universal practice of Christendom?

We may smile indeed at a theological opinion, no matter how novel or erroneous it may be, so long as it does not involve any dangerous consequences. But when it is given in a case of life and death, how terrible is the responsibility of those who propagate doctrines so erroneous!

The opposite practice of the Catholic and the Baptist churches, in their treatment of the new-born infant, may be well compared to the conduct of the true and the false mother who both claimed the child at the tribunal of Solomon. The king exclaimed: "Divide the living child in two, and give half to the one and half to the other." The pretended mother consented, saying: Let it be neither mine nor thine, but divide it. "But the woman whose child was alive, said to the king (for her bowels were moved upon her child): I beseech thee, my lord, give her the child alive, and do not kill it." While the Baptist church is willing that the child should die a spiritual death, the true mother, the Catholic Church, cries out: Keep the child, provided its spiritual life is saved, even at your hands. Let it be clothed with the robe of innocence even by a stranger. Let it be nursed at the breasts even of a step-mother. Better it should live without me than perish before my face. I will still be its mother, though it know me not.

Ah! my Baptist friend, you think that Baptism is not necessary for your child's salvation. The old Church teaches the contrary. You admit that you may be wrong, and it is a question of life and death. Take the safe side. Give your child the benefit of the doubt. Let it be baptized.

Baptism washes away *original sin, and also actual sins* from the adult who may have contracted them. The cleansing efficacy of Baptism was clearly foreshadowed by the prophet Ezechiel in these words: "I will pour upon you clean water, and you shall be cleansed from all your filthiness. And I will give you a new heart and will put a new spirit within you." [22]

When the Jews asked St. Peter what they should do to be saved the Apostle replied: "Repent, and let everyone of you be baptized in the name of Jesus Christ for the remission of your sins." [23]

And Ananias said to Saul, after his conversion: "Rise up and be baptized, and wash away thy sins." [24]

"We were by nature," says St. Paul, "children of wrath," but by our regeneration, or new birth in Baptism, we become *Christians and children of God*. "For, ye are all the children of God by faith in Christ Jesus. For as many of you as have been baptized in Christ have put on Christ." [25] We are adopted into the same family with Jesus Christ. What He is by nature we are by grace— children of God, and consequently brethren of Christ. Nay, our union with Jesus is still more close. We become true members of

[22] Ezech. xxxvi. 25, 26.
[24] Ibid. xxii. 16.
[23] Acts ii. 38.
[25] Gal. iii. 26, 27.

His mystical body, which is His Church, and His Divine image is stamped upon our soul.

Baptism also clothes us with the *garment of sanctity,* so that our soul becomes a fit dwelling-place for the Holy Ghost. The Apostle, after giving a fearful catalogue of the vices of the Pagans, says to the Corinthians: "And such some of you were; but ye are washed, but ye are sanctified, but ye are justified in the name of our Lord Jesus Christ, and in the Spirit of God." [26]

Baptism, in fine, makes us *heirs of heaven* and co-heirs with Jesus Christ. "We ourselves also," says St. Paul, "were sometimes unwise, incredulous, erring, slaves to divers desires and pleasures, living in malice and envy, hateful, and hating one another. But when the goodness and kindness of God our Savior appeared, . . . He saved us by the laver of regeneration and renovation of the Holy Ghost, whom He hath poured forth abundantly upon us, through Jesus Christ our Savior, that being justified by His grace, we may be heirs, according to the hope of life everlasting." [27]

Here we plainly see that the forgiveness of sin, the adoption into the family of God, the sanctification of the soul and the pledge of eternal life are ascribed to the due reception of Baptism —not, indeed, that water or the words of the minister have any intrinsic virtue to heal the soul, but because Jesus Christ, whose word is creative power, is pleased to attach to this rite its wonderful efficacy of healing the soul, as He imparted to the pool of Bethsaida the power of healing the body." [28]

From what has been said, I ask you candidly what are you to think of the decision rendered in 1872 by the Bishops of the Protestant Episcopal Church, who, in their convention in Baltimore, declared that by the word *regeneration* we are not to understand *a moral change.* If no moral change is effected by Baptism, then there is no change at all; for certainly Baptism produces no physical change in the soul.

Is it no change to pass from sin to virtue, from a "child of wrath" to be a "child of God;" from corruption to sanctification;

[26] I. Cor. vi. 11. [27] Tit. iii. 3-7. [28] John v.

from the condition of heirs of death to the inheritance of heaven? If all this implies no moral change, then these words have lost their meaning.

Modes of baptizing. The Baptists err in asserting that Baptism by immersion is the only valid mode. Baptism may be validly administered in either of three ways, viz.: by *immersion,* or by plunging the candidate into the water; by *infusion,* or by pouring the water; and by *aspersion,* or sprinkling.

As our Lord nowhere prescribes any special form of administering the Sacrament, the Church exercises her discretion in adopting the most convenient mode, according to the circumstances of time and place.

For several centuries after the establishment of Christianity Baptism was *usually* conferred by immersion; but since the twelfth century the practice of baptizing by infusion has prevailed in the Catholic Church, as this manner is attended with less inconvenience than Baptism by immersion.

To prove that Baptism by infusion or by sprinkling is as legitimate as by immersion, it is only necessary to observe that, though immersion was the more common practice in the Primitive Church, the Sacrament was frequently administered even then by infusion and aspersion.

After St. Peter's first discourse three thousand persons were baptized.[29] It is not likely that so many could have been immersed in one day, especially when we consider the time occupied in instructing the candidates.

On reading the account of the Baptism of St. Paul and the jailer the context leaves a strong impression on the mind that both received the Sacrament by aspersion or by infusion.

Early ecclesiastical history records a great many instances in which Baptism was administered to *sick persons* in their beds, to *prisoners* in their cells, and to persons on *shipboard*. The Fathers of the Church never called in question the validity or the legitimacy of such Baptisms. Now, it is almost impossible to believe

[29] Acts ii. 41.

that candidates in such situations could receive the rite by immersion.

We have seen, moreover, that Baptism has always been declared necessary for salvation. It is reasonable, hence, to believe that our Lord would have afforded the greatest facility for the reception of so essential a Sacrament.

But if Baptism by immersion only is valid, how many sick and delicate persons, how many prisoners and seafaring people, how many thousands living in the frigid zone, or even in the temperate zone, in the depth of an inclement winter, though craving the grace of regeneration, would be deprived of God's seal, or would receive it at the risk of their lives! Surely God does not ordinarily impose His ordinances upon us under such a penalty.

Moreover, if immersion is the only valid form of Baptism, what has become of the millions of souls who, in every age and country, have been regenerated by the infusion or the aspersion of water in the Christian Church?

CHAPTER XX

THE SACRAMENT OF CONFIRMATION

CONFIRMATION is a Sacrament in which, through the imposition of the Bishop's hands, unction and prayer, baptized persons receive the Holy Ghost, that they may steadfastly profess their faith and lead upright lives.

This Sacrament is called *Confirmation,* because it *confirms* or strengthens the soul by Divine grace. Sometimes it is named *the laying on of hands,* because the Bishop imposes his hands on those whom he confirms. It is also known by the name of *Chrism,* because the forehead of the person confirmed is anointed with chrism in the form of a cross.

Frequent mention is made of this Sacrament in the Holy Scripture. In the Acts it is written that "When the Apostles who were in Jerusalem had heard that Samaria had received the Word of God they sent unto them Peter and John, who, when they were come, prayed for them that they might receive the Holy Ghost; for He was not yet come upon any of them, but they were only baptized in the name of the Lord Jesus. Then they laid their hands on them, and they received the Holy Ghost." [1]

It is also related that the disciples at Ephesus "were baptized in the name of the Lord Jesus, and when Paul had imposed his hands upon them the Holy Ghost came upon them and they spoke tongues and prophesied." [2]

In his Epistle to the Hebrews St. Paul enumerates Confirmation, or the laying on of hands, together with Baptism and Penance, among the fundamental truths of Christianity. [3]

[1] Acts viii. 14-17.   [2] Acts xix. 5, 6.   [3] Heb. vi. 1, 2.

To the Corinthians he writes: "He that confirmeth us with you in Christ, and that hath anointed us, is God; who also hath sealed us and given the pledge of the Spirit in our hearts." [4] God *confirmeth* us in faith; He hath *anointed* us by spiritual unction, typified by the sacred chrism which is marked on our foreheads. He hath *sealed* us by the indelible character stamped on our souls, which is indicated by the sign of the cross impressed on us. He hath given the *pledge* of the Holy Ghost in our hearts, by the testimony of a good conscience, as an earnest of future glory. The Bishop performs the external unction, but God, "who worketh all in all," sanctifies the soul by His secret operation.

It cannot be asserted that the laying on of hands and the graces which followed from it, as recorded in the Acts, were not intended to be continued after the Apostles' times, for there is no warrant for such an assumption. This function of imposing hands formed as regular and imperative a part of the Apostolic ministry as the duties which they exercised in preaching, baptizing, ordaining, etc. Hence the successors of the Apostles in the nineteenth century have precisely the same authority and obligation to confirm as they have to preach, to baptize or to ordain.

Those who were confirmed by the Apostles usually gave evidence of the grace which they received by prophecy, the gift of tongues and the manifestation of other miraculous powers. It may be asked: Why do not these gifts accompany now the imposition of hands? I answer: Because they are no longer needed. The grace which the Apostolic disciples received was for their personal sanctification. The gift of tongues which they exercised was intended by Almighty God to edify and enlighten the spectators, and to give Divine sanction to the Apostolic ministry. But now that the Church is firmly established, and the Divine authority of her ministry is clearly recognized, these miracles are no longer necessary. St. Gregory illustrates this point by a happy comparison: As the sapling, he says, when it is first planted is regularly watered by the gardener, who softens the earth around it, that the sun and the moisture may nourish its roots until it

[4] II. Cor. i. 21.

takes deep root and it no longer requires any special care, so the Church in her infancy had to be nourished by the miraculous power of God. But after it had taken root in the hearts of the people and spread its branches over the earth it was left to the ordinary agencies of Providence.

St. Augustine writes also on the same subject: "In the first days (of the Church) the Holy Ghost came down on believers, and they spoke in tongues which they had not learned. . . . . These were miracles suited to the times. . . . . Is it now expected that they upon whom hands are laid should speak with tongues? Or, when we imposed hands on these children, did each of you wait to see whether they would speak with tongues? . . . . If, then, there be not now a testimony to the presence of the Holy Spirit by means of these miracles, whence is it proved that he has received the Holy Spirit? Let him ask his own heart; if he loves his brother, the Spirit of God abides in him." [5]

Following in the footsteps of the Apostles we find the Fathers of the Church, from the earliest age, recognizing Confirmation as a Divine and sacramental institution and proclaiming its salutary effects.

"The flesh," says Tertullian, "is *anointed,* that the soul may be consecrated; the flesh is marked, that the soul may be fortified; the flesh is overshadowed *by the imposition of hands,* that the soul may be enlightened with the Spirit." [6]

St. Cyprian, speaking of the Christians baptized in Samaria, says: "Because they had received the legitimate baptism, ... what was wanting, that was done by Peter and John, that prayer being made for them and hands imposed, the Holy Ghost should be invoked and poured forth upon them. *Which now also is done amongst us,* so that they who are baptized in the Church are presented to the Bishops of the Church, and by our prayer and imposition of hands they receive the Holy Ghost and are perfected with the seal of the Lord." [7]

St. Cyril of Jerusalem compares the sacred Chrism in Con-

[5] Tract VI. in Ep. Joan.   [6] De Resur. car.   [7] Epist. lxxiii.

firmation to the Eucharist: "You were anointed with oil, being made sharers and partners of Christ. And see well that you regard it not as mere ointment; for, as the bread of the Eucharist, after the invocation of the Holy Ghost, is no longer mere bread but the body of Christ, so likewise this holy ointment is no longer common ointment after the invocation, but the gift of Christ and of the Holy Ghost, being rendered efficient by His Divinity. You were anointed on the forehead, that you might be delivered from the shame which the first transgressor always experienced, and that you might contemplate the glory of God with an unveiled countenance. . . . . As Christ, after His baptism and the descent of the Holy Ghost upon Him, going forth overcame the adversary, so you likewise, after holy baptism and the mysterious unction, clothed with the panoply of the Holy Ghost, stand against the adverse power and subdue it, saying: 'I can do all things in Christ, who strengtheneth me.' " [8]

St. Ambrose, commenting on these words of the Apostle, "God . . . . hath given us the pledge of the Spirit," (II. Cor. i. 22) expressly applies the text to the seal of Confirmation: "Remember," he says, "that you have received the spiritual seal, the spirit of wisdom and understanding, the spirit of counsel and fortitude, the spirit of knowledge and piety, the spirit of holy fear. God the Father hath sealed you; Christ the Lord hath *confirmed* you, and hath given the pledge of the Spirit in your hearts, *as you have learned from the lesson read from the Apostle.*" [9]

St. Ambrose here speaks of the sevenfold gifts of the Holy Ghost which are received in Confirmation, and every Bishop in our day invokes these same gifts on those whom he is about to confirm.

"Do you know," writes St. Jerome against the sect of Luciferians of his time, "that it is the practice of the churches that the imposition of hands should be performed over baptized persons and the Holy Ghost thus invoked? Do you ask where it is written? In the Acts of the Apostles; but were there no Scriptural

---

[8] Cat. xxi. Mys. iii. De S. Chrism.   [9] De Myst. cvii. n. 42.

authority at hand the consent of the whole world in this regard would have the force of law." [10]

"You willingly understand," says St. Augustine, "by this ointment the Sacrament of Chrism, which, indeed, in the class of visible seals is as sacred as Baptism itself." [11]

The Oriental schismatic churches recognize Confirmation as a Sacrament, and administer the rite as we do, by the imposition of hands and the application of chrism. Now, some of these churches have been separated from the Catholic Church since the fourth and fifth centuries. This fact is an eloquent vindication of the Apostolic antiquity of Confirmation, and is an ample refutation of those who would ascribe to it a more recent origin.

Protestantism, which made such havoc of the other Sacraments, did not fail to abolish Confirmation in its sweeping revolution.

The Episcopal church retains, indeed, the name of Confirmation in its ritual, and even borrows a portion of our prayers and ceremonial. But, in opposition to the uniform teaching of the Catholic, as well as of all the Oriental churches, both orthodox and schismatic, it declares Confirmation to be a mere rite and not a Sacrament.

In violation of the practice of all antiquity it mutilates the rite by omitting the sacred unction. It retains the shadow without the substance.

It raises, indeed, its hands over the candidates; but they are not the anointed hands of Peter or John, or Cyprian or Augustine, to whom it is said: "Whatsoever thou shalt bless, let it be blessed; whatsoever thou shalt sanctify, let it be sanctified." [12] Their hands were lifted up with authority and clothed with supernatural power; but the hands of the Episcopal Bishops are spiritually paralyzed by the suicidal act of the Reformers, and they expressly disclaim any sacramental efficacy in the rite which they administer.

[10] Dial. adv. Lucifer.
[11] L. II., contra lit. Petil.
[12] Roman Pontifical.

CHAPTER XXI

THE HOLY EUCHARIST

AMONG the various dogmas of the Catholic Church there is none which rests on stronger Scriptural authority than the doctrine of the Real Presence of Jesus Christ in the Holy Eucharist. So copious, indeed, and so clear are the passages of the New Testament which treat of this subject that I am at a loss to determine which to select, and find it difficult to compress them all within the compass of this short chapter.

The Evangelists do not always dwell upon the same mysteries of religion. Their practice is rather to supplement each other, so that one of them will mention what the others have omitted or have touched in a cursory way. But in regard to the Blessed Eucharist the sacred writers exhibit a marked deviation from this rule. We find that the four Evangelists, together with St. Paul, have written so explicitly and abundantly on this subject that one of them alone would be amply sufficient to prove the dogma without taking them collectively.

These five inspired writers gave the weight of their individual testimony to the doctrine of the Eucharist because they foresaw —or rather the Holy Ghost, speaking through them, foresaw— that this great mystery, which exacts so strong an exercise of our faith, and which bids us bow down our "understanding unto the obedience of Christ," [1] would meet with opposition in the course of time from those who would measure the infallible Word of God by the erring standard of their own judgment.

[1] II. Cor. x. 5.

I shall select three classes of arguments from the New Testament which satisfactorily demonstrate the Real Presence of Christ in the Blessed Sacrament. The first of these texts speaks of the promise of the Eucharist, the second of its institution and the third of its use among the faithful.

To begin with the words of the promise. While Jesus was once preaching near the coast of the Sea of Galilee He was followed, as usual, by an immense multitude of persons, who were attracted to Him by the miracles which He wrought and the words of salvation which He spoke. Seeing that the people had no food, He multiplied five loaves and two fishes to such an extent as to supply the wants of five thousand men, besides women and children.

Our Lord considered the present a favorable occasion for speaking of the Sacrament of His body and blood, which was to be distributed, not to a few thousands, but to millions of souls; not in one place, but everywhere; not at one time, but for all days, to the end of the world. "I am," He says to His hearers, "the bread of life. Your fathers did eat manna in the desert and died. . . . I am the living bread which came down from heaven. If any man eat of this bread he shall live forever, and the bread which I will give is my flesh for the life of the world. The Jews, therefore, disputed among themselves, saying: How can this man give us His flesh to eat? Then Jesus said to them: Amen, amen, I say to you: Unless ye eat the flesh of the Son of Man and drink His blood, ye shall not have life in you. He that eateth My flesh and drinketh My blood hath everlasting life, and I will raise him up on the last day. For My flesh is meat indeed, and My blood is drink indeed." [2]

If these words had fallen on your ears for the first time, and if you had been among the number of our Savior's hearers on that occasion, would you not have been irresistibly led, by the noble simplicity of His words, to understand Him as speaking truly of His body and blood? For His language is not susceptible of any other interpretation.

When our Savior says to the Jews: "Your fathers did eat

[2] John vi. 48-56.

manna and died, . . . but he that eateth this (Eucharistic) bread shall live forever," He evidently wishes to affirm the superiority of the food which He would give, over the manna by which the children of Israel were nourished.

Now, if the Eucharist were merely commemorative bread and wine, instead of being superior, it would be really inferior to the manna; for the manna was supernatural, heavenly, miraculous food, while bread and wine are a natural, earthly food.

But the best and the most reliable interpreters of our Savior's words are certainly the multitude and the disciples who are listening to Him. They all understood the import of His language precisely as it is explained by the Catholic Church. They believed that our Lord spoke literally of His body and blood. The Evangelist tells us that the Jews "disputed among themselves, saying: How can this man give us His flesh to eat?" Even His disciples, though avoiding the disrespectful language of the multitude, gave expression to their doubt in this milder form: "This saying is hard, and who can hear it?" [3] So much were they shocked at our Savior's promise that "after this many of His disciples went back and walked no more with Him." [4] They evidently implied, by their words and conduct, that they understood Jesus to have spoken literally of His flesh; for, had they interpreted His words in a figurative sense, it would not have been a hard saying, nor have led them to abandon their Master.

But, perhaps, I shall be told that the disciples and the Jews who heard our Savior may have misinterpreted His meaning by taking His words in the literal acceptation, while He may have spoken in a figurative sense. This objection is easily disposed of. It sometimes happened, indeed, that our Savior was misunderstood by His hearers. On such occasions He always took care to remove from their mind the wrong impression they had formed by stating His meaning in simpler language. Thus, for instance, having told Nicodemus that unless a man be born again he cannot enter the kingdom of heaven, and having observed that His

[3] John vi. 61.
[4] Ibid. vi. 67.

meaning was not correctly apprehended by this disciple our Savior added: "Unless a man be born again of water and the Holy Ghost he cannot enter the kingdom of heaven." [5] And again, when He warned His disciples against the leaven of the Pharisees, and finding that they had taken an erroneous meaning from His word, He immediately subjoined that they should beware of the doctrine of the Pharisees.[6]

But in the present instance does our Savior alter His language when He finds His words taken in the literal sense? Does He tell His hearers that He has spoken figuratively? Does He soften the tone of His expression? Far from weakening the force of His words He repeats what He said before, and in language more emphatic: "Amen, amen, I say unto you, Unless ye eat the flesh of the Son of man, and drink His blood, ye shall not have life in you."

When our Savior beheld the Jews and many of His disciples abandoning Him, turning to the chosen twelve, He said feelingly to them: "Will ye also go away? And Simon Peter answered Him: Lord, to whom shall we go? Thou hast the words of eternal life." [7] You, my dear reader, must also take your choice. Will you reply with the Jews, or with the disciples of little faith, or with Peter? Ah! let some say with the unbelieving Jews: "How can this man give us His flesh to eat?" Let others say with the unfaithful disciples: "This is a hard saying. Who can hear it?" But do you say with Peter: "Lord, to whom shall we go? Thou hast the words of eternal life."

So far I have dwelt on the words of the Promise. I shall now proceed to the words of the Institution, which are given in almost the same expressions by St. Matthew, St. Mark and St. Luke. In the Gospel according to St. Matthew we read the following narrative: "And while they were at supper, Jesus took bread, and blessed and broke and gave to His disciples and said: Take ye and eat. This is My body. And taking the chalice, He gave thanks and gave to them, saying: Drink ye all of this; for this is My

[5] John. iii.   [6] Matt. xvi.   [7] John vi. 68, 69.

blood of the New Testament, which shall be shed for many unto remission of sins." [8]

I beg you to recall to mind the former text relative to the Promise and to compare it with this. How admirably they fit together, like two links in a chain! How faithfully has Jesus fulfilled the Promise which He made! Could any idea be expressed in clearer terms than these: This is My body; this is My blood?

Why is the Catholic interpretation of these words rejected by Protestants? Is it because the text is in itself obscure and ambiguous? By no means; but simply because they do not comprehend how God could perform so stupendous a miracle as to give His body and blood for our spiritual nourishment.

Is, then, the power or the mercy of God to be measured by the narrow rule of the human understanding? Is the Almighty not permitted to do anything except what we can sanction by our reason? Is a thing to be declared impossible because we cannot see its possibility?

Has not God created the heavens and the earth *out of nothing* by the fiat of His word? What a mystery is this! Does He not hold this world in the midst of space? Does He not transform the tiny blade into nutritious grain? Did He not feed upwards of five thousand persons with five loaves and two fishes? What a mystery! Did He not rain down manna from heaven for forty years to feed the children of Israel in the desert? Did He not change rivers into blood in Egypt, and water into wine at the wedding of Cana? Does He not daily make devout souls the tabernacles of the Holy Ghost? And shall we have the hardihood to deny, in spite of our Lord's plain declaration, that God, who works these wonders, is able to change bread and wine into His body and blood for the food of our souls?

You tell me it is a mystery above your comprehension. A mystery, indeed. A religion that rejects a revealed truth because it is incomprehensible contains in itself the seeds of dissolution

[8] Matt. xxvi. 26-28.

and will end in rationalism. Is not everything around us a mystery. Are we not a mystery to ourselves? Explain to me how the blood circulates in your veins, how the soul animates and permeates the whole body, how the hand moves at the will of the soul. Explain to me the mystery of life and death.

Is not the Scripture full of incomprehensible mysteries? Do you not believe in the Trinity—a mystery not only above, but apparently contrary to, reason? Do you not admit the Incarnation—that the helpless infant in Bethlehem was God? I understand why Rationalists, who admit nothing above their reason, reject the Real Presence; but that Bible Christians should reject it is to me incomprehensible.

But do those who reject the Catholic interpretation explain this text to their own satisfaction: "This is My body, etc?" Alas! here their burden begins. Only a few years after the early Reformers had rejected the Catholic doctrine of the Eucharist no fewer than one hundred meanings were given to these words: "This is My body." It is far easier to destroy than to rebuild.

Let me now offer you some additional reasons in favor of the Catholic or literal sense. According to a common rule observed in the interpretation of the Holy Scripture, we must always take the words in their literal signification, unless we have some special reason which obliges us to accept them in a figurative meaning. Now, in the present instance, far from being forced to employ the words above quoted in a figurative sense, every circumstance connected with the delivery of them obliges us to interpret them in their plain and literal acceptation.

To whom did our Savior address these words? At what time and under what circumstances did He speak? He was addressing His few chosen disciples, to whom He promised to speak in future, not in parables nor in obscure language, but in the words of simple truth. He uttered these words the night before His Passion. And when will a person use plainer speech than at the point of death?

These words: "This is My body; this is My blood," embodied a new dogma of faith which all were obliged to believe, and a new law which all were obliged to practice. They were the last will and testament of our blessed Savior. What language should be plainer than that which contains an article of faith? What words should be more free from tropes and figures than those which enforce a Divine law? But, above all, where will you find any words more plain and unvarnished than those contained in a last will?

Now, if we understand these words in their plain and obvious, that is, in their Catholic, sense, no language can be more simple and intelligible. But if we depart from the Catholic interpretation, then it is impossible to attach to them any reasonable meaning.

We now arrive at the third class of Scripture texts which have reference to the use or reception of the Sacrament among the faithful.

When Jesus, as you remember, instituted the Eucharist at His last Supper He commanded His disciples and their successors to renew, till the end of time, in remembrance of Him, the ceremony which He performed. What I have done, do ye also "for a commemoration of Me." [9]

We have a very satisfactory means of ascertaining the Apostolic belief in the doctrine of the Eucharist by examining what the Apostles did in commemoration of our Lord. Did they bless and distribute mere bread and wine to the faithful, or did they consecrate, as they believed, the body and blood of Jesus Christ? If they professed to give only bread and wine in memory of our Lord's Supper, then the Catholic interpretation falls to the ground. If, on the contrary, we find the Apostles and their successors, from the first to the nineteenth century, professing to consecrate and dispense the body and blood of Christ, and doing so by virtue of the command of their Savior, then the Catholic interpretation alone is admissible.

Let St. Paul be our first witness. Represent yourself as a member of the primitive Christian congregation assembled in Corinth. About eighteen years after St. Matthew wrote his Gospel, a letter is read from the Apostle Paul, in which the following words

[9] Luke xxii. 19.

occur: "The chalice of benediction which we bless, is it not the communion of the blood of Christ? and the bread which we break, is it not the partaking of the body of the Lord? . . . For, I have received of the Lord that which also I delivered to you, that the Lord Jesus, on the night in which he was betrayed, took bread, and giving thanks, brake it, and said: Take and eat: this is My body which shall be delivered for you. This do for the commemoration of Me. In like manner also the chalice, after the supper, saying: This cup is the New Covenant in My blood. This do ye, as often as ye shall drink, for the commemoration of Me. For, as often as ye shall eat this bread, and drink the cup, ye shall show the death of the Lord until He come. Therefore, whoever shall eat this bread, or drink the chalice of the Lord unworthily, *shall be guilty of the body and of the blood of the Lord*. But let a man prove himself; and so let him eat of that bread and drink of the chalice. For, he who eateth and drinketh unworthily, eateth and drinketh judgment to himself, *not discerning the body of the Lord*." [10]

Could St. Paul express more clearly his belief in the Real Presence than he has done here? The Apostle distinctly affirms that the chalice and bread which he and his fellow Apostles bless is a participation of the body and blood of Christ. And surely no one could be said to partake of that divine food by eating ordinary bread. Mark these words of the Apostle: Whosoever shall take the Sacrament unworthily "shall be guilty of the body and blood of the Lord." What a heinous crime! For these words signify that he who receives the Sacrament unworthily shall be guilty of the sin of high treason, and of shedding the blood of his Lord in vain. But how could he be guilty of a crime so enormous, if he had taken in the Eucharist only a particle of bread and wine. Would a man be accused of homicide, in this common-wealth, if he were to offer violence to the statue or painting of the governor? Certainly not. In like manner, St. Paul would not be so unreasonable as to declare a man guilty of trampling on

[10] I. Cor. x. 16, and xi. 23-29.

the blood of his Savior by drinking in an unworthy manner a little wine in memory of Him.

Study also these words: "He who eateth and drinketh unworthily eateth and drinketh condemnation to himself, *not discerning the body of the Lord.*" The unworthy receiver is condemned for not recognizing or discerning in the Eucharist the body of the Lord. How could he be blamed for not discerning the body of the Lord, if there were only bread and wine before him? Hence, if the words of St. Paul are figuratively understood, they are distorted, forced and exaggerated terms, without meaning or truth. But, if they are taken literally, they are full of sense and of awful significance, and an eloquent commentary on the words I have quoted from the Evangelist.

The Fathers of the Church, without an exception, re-echo the language of the Apostle of the Gentiles by proclaiming the Real Presence of our Lord in the Eucharist. I have counted the names of sixty-three Fathers and eminent Ecclesiastical writers flourishing between the first and sixth century all of whom proclaim the Real Presence—some by explaining the mystery, others by thanking God for his inestimable gift, and others by exhorting the faithful to its worthy reception. From such a host of witnesses I can select here only a few at random.

St. Ignatius, a disciple of St. Peter, speaking of a sect called Gnostics, says: "They abstain from the Eucharist and prayer, because they confess not that the Eucharist and prayer is the flesh of our Savior Jesus Christ."

St. Justin Martyr, in an apology to the Emperor Antoninus, writes in the second century: "We do not receive these things as common bread and drink; but as Jesus Christ our Savior was made flesh by the word of God, even so we have been taught that the Eucharist is *both the flesh and the blood of the same incarnate Jesus.*"

Origen (third century) writes: "If thou wilt go up with Christ to celebrate the Passover, He will give to thee that bread of benediction, His own body, and will vouchsafe to thee His own blood."

St. Cyril, of Jerusalem (fourth century), instructing the Catechumens, observes: "He Himself having declared, *This is My body,* who shall dare to doubt henceforward? And He having said, *This is My blood,* who shall ever doubt, saying: This is not His blood? He once at Cana turned water into wine, which is akin to blood; and is He undeserving of belief when He turned wine into blood?" He seems to be arguing with modern unbelief.

St. John Chrysostom, who died in the beginning of the fifth century, preaching on the Eucharist, says: "If thou wert indeed incorporeal, He would have delivered to thee those same incorporeal gifts without covering. But since the soul is united to the body, He delivers to thee in things perceptible to the senses the things to be apprehended by the understanding. How many nowadays say: 'Would that they could look upon His (Jesus') form, His figure, His raiment, His shoes. Lo! thou seest Him, touchest Him, eatest Him.' "

St. Augustine (fifth century), addressing the newly-baptized, says: "I promised you a discourse wherein I would explain the sacrament of the Lord's table, which sacrament you even now behold, and of which you were last night made partakers. You ought to know what you have received. The bread which you see on the altar, after being sanctified by the word of God, is the body of Christ. That chalice, after being sanctified by the word of God, is the blood of Christ." [11]

But why multiply authorities? At the present day every Christian communion throughout the world, with the sole exception of Protestants, proclaims its belief in the Real Presence of Christ in the Sacrament.

The Nestorians and Eutychians, who separated from the Catholic Church in the fifth century, admit the corporeal presence of our Lord in the Eucharist. Such also is the faith of the Greek church, which seceded from us a thousand years ago, of the Present Russian church, of the schismatic Copts, the Syrians, Chaldeans, Armenians, and, in short, of all the Oriental sects no longer in communion with the See of Rome.

[11] "See Faith of Catholics." Vol. II.

CHAPTER XXII

COMMUNION UNDER ONE KIND

OUR Savior gave communion under both forms of bread and wine to His Apostles at the last Supper. Officiating Bishops and Priests are always required, except on Good Friday, to communicate under both kinds. But even the clergy of every rank, including the Pope, receive only of the consecrated bread unless when they celebrate Mass.

The Church teaches that Christ is contained whole and entire under each species; so that whoever communicates under the form of bread *or* of wine receives not a mutilated Sacrament or a divided Savior, but shares in the whole Sacrament as fully as if he participated in both forms. Hence, the layman who receives the consecrated Bread partakes as copiously of the body and blood of Christ as the officiating Priest who receives both consecrated elements.

Our Lord says: "I am the living bread which came down from Heaven. If any man eat of this bread, he shall live forever; and the bread which I will give is My flesh, for the life of the world. . . . He that eateth Me the same also shall live by Me. He that eateth this bread shall live forever." [1]

From this passage it is evident that whoever partakes of the form of bread partakes of the living flesh of Jesus Christ, which is inseparable from His blood, and which, being now in a glorious state, cannot be divided; for, "Christ rising from the dead, dieth now no more." [2] Our Lord, in His words quoted, makes no reference to the sacramental cup, but only to the Eucharistic

---

[1] John vi. 51, and seq.   [2] Rom. vi. 9.

bread, to which He ascribes all the efficacy which is attached to communion under both kinds, viz., union with Him, spiritual life, eternal salvation.

St. Paul, writing to the Corinthians, says: "Whosoever shall eat this bread, *or* drink the chalice of the Lord unworthily, shall be guilty of the body *and* of the blood of the Lord." [3] The Apostle here plainly declares that, by an unworthy participation in the Lord's Supper, under the form of either bread or wine, we profane both the body and the blood of Christ. How could this be so, unless Christ is entirely contained under each species? So forcibly, indeed, did the Apostle assert the Catholic doctrine that the Protestant translators have perverted the text by rendering it: "Whosoever shall eat this bread *and* drink the chalice," substituting *and* for *or,* in contradiction to the Greek original, of which the Catholic version is an exact translation.

It is also the received doctrine of the Fathers that the Eucharist is contained in all its integrity either in the consecrated bread or in the chalice. St. Augustine, who may be taken as a sample of the rest, says that "each one receives Christ the Lord *entire* under each particle." [4]

Luther himself, even after his revolt, was so clearly convinced of this truth that he was an uncompromising advocate of communion under one kind. "If any Council," he says, "should decree or permit both species, we would by no means acquiesce; but, in spite of the Council and its statute, we would use one form, or neither, and never both." [5]

Leibnitz, the eminent Protestant divine, observes: "*It cannot be denied* that Christ is received entire by *virtue* of concomitance, under each species; nor is His flesh separated from His blood." [6]

As the same virtue is contained in the Sacrament, whether administered in one or both forms, the faithful gain nothing by receiving under both kinds, and lose nothing by receiving under one form. Consequently, we nowhere find our Savior requiring the communion to be administered to the faithful under both

[3] I. Cor. xi. 27.　　　　　　[4] Aug. De consec. dist.
[5] De formula Missæ.　　　　[6] Systema Theol., p. 250.

forms; but He has left this matter to be regulated by the wisdom and discretion of the Church, as He has done with regard to the manner of administering Baptism.

Our Redeemer, it is true, has said: "Drink ye all of this." But it should be remembered that these words were addressed not to the people at large, but only to the Apostles, who alone were also commanded, on the same occasion, to consecrate His body and blood in remembrance of Him. Now we have no more right to infer that the faithful are obliged to drink of the cup, because the Apostles were commanded to drink of it, than we have to suppose that the laity are required or allowed to consecrate the bread and wine, because the power of doing so was at the last Supper conferred on the Apostles.

It is true also that our Lord said to the people: "Unless ye eat the flesh of the Son of man, and drink His blood, ye shall not have life in you." But this command is literally fulfilled by the laity when they partake of the consecrated bread, which, as we have seen, contains Christ the Lord in all His integrity. Hence, if our Savior has said: "Whoso eateth My flesh, and drinketh My blood, hath everlasting life," He has also said: "The bread which I will give is My flesh, for the life of the world."

It seems to me that the charge of withholding the cup comes with very bad grace from Protestant teachers, who destroy the whole intrinsic virtue of the Sacrament by giving to their followers nothing but bread and wine. The difference between them and us lies in this—that under one form we give the *substance,* while they under two forms confessedly give only the *shadow.*

In examining the history of the Church on the subject we find that up to the twelfth century communion was sometimes distributed in one form, sometimes in another, commonly in both.

First—St. Luke tells us that the converts of Jerusalem "were persevering in the doctrine of the Apostles, and in the communion of bread (as the Eucharist was sometimes familiarly called), and in prayer." [7] Again he speaks of the Christian

[7] Acts ii. 42.

disciples assembled at Troas on the Lord's day, "to break bread." [8]
We are led to conclude from these passages that the Apostles
sometimes distributed the communion in the form of bread alone,
as no reference is made to the cup.

It was certainly the custom to carry to the sick only the
consecrated Host. Surely if there is any period of life when nothing should be neglected which conduces to salvation it is the
time of approaching death. Eusebius tells us that the aged Sera-
pion received only the Sacred Bread at the hands of the Priest.
In the *Life* of St. Ambrose we are told that in his last illness the
consecrated Host alone was given to Him.

The Christians in time of persecution, confessors of the faith
confined in prison, travellers on their journey, soldiers before
engaging in battle and hermits living in the desert were permitted
to keep with them and to fortify themselves with the consecrated
Bread—as Tertullian, Cyprian, Basil, Ambrose and other Fathers
of the Church testify.

Moreover, the Mass of the *Presanctified,* celebrated in the Latin
church on Good Friday only, and in the Greek church on every
day in Lent, except Saturdays and Sundays, the officiating Priest
receives the consecrated Bread alone.[9]

In all these instances the communicants never doubted that they
received the Lord's Supper in its integrity. Surely the conscientious guides of the faith would sooner withhold altogether the
Sacred Host from their flocks than permit them to partake of a
mutilated Sacrament.

Second—In the primitive days of the Church the Holy Communion used to be imparted to infants, but only in the form of
wine. The Priest dipped his fingers in the consecrated chalice and
gave it to be sucked by the infant. This custom prevails to this day
among the schismatic Christians of all Oriental rites. In some
instances the Sacred Host, saturated in the cup, is given to the
child.[10]

Third—Public Communion was, indeed, usually administered

[8] Ibid. xx. 7. [9] Alzog's Hist., Vol. I., p. 721.
[10] Denziger, Rit. Orientales.

in the first ages under both forms. The faithful, however, had the privilege of dispensing with the cup and of partaking only of the bread until the time of Pope Gelasius, in the fifth century, when this general, but hitherto optional, practice of receiving under both kinds was enforced as a law for the following reason:

The Manichean sect abstained from the cup on the erroneous assumption that the use of wine was sinful. Pope Gelasius, in order to detect and condemn the error of those sectaries, left it no longer optional with the faithful to receive under one or both forms, but ordained that all should communicate under both kinds.

This law continued in force for several ages, but towards the thirteenth century, for various causes, it had gradually grown into disuse, with the tacit approval of the Church. The Council of Constance, which convened in 1414, established a law requiring the faithful to communicate under the form of bread only; and in taking this step, the Council was actuated both by reasons of propriety and of religion.

The wide-spread diffusion of Christianity throughout the world had rendered it very difficult to supply all the faithful with the consecrated wine. Such inconvenience is scarcely felt by Protestant communicants, whose numbers are limited and who ordinarily communicate only on certain Sundays of each month. The Catholics of the world, on the contrary, number about three hundred millions; and as communion is administered to some of the faithful almost every day in most of our churches and chapels, and as the annual communions in every parish church are generally at least twice as numerous as its aggregate Catholic population, the sum total of annual communions throughout the globe may be estimated in round numbers at not less than five hundred millions. What effort would be required to procure altar-wine for such a multitude? In my missionary journeys through North Carolina I have often found it no easy task to provide for the celebration of Mass a sufficiency of pure wine, which is essential for the validity of the sacrifice. This embarrassment would be increased beyond measure if the cup had to be extended to the laity, and still more in the coal regions, where the cultivation of the grape is unknown and where imported wine is exclusively used.[11]

It would be very distasteful, besides, for so many communicants to drink successively out of the same chalice, which would be unavoidable if the Sacrament were administered in both forms. In our larger churches, where communion is distributed every Sunday to hundreds, there would be great danger of spilling a portion of the consecrated chalice and of thus exposing it to profanation.

But above all, as the Church in the fifth century, through her chief Pastor, Gelasius, enforced the use of the cup to expose and reprobate the error of the Manichees, who imagined that the use of wine was sinful; so in the fifteenth century she withdrew the cup to condemn the novelties of the Calixtines, who taught that the consecrated wine was necessary for a valid communion. Should circumstances ever justify or demand a change from the present discipline the Church will not hesitate to restore the cup to the laity.

[11] While Protestants consider the cup as an indispensable part of the communion service, they do not seem, in many instances, to be very particular as to what the cup will contain. And the New York *Independent,* of September 21, 1876, relates the following incident: "A late English traveler found a Baptist mission church, in far-off Burmah, using for the communion service Bass's pale ale instead of wine. The opening of the frothing bottle on the communion table seemed not quite decorous to the visitor, who presented the pastor with a half-dozen bottles of claret for sacramental use."

CHAPTER XXIII

THE SACRIFICE OF THE MASS

SACRIFICE is the oblation or offering made to God of some sensible object, with the destruction or change of the object, to denote that God is the Author of life and death. Thus, in the Old Law, before the coming of Christ, when the Hebrew people wished to offer sacrifice to God they took a lamb or some other animal, which they slew and burned its flesh, acknowledging by this act that the Lord was the supreme Master of life and death. The ancients offered to God two kinds of sacrifices, viz., living creatures, such as bulls, lambs and birds; and inanimate objects, such as wheat and barley, and, in general, the first fruits of the earth.

All nations—whether Jews, idolaters or Christians, except Mahometans and modern Protestants—have made sacrifice their principal act of worship. If you go back to the very dawn of creation, you will find the children of Adam offering sacrifices to God. Abel offered to the Lord the firstlings of his flock, and Cain offered of the fruits of the earth.[1]

When Noe and his family are rescued from the deluge which had spread over the face of the earth his first act on issuing from the ark, when the waters disappear, is to offer holocausts to the Lord, in thanksgiving for his preservation.[2] Abraham, the great father of the Jewish race, offered victims to the Almighty at His express command.[3] We read that Job was accustomed to offer holocausts to the Lord, to propitiate His favor in behalf of his

---

[1] Gen. iv. [2] Gen. viii. [3] Ibid. xv.

children, and to obtain forgiveness for the sins they might have committed.[4]

When Jehovah delivered to Moses the written law on Mount Sinai He gave His servant the most minute details with regard to all the ceremonies to be observed in the sacrifices which were to be offered to Him. He prescribed the kind of victims to be immolated, the qualifications of the Priests who were to minister at the altar, and the place and manner in which the victims were to be offered. Hence, it was the custom of the Jewish Priests to slay every day two lambs as a sacrifice to God,[5] and in doing this they were prefiguring the great sacrifice of the New Law, in which we daily offer up on the altar "the Lamb of God, who taketh away the sins of the world."

In a word, in all their public calamities—whenever they were threatened by their enemies; whenever they were about to engage in war; whenever they were visited by any plague or pestilence— the Jews had recourse to God by solemn sacrifices. Like the Catholic Church of the present day, they had sacrifices not only for the living, but also for the dead; for we read in Sacred Scripture that Judas Machabeus ordered sacrifice to be offered up for the souls of his men who were slain in battle.[6]

We find sacrifices existing not only among the Jews, who worshiped the true God, but also among Pagan and idolatrous nations.

No matter how confused, imperfect or erroneous was their knowledge of the Deity, the Pagan nations retained sufficient vestiges of primitive tradition to admonish them of their obligation of appeasing the anger and invoking the blessings of the Divinity by victims and sacrifices. Plutarch, an ancient writer of the second century, says of these heathen people: "You may find cities without walls, without literature and without the arts and sciences of civilized life; but you will never find a city without Priests and altars, or which has not sacrifices offered to the gods."

The Indians of our own country were accustomed to offer sacrifice to the Great Spirit, as Father Jogues and other pioneer

---

[4] Job i. [5] Numb. xxviii. [6] II. Mac. xii. 43-46.

missionaries inform us. But all those ancient sacrifices were only the types and figures of the great Sacrifice of the New Law, from which they derived all their efficacy, just as the Old Law itself was the type of the New Law of grace. Since the ancient sacrifices were but figures and shadows, they were imperfect and insufficient; for "it is impossible," says St. Paul, "that by the blood of oxen and of goats sins should be taken away. Wherefore, when He (Jesus) cometh into the world, He saith: Sacrifice and oblation Thou wouldst not, but a body Thou hast fitted to me. Holocausts for sin did not please Thee. Then said I: Behold, I come." [7] As if He should say: The blood of oxen and of goats is not sufficient to appease Thy vengeance, and to cleanse Thy people from their sins; therefore I come, that I may offer Myself an acceptable sacrifice for the sins of the world.

The Prophet Isaiah declared that the Jewish sacrifices had become displeasing to God and would be abolished. "To what purpose," says the Lord by His prophet, "do you offer Me the multitude of your victims? . . . I desire not holocausts of rams, . . . and blood of calves and lambs and buck-goats . . . Offer sacrifice no more in vain." [8]

But did God, in rejecting the Jewish oblations, intend to abolish sacrifices altogether? By no means. On the contrary, He clearly predicts, by the mouth of the Prophet Malachias, that the immolations of the Jews would be succeeded by a clean victim, which would be offered up not on a single altar, as was the case in Jerusalem, but in every part of the known world. Listen to the significant words addressed to the Jews by this prophet: "I have no pleasure in you, saith the Lord of hosts, and I will not receive a gift of your hand. For, from the rising of the sun, even to the going down, My name is great among the Gentiles, and in every place there is sacrifice, and there is offered to My name a clean oblation; for My name is great among the Gentiles, saith the Lord of hosts." [9] The prophet here clearly foretells that an acceptable oblation would be offered to God not by Jews, but by Gentiles; not merely in Jerusalem, but in every place from the rising to the

[7] Heb. x. 4, 7.　　　　[8] Isaiah i. 11-13.　　　　[9] Mal. i. 10, 11.

setting of the sun. These prophetic words must have been ful-filled. Where shall we find the fulfilment of the prophecy?

We may divide the inhabitants of the world into five different classes of people, professing different forms of religion—Pagans, Jews, Mohammedans, Protestants and Catholics. Among which of these shall we find the clean oblation of which the prophet speaks? Not among the Pagan nations; for they worship false gods, and consequently cannot have any sacrifice pleasing to the Almighty. Not among the Jews; for they have ceased to sacrifice altogether, and the words of the prophet apply not to the Jews, but to the Gentiles. Not among the Mohammedans; for they also reject sacrifices. Not among any of the Protestant sects; for they all distinctly repudiate sacrifices. Therefore, it is only in the Catholic Church that is fulfilled this glorious prophecy; for whithersoever you go, you will find the clean oblation offered on Catholic altars. If you travel from America to Europe, to Oceanica, to Africa, or Asia, you will see our altars erected, and our Priests daily fulfilling the words of the prophets by offering the "clean oblation" of the body and blood of Christ.

This oblation of the New Law is commonly called *Mass*. The word Mass is derived by some from the Hebrew term *Missach* (Deut. xvi.), which means a free offering. Others derive it from the word *Missa*, which the Priest uses when he announces to the congregation that Divine Service is over. It is an expression indelibly marked on our English tongue from the origin of our language, and we find it embodied in such words as *Candlemas*, *Michaelmas*, *Martin-mas* and *Christmas*.

The sacrifice of the Mass is the consecration of the bread and wine into the body and blood of Christ, and the oblation of this body and blood to God, by the ministry of the Priest, for a per-petual memorial of Christ's sacrifice on the cross. The Sacrifice of the Mass is identical with that of the cross, both having the same victim and High Priest—Jesus Christ.

The only difference consists in the manner of the oblation. Christ was offered up on the cross in a bloody manner, and in the Mass He is offered up in an unbloody manner. On the cross

He purchased our ransom, and in the Eucharistic Sacrifice the price of that ransom is applied to our souls. Hence, all the efficacy of the Mass is derived from the sacrifice of Calvary.

It was on the night before He suffered that our Lord Jesus Christ instituted the Sacrifice of the New Law. "Jesus," says St. Paul, "the night in which He was betrayed took bread, and, giving thanks, broke and said: Take ye and eat; this is My body which shall be delivered for you. This do for the commemoration of Me. In like manner also the chalice, after He had supped, saying: This chalice is the new testament in My blood. This do ye, as often as you shall drink, for the commemoration of Me; for as often as ye shall eat this bread, and drink the chalice, ye shall show the death of the Lord until He come." [10]

From these words we learn that the principal motive which our Savior had in view in instituting the Sacrifice of the Altar was to keep us in perpetual remembrance of His sufferings and death. He wished that the scene of Calvary should ever appear in panoramic view before our eyes, and that our heart, memory and intellect should be filled with the thoughts of His Passion. He knew well that this would be the best means of winning our love and exciting sorrow for sin in our soul; therefore, He designed that in every church throughout the world an altar should be erected, to serve as a monument of His mercies to His people, as the children of Israel erected a monument, on crossing the Jordan, to commemorate His mercies to His chosen people. The Mass is truly the memorial service of Christ's Passion.

In compliance with the command of our Lord the adorable Sacrifice of the Altar has been daily renewed in the Church, from the death of our Savior till the present time, and will be perpetuated till time shall be no more.

In the Acts it is said that while Saul and others were ministering (or, as the Greek text expresses it, *sacrificing*) to the Lord, and fasting, the Holy Spirit said to them: "Set apart for Me Saul and Barnabas." St. Paul, in his Epistle to the Hebrews, frequently alludes to the Sacrifice of the Mass. "We have an altar," he says,

[10] I. Cor. xi. 23-26.

"whereof they cannot eat who serve the tabernacle."[11] The Apostle here plainly declares that the Christian church has its altars as well as the Jewish synagogue. An altar necessarily supposes a sacrifice, without which it has no meaning. The Apostle also observes that the priesthood of the New Law was substituted for that of the Old Law.[12] Now, the principal office of Priests has always been to offer sacrifice. Priest and sacrifice are as closely identified as judge and court.

St. Paul, after David, calls Jesus "a Priest forever, according to the order of Melchisedech."[13] He is named a *Priest* because He offers sacrifice; a Priest *forever* because His sacrifice is perpetual; *according to the order of Melchisedech* because He offers up consecrated bread and wine, which were prefigured by the bread and wine offered by "Melchisedech, the Priest of the Most High God."[14]

Tradition, with its hundred tongues, proclaims the perpetual oblation of the Sacrifice of the Mass, from the time of the Apostles to our own days. If we consult the Fathers of the Church, who have stood like faithful sentinels on the watch-towers of Israel, guarding with a jealous eye the deposit of faith, and who have been the faithful witnesses of their own times and the recorders of the past; if we consult the General Councils, at which were assembled the venerable hierarchy of Christendom, they will all tell us, with one voice, that the Sacrifice of the Mass is the centre of their religion and the acknowledged institution of Jesus Christ.

Another remarkable evidence in favor of the Divine institution of the Mass is furnished by the Nestorians and Eutychians, who separated from the Catholic Church in the fifth century, and who still exist in Persia and in other parts of the East, as well as by the Greek schismatics, who severed their connection with the Church in the ninth century. All these sects, as well as the numerous others scattered over the East, retain to this day the oblation of the Mass in their daily service. As these Christian communities have had no communication with the Catholic

[11] Heb. xiii. 10.
[13] Ps. cix. 4; Heb. v. 6.
[12] Ibid. vii. 12.
[14] Gen. xiv. 18.

Church since the period of their separation from her, they could not, of course, have borrowed from her the doctrine of the Eucharistic Sacrifice; consequently they must have received it from the same source from which the Church derived it, viz., from the Apostles themselves.

But of all proofs in favor of the Apostolic origin of the Sacrifice of the Mass, the most striking and the most convincing is found in the Liturgies of the Church. The Liturgy is the established Ritual of the Church. It is the collection of the authorized prayers of divine worship. These prayers are fixed and immovable. Among others we have the Liturgy of Jerusalem, ascribed to the Apostle St. James; the Liturgy of Alexandria, attributed to St. Mark the Evangelist, and the Liturgy of Rome, referred to St. Peter. There are various other Liturgies accredited to the Apostles or to their immediate successors. Now I wish to call your attention to this remarkable fact, that all these Liturgies, though compiled by different persons, at different times, in various places, and in divers languages, contain, without exception, in clear and precise language, the prayers to be said at the celebration of Mass; prayers in substance the same as those found in our prayer books at the Canon of the Mass.

We cannot account for this wonderful uniformity except by supposing that the doctrine respecting the Mass was received by the Apostles from the common fountain of Christianity—Jesus Christ Himself.

It was such facts as these that opened the eyes of those eminent English divines who, during the present century, have abandoned heresy and schism and rich preferments and who have embraced the Catholic faith, though, by taking such a step, they had to sacrifice all that was dear to them on earth.

The following passages from St. Paul's Epistle to the Hebrews are sometimes urged as an argument against the sacrifice of the Mass: "Christ, . . . neither by the blood of goats, or of calves, but by His own blood, entered once into the Holies, having obtained eternal redemption." "Nor yet that He should offer Himself often, as the High Priest entereth into the Holies every year." [15] Again: "Every Priest standeth, indeed, daily ministering, and often offering the same sacrifices, which can never take away sins, but this Man, offering one sacrifice for sin, forever sitteth at the right hand of God." [16]

St. Paul says that Jesus was offered once. How, then, can we offer Him daily? I answer, that Jesus was offered once in a bloody manner, and it is of this sacrifice that the Apostle speaks. But in the Sacrifice of the Mass He is offered up in an unbloody manner. Though He is daily offered on ten thousand altars, the Sacrifice is the same as that of Calvary, having the same High Priest and victim—Jesus Christ. The object of St. Paul is to contrast the Sacrifice of the New Law, which has only one victim, with the sacrifices of the Old Law, where the victims were many; and to show the insufficiency of the ancient sacrifices and the all-sufficiency of the Sacrifice of the new dispensation.

But if the sacrifice of the cross is all-sufficient what need then, you will say, is there of a commemorative Sacrifice of the Mass? I would ask a Protestant in return, Why do you pray, and go to church, and why were you baptized, and receive Communion, and the rite of Confirmation? What is the use of all these exercises, if the sacrifice of the cross is all-sufficient? You will tell me that in all these acts you apply to yourself the merits of Christ's Passion. I will tell you, in like manner, that in the Sacrifice of the Mass I apply to myself the merits of the sacrifice of the cross, from which the Mass derives all its efficacy. Christ, indeed, by His death made full atonement for our sins, but He has not released us from the obligation of co-operating with Him by applying His merits to our souls. What better or more efficacious way can we have of participating in His merits than by assisting at the Sacrifice of the Altar, where we vividly recall to mind His sufferings, where Calvary is represented before us, where "we show the death of the Lord until He come," and where we draw abundantly to our souls the fruit of His Passion by drinking of the same blood that was shed on the cross?

In the Old Law there were different kinds of sacrifices offered

[15] Heb. ix. 25.   [16] Ibid. x. 11, 12.

up for different purposes. There were sacrifices of praise and thanksgiving to God for His benefits, sacrifices of propitiation to implore His forgiveness for the sins of the people, and sacrifices of supplication to ask His blessing and protection. The Sacrifice of the Mass fulfils all these ends. It is a sacrifice of praise and thanksgiving, a sacrifice of propitiation and of supplication; hence that valued book, the *"Following of Christ,"* says: "When a Priest celebrates Mass he honors God, he rejoices the angels, he edifies the church, he helps the living, he obtains rest for the dead, and makes himself a partaker of all that is good." To form an adequate idea of the efficiency of the Divine Sacrifice of the Mass we have only to bear in mind the Victim that is offered— Jesus Christ, the Son of the living God.

First—The Mass is a sacrifice of praise and thanksgiving. If all human beings in this world, and all living creatures, and all inanimate objects were collected and burned as a holocaust to the Lord, they would not confer as much praise on the Almighty as a single Eucharistic sacrifice. These earthly creatures—how numerous and excellent soever—are finite and imperfect; while the offering made in the Mass is of infinite value, for it is our Lord Jesus, the acceptable Lamb without blemish, the beloved Son in whom the Father is well pleased, and who "is always heard on account of His reverence."

With what awe and grateful love should we assist at this Sacrifice? The angels were present at Calvary. Angels are present also at the Mass. If we cannot assist with the seraphic love and rapt attention of the angelic spirits, let us worship, at least, with the simple devotion of the shepherds of Bethlehem and the unswerving faith of the Magi. Let us offer to our God the golden gift of a heart full of love and the incense of our praise and adoration, repeating often during the holy oblation the words of the Psalmist: "The mercies of the Lord I will sing forever."

Second—The Mass is also a sacrifice of propitiation. Jesus daily pleads our cause in this Divine oblation before our Heavenly Father. "If any man sin," says St. John, "we have an Advocate with the Father, Jesus Christ the just; and He is the propitiation for our sins; and not for ours only, but also for those of the whole world." [17] Hence the Priest, whenever he offers up the holy sacrifice, recites this prayer at the offertory: "Receive, O holy Father, almighty, eternal God, this immaculate victim which I, Thy unworthy servant, offer to Thee, my living and true God, for my innumerable sins, offences and negligences, for all here present, and for all the faithful living and dead, that it may avail me and them to life everlasting."

Whenever, therefore, we assist at Mass let us unite with Jesus Christ in imploring the mercy of God for our sins. Let us represent to ourselves the Mass as another Calvary, which it is in reality. Like Mary, let us stand in spirit beneath the cross, and let our souls be pierced with grief for our transgressions. Let us acknowledge that our sins were the cause of that agony and of the shedding of that precious blood. Let us follow in mind and heart that crowd of weeping penitents who accompanied our Savior to Calvary, striking their breasts, and let us say: "Spare, O Lord, spare Thy people." Or let us repeat with the publican this heartfelt prayer: "O God, be merciful to me a sinner." At the death of Jesus the sun was darkened, the earth trembled, the very rocks were rent, as if to show that even inanimate nature sympathized with the sufferings of its God. And should not we tremble for our sins? Should not our hearts, though cold and hard as rocks, be softened at the spectacle of our God suffering for love of us, and in expiation for our offences?

Third—The Sacrifice of the Mass is, in fine, a sacrifice of supplication: "For, if the blood of goats and of oxen, and the ashes of a heifer being sprinkled, sanctify such as are defiled to the cleansing of the flesh, how much more shall the blood of Christ, who, through the Holy Ghost, offered himself without spot to God, cleanse our conscience from dead works to serve the living God?" [18] If the prayers of Moses and David and the Patriarchs were so powerful in behalf of God's servants, what must be the influence of Jesus' intercession? If the wounds of the

[17] I. John ii. 1, 2.
[18] Heb. ix. 13, 14.

Martyrs plead so eloquently for us, how much more eloquent is the blood of Jesus shed daily upon our altars? His blood cries louder for mercy than the blood of Abel cried for vengeance. If God inclines His ear to us miserable sinners, how can He resist the pleadings in our behalf of the "Lamb of God who taketh away the sins of the world."

"Let us go, therefore, with confidence to the throne of grace, that we may obtain mercy and find grace in seasonable aid." [19]

[19] Heb. iv. 16.

CHAPTER XXIV

THE USE OF RELIGIOUS CEREMONIES DICTATED BY RIGHT REASON—APPROVED BY ALMIGHTY GOD IN THE OLD LAW—SANCTIONED BY JESUS CHRIST IN THE NEW

BY RELIGIOUS ceremonies we mean certain expressive signs and actions which the Church has ordained for the worthy celebration of the Divine service.

True devotion must be interior and come from the heart, for "the true adorers shall adore the Father in spirit and in truth. For the Father indeed seeketh such to worship Him. God is a spirit; and they who worship Him must worship Him in spirit and in truth." [1] But we are not to infer from this that exterior worship is to be contemned because interior worship is prescribed as essential. On the contrary, the rites and ceremonies enjoined in the worship of God and the administration of the Sacraments are dictated by right reason, are sanctioned by Almighty God in the Old Law, and by Christ and His Apostles in the New.

The angels, being pure spirits without a body, render to God a purely spiritual worship. The sun, moon and stars of the firmament pay Him a kind of external homage. In the Prophet Daniel we read: "Sun and moon bless the Lord. . . . stars of heaven bless the Lord, praise and exalt Him above all forever." [2] "The heavens show forth the glory of God, the firmament announces the work

[1] John iv. 23, 24.
[2] Dan. iii. 62, 63. Though this passage is omitted in the Protestant Bible, it is retained in the Book of Common Prayer.

of His hands." [3] Man, by possessing a soul of spiritual substance, partakes of the nature of angels, and by possessing a body partakes of the nature of the heavenly bodies. It is, therefore, his privilege, as well as his duty, to offer to God the twofold homage of body and soul; in other words, to honor Him by internal and external worship.

Genuine piety cannot long be concealed in the heart without manifesting itself by exterior practices of religion; hence, though interior and exterior worship are distinct, they cannot be separated in the present life. Fire cannot burn without sending forth flame and heat. Neither can the fire of devotion burn in the soul without being reflected on the countenance and even in speech. It is natural for man to express his sentiments by signs and ceremonies, for "from the fulness of the heart the mouth speaketh;" and as fuel is necessary to keep fire alive, even so the flame of piety is nourished by the outward forms of religion.

A devoted child will not be content with loving his father in his heart, but will manifest that love by affectionate language, and by the service of his body, if necessary. So will the child of God show his affection for his heavenly Father not only by interior devotion, but also by the homage of his body. "I beseech you," says the Apostle, "by the mercy of God, that you present your bodies, a living sacrifice, holy pleasing unto God, your reasonable service." [4]

The fruit of a tree does not consist in its bark, its leaves and its branches. Nevertheless, you never saw a tree bearing fruit unless when clothed with bark, adorned with branches and covered with leaves. These are necessary for the protection of the fruit. In like manner, though the fruit of piety does not consist in exterior forms, it must, however, be fostered by some outward observances or it will soon decay. There is as close a relation between devotion and ceremonial as exists between the bark and the fruit of a tree.

The man who daily bends his knee to the Maker, who recites or sings His praises, who devoutly makes the sign of the cross, who

[3] Psalm. xviii. 1.   [4] Rom. xii. 1.

assists without constraint at the public services of the Church, who observes an exterior decorum in the house of God, who gives to the needy according to his means and duly attends to the other practices and ceremonies of religion, will generally be one whose heart is united to God, and who yields to Him a ready obedience. Show me, on the contrary, a man who habitually neglects these outward observances of religion and charity, and I will show you one in whose soul the fire of devotion, if not quite extinguished, at least burns very faintly.

The ceremonies of the Church not only render divine service more solemn, but also rivet our attention and lift it up to God. Our mind is so active, so volatile, so full of distractions, our imagination so fickle, that we have need of some external objects on which to fix our thoughts.

Almighty God considered ceremonial so indispensable to interior worship that we find Him in the Old Law prescribing in minute detail the various rites, ceremonies and ordinances to be observed by the Jewish Priests and people in their public worship. What is the entire book of Leviticus but an elaborate ritual of the Jewish church. Not, indeed, that external rites are to be compared in merit with interior worship, but because they are as necessary for nourishing internal devotion as food is necessary for our animal life.

Our Savior, though He came to establish a more spiritual religion than that of the Hebrew people, did not discard the outward forms of worship. He was accustomed to accompany His religious acts by appropriate ceremonies.

In the garden of Gethsemani "He fell upon His face"[5] in humble supplication.

He went in procession to Jerusalem, accompanied by a great multitude, who sang Hosanna to the Son of David.[6]

At the Last Supper He invoked a blessing on the bread and wine, and afterward chanted a hymn with His disciples.[7]

When the deaf and dumb man was brought to Him, before healing Him, He put His fingers into his ears and touched his

[5] Matt. xxvi.   [6] Ibid. xxi.   [7] Ibid. xxvi.

tongue with spittle, "and, looking up to heaven, He groaned and said: Ephpheta, which is, Be thou opened." [8]

When He imparted the Holy Ghost to His disciples, He breathed on them[9] and the same Apostles afterward communicated the Holy Ghost to others by laying hands on them.[10]

The Apostle St. James directs that if any man is sick he shall call in the Priest, who will anoint him with oil.[11]

Now, are not all these acts which I have just recorded—the prostration and procession, the prayerful invocation, the chanting of a hymn, the touching of the ears, the lifting up of the eyes to heaven, the breathing on the Apostles, the laying on of hands and the unction of the sick—are not all these acts so many ceremonies serving as models to those which the Catholic Church employs in her public worship, and in the administration of her Sacraments?

The ceremonies now accompanying our public worship are, indeed, usually more impressive and elaborate than those recorded of our Savior; but it is quite natural that the majesty of ceremonial should keep pace with the growth and development of Christianity.

But where shall we find a ritual so gorgeous as that presented to us in the Book of Revelation, which is descriptive of the worship of God in the heavenly Jerusalem? Angels with golden censers stand before the throne, while elders cast their crowns of gold before the Lamb once slain. Then that unnumbered multitude of all nations, tongues and people, clothed in white raiment, bearing palms of victory. Virgins, too, with harp and canticle, follow near the Lamb, singing the new song which they alone can utter.[12]

How glorious the pageant! How elaborate in detail!

Surely there ought to be some analogy and resemblance, some proportion and harmony between the public worship which is paid to God in the Church militant on earth, and that which is offered to Him in the Church triumphant in heaven.

[8] Mark vii. [9] John xx. [10] Acts viii.
[11] James v. [12] Apocalypse, passim.

Strange would it be if God, who, in the dispensation past and that to come, is seen delighting in external majesty, should have deprived the Christian Church (the living link between the past and the future) of all external glory. "For," as St. Paul says, "if the ministry of condemnation is glory, much more the ministry of justice aboundeth in glory." [13]

It is true that God uttered this complaint against the children of Israel: "This people draw near Me with their mouth and honor Me with their lips, but their heart is far from Me." [14] It is also true that He was displeased with their sacrifices and religious festivals.[15] But He blamed them not because they praised Him with their voice, but because their hearts felt not what their lips uttered. He rejected their sacrifices because they were not accompanied by the more precious sacrifice of a penitent spirit.

The same Lord who declares that the true adorer shall adore the Father in spirit commands also that public praise be given to Him in His holy temple: "Praise ye the Lord," He says, "in His holy places. . . . Praise Him with sound of trumpet. Praise Him with psaltery and harp. Praise Him with timbrel and choir. Praise Him with strings and organs." [16]

If He says in one place: "Rend your hearts and not your garments," [17] immediately after He adds: "Blow the trumpet in Sion, sanctify a fast, call a solemn assembly. Gather together the people, sanctify the Church. . . . Between the porch and the altar the Priests, the Lord's ministers, shall weep and shall say: Spare, O Lord, spare Thy people!" [18] The Prophet first points out the absolute necessity of interior sorrow and contrition of heart, and then he insists on the duty of performing some acts of expiation, penance and humiliation, as you do when you have your forehead marked with ashes on Ash Wednesday, and when you observe the fast and abstinence of Lent.

When St. Paul says that though he speak with the tongues of angels and of men, and distribute all his goods to feed the poor, and deliver his body to be burned, and have not the love of God,

---

[13] II. Cor. iii. 9.   [14] Isaiah xxix. 13.   [15] Ibid. i. 13.
[16] Ps. cl.   [17] Joel ii. 13.   [18] Ibid. ii. 15-17.

it profiteth him nothing,[19] he points out the necessity of interior worship. And when he says elsewhere that "in the name of Jesus every knee should bend of those that are in heaven, on earth and under the earth," [20] he shows us the duty of exterior or ceremonial worship.

When political leaders desire to influence the masses in their favor they are not content with addressing themselves to the intellect. They appeal also to the feelings and imagination. They have torchlight processions, accompanied by soul-stirring music discoursing popular airs. They have flags and banners floating in the breeze. They have public meetings, at which they deliver patriotic speeches to arouse the enthusiasm of the people.

What these men do for political reasons the Church performs from the higher motives of religion. Therefore, she has her solemn processions. She has her heavenly music to soften the heart and raise it to God. She consecrates her sacred banners, especially the cross, the banner of salvation. She preaches with a hundred tongues, speaking not only to our head and heart by the Word of God, but to our feelings and imagination by her grand and imposing ceremonial.

[19] I. Cor. xiii.
[20] Phil. ii. 10.

CHAPTER XXV

CEREMONIES OF THE MASS—THE MISSAL—LATIN LANGUAGE—LIGHTS—FLOWERS—INCENSE —VESTMENTS

LET us now, dear reader, walk together into a Catholic Church in time to assist at the late Mass, which is the most solemn service of the Catholic Liturgy. Meantime, I shall endeavor to explain to you the principal objects which attract your attention.

As we enter I dip my fingers into a vase placed at the church door, and filled with holy water, and I make the sign of the cross, praying at the same time to be purified from all defilement, so that with a clean heart I may worship in God's holy temple.

The Church, through her ministers, blesses everything used in her service; for, St. Paul says, that "Every creature of God is good, . . . that is received with thanksgiving, for it is sanctified by the word of God and by prayer." [1]

Before Mass begins the Priest sprinkles the assembled congregation with holy water, reciting at the same time these words of the fiftieth Psalm: "Thou shalt sprinkle me with hyssop, and I shall be cleansed; Thou shalt wash me, and I shall be made whiter than snow."

The practice of using blessed water dates back to a very remote antiquity, and is alluded to by several Fathers of the primitive Church.

As we advance up the aisle you observe lying open on the altar a large book, which is called a *Missal,* or Mass-book, because it

[1] I. Tim. iv. 4.

contains the prayers said at Mass. The office of the Mass consists of selections from the Old and the New Testament, the Canon and other appropriate prayers. The Canon of the Mass never varies throughout the year, and descends to us from the first ages of the Church with scarcely the addition of a word. Nearly all the collects are also very old, many of them dating back to a period prior to the seventh century. I am acquainted with no prayers that can compare with the collects of the Missal in earnestness and vigor of language, in conciseness of style and unction of piety. It is evident that their authors were men who felt what they said and were filled with the spirit of God, despising "the persuasive words of human wisdom," unlike so many modern prayer-composers whose rounded periods are directed rather to tickle the ears of men than to pierce the clouds.

You are probably familiar with the Episcopal *Book of Common Prayer,* and have no doubt admired its beautiful simplicity of diction. But perhaps you will be surprised when I inform you that this Prayer-Book is for the most part a translation from our Missal.

Let us now reverently follow the officiating Priest through the service of the Mass.

You see him advance from the sacristy and stand at the foot of the altar, where he makes an humble confession of his sins to God and His saints. He then ascends the altar, and nine times the Divine clemency is invoked in the *Kyrie Eleison, Christe Eleison.* He intones the sublime doxology, *Gloria in Excelsis Deo,* sings the collects of the day, reads the Lesson or Epistle and chants the Gospel, after which the sermon is usually preached. Next he recites the Nicene Creed, which for upwards of fifteen centuries has been resounding in the churches of Christendom. Then you perceive him making the oblation of the bread and wine. He washes the tips of his fingers, reciting the words of the Psalmist: "I will wash my hands among the innocent and will encompass Thy altar, O Lord." He is admonished, by this ceremony, to be free from the least stain, in view of the sacred act he is going to perform. The Preface and Canon follow, including the solemn words of consecration, during which the bread and wine are changed by the power of Jesus Christ into His body and blood. He proceeds with other prayers, including the best of all, the *Our Father,* as far as the Communion, when he partakes of the consecrated Bread and chalice, giving the Holy Communion afterward to such as are prepared to receive it. He continues the Mass, gives his blessing to the kneeling congregation, and concludes with the opening words of the sublime Gospel of St. John.

Here you have not merely a number of prayers strung together, but you witness a scene which rivets pious attention and warms the heart into fervent devotion. You participate in an act of worship worthy of God, to whom it is offered.

But you are anxious that I should explain to you the reason why the Mass is said in Latin. When Christianity was first established the Roman Empire ruled the destinies of the world. Pagan Rome had dominion over nearly all Europe and large portions of Asia and Africa. The Latin was the language of the Empire. Wherever the Roman standard was planted, there also was spread the Latin tongue; just as at the present time the English language is spoken wherever the authority of Great Britain or of the United States is established.

The Church naturally adopted in her Liturgy, or public worship, the language which she then found prevailing among the people. The Fathers of the early Church generally wrote in the Latin tongue, which thus became the depository of the treasures of sacred literature in the Church.

In the fifth century came the disruption of the Roman Empire. New kingdoms began to be formed in Europe out of the ruins of the old empire. The Latin gradually ceased to be a living tongue among the people, and new languages commenced to spring up like so many shoots from the parent stock. The Church, however, retained in her Liturgy, and in the administration of the Sacraments, the Latin language for very wise reasons, some of which I shall briefly mention:

First—The Catholic Church has always *one and the same faith,* the same form of public worship, the same spiritual government.

As her doctrine and liturgy are unchangeable, she wishes that the language of her Liturgy should be fixed and uniform. Faith may be called the jewel, and language is the casket which contains it. So careful is the Church of preserving the jewel intact that she will not disturb even the casket in which it is set. Living tongues, unlike a dead language, are continually changing in words and meaning. The English language as written four centuries ago would be now almost as unintelligible to an English reader as the Latin tongue. In an old Bible published in the fourteenth century St. Paul calls himself *the villain of Jesus Christ.* The word *villain* in those days meant a servant, but the term would not be complimentary now to one even less holy than the Apostle. This is but one instance, out of many which I might adduce, to show the mutations which our language has undergone. But the Latin, being a dead language, is not liable to these changes.

Second—The Catholic Church is spread over the whole world, embracing in its fold children of all climes and nations, and peoples and tongues under the sun. How, I ask, could the Bishops of these various countries communicate with one another in council if they had not one language to serve as a common medium of communication? It would be simply impossible. A church that is universal must have a universal tongue; whilst a national church, or a church whose members speak one and the same language, and whose doctrines conveniently change to suit the times, can safely adopt the vernacular tongue in its liturgy.

A few years ago a Convocation was held in England, composed of British and American Episcopal Bishops. They had no difficulty in communicating with one another because all spoke their mother tongue. But suppose they had representatives from Spain, France and Germany. The lips of those Continental Bishops would be sealed because they could not speak to their English brothers; their ears also would be sealed because they could not comprehend what was said to them.

In 1869, at the Ecumenical Council of the Vatican, were assembled Bishops from all parts of the world speaking all the civilized languages of Christendom. Had those Bishops no uniform language to express their thoughts, public debates and familiar conversation among them would have been impracticable. The Council Chamber would have been a confused Babel of tongues. But, thanks to the Latin language, which they all spoke (except a few Orientals), their speeches were as plainly understood as if each had spoken in his native dialect.

Third—Moreover, the Bishops and Clergy of the Catholic Church are in frequent correspondence with the Holy See. This requires that they should communicate in one uniform language, otherwise the Pope would be compelled to employ secretaries speaking every language in Christendom.

But if the Priest says Mass in an unknown tongue, are not the people thereby kept in ignorance of what he says, and is not their time wasted in Church? We are forced to smile at such charges, which are flippantly repeated from year to year. These assertions arise from a total ignorance of the Mass. Many Protestants imagine that the essence of public worship consists in a sermon. Hence, to their minds, the primary duty of a congregation is to listen to a discourse from the pulpit. Prayer, on the contrary, according to Catholic teaching, is the most essential duty of a congregation, though they are also regularly instructed by sermons. Now, what is the Mass? It is not a sermon, but it is a sacrifice of prayer which the Priest offers up to God for himself and the people. When the Priest says Mass he is speaking not to the people, but to God, to whom all languages are equally intelligible.

The congregation, indeed, could not be expected to hear the Priest, even if he spoke in English, since his face is turned from them, and the greater part of what he says is pronounced in an undertone. And this was the system of worship God ordained in the ancient dispensation, as we learn from the Old Testament and from the first chapter of St. Luke. The Priest offered sacrifice and prayed for the people in the sanctuary, while they prayed at a distance in the court. In all the schismatic churches of the East the Priest in the public service prays not in the vulgar, but in a dead language. Such, also, is the practice in the Jewish synagogues at this day. The Rabbi reads the prayers in Hebrew, a language with which many of the congregation are not familiar.

But is it true that the people do not understand what the Priest says at Mass? Not at all. For, by the aid of an English Missal, or any other Manual, they are able to follow the officiating clergyman from the beginning to the end of the service.

You also observe *lighted tapers* on the altar, and you desire to know for what purpose they are used.

In the Old Law the Almighty Himself ordained that lighted chandeliers should adorn the tabernacle.[2] Assuredly, that cannot be improper in the New Dispensation which God sanctioned in the Old.

The lights upon our altars have both a historical and a symbolical meaning. In the primitive days of the Church Christianity was not tolerated by the Pagan world. The Christians were, consequently, obliged to assemble for public worship in the Catacombs of Rome and other secret places. These Catacombs, or subterranean rooms, still exist, and are objects of deep interest to the pious stranger visiting the Eternal City. As these hidden apartments did not admit the light of the sun, the faithful were obliged to have lights even in open day. In commemoration of the event the Church has retained the use of lights on her altars.

Lighted candles have also a symbolical meaning. They represent our Savior, who is "the light of the world," "who enlighteneth every man that cometh into the world," without whom we should be wandering in darkness and in the shadow of death.

They also serve to remind us to "let our light so shine before men (by our good example) that they may see our good works and glorify our Father who is in heaven."

Lights are used, too, as a sign of spiritual joy. St. Jerome, who lived in the fourth century, remarks: "Throughout all the Churches of the East, before the reading of the Gospel, candles are lighted at mid-day, not to dispel darkness, but as a sign of joy."

You also noticed the Priest incensing the altar. Incense is a

[2] Exod. xxv. 31, and seq.

striking emblem of prayer, which should ascend to heaven from hearts burning with love, just as the fragrant smoke ascends from the censer. "Let my prayer," says the Royal Prophet, "ascend like incense in Thy sight." [3] God enjoined in the Old Law the use of incense: "Aaron shall burn sweet-smelling incense upon the altar in the morning." [4] Hence we see the Priest Zachariah "offer incense on going into the temple of the Lord. And all the multitude were praying without at the hour of incense." [5]

You perceive that the altar is decorated today with *vases and flowers* because this is a festival of the Church. There is one spot on earth which can never be too richly adorned, and that is the sanctuary in which our Lord vouchsafes to dwell among us. Nothing is too good, nothing too beautiful, nothing too precious for God. He gives us all we possess, and the least we can do in return is to ornament that spot which He has chosen for His abode upon earth. The Almighty, it is true, has no need of our gifts. He is rich without them. "The earth is the Lord's and the fulness thereof." Nevertheless, He is pleased to accept our offerings when they are bestowed upon Him as a mark of our affection, just as a father joyfully receives from his child a present bought with his own means. Our Savior gratefully accepted the treasures of the Magi, though he could have done without such gifts. Some persons, when they see our sanctuary sumptuously decorated, will exclaim: Would it not have been better to give to the poor the money spent in purchasing these things? So complained Judas (though caring not for the poor[6]) when Mary poured from an alabaster vase the precious ointment on the feet of an approving Savior. Why should not we imitate Mary by placing at His feet, around His sanctuary, our vases with their chaste and fragrant flowers, that the Church may be filled with their perfume, as Simon's house was filled with the odor of the ointment?

Does not the Almighty at certain seasons adorn with lilies and flowers of every hue this earth, which is the great temple of

[3] Ps. cxl.   [4] Exod. xxx, 7.
[5] Luke i. 9, 10.   [6] John xii. 6.

nature? And what is more appropriate than that we should on special occasions embellish our sanctuary, the place which He has chosen for His habitation among us? It is sweet to snatch from the field its fairest treasures wherewith to beautify the temple made with hands.

The *sacred vestments* which you saw worn by the officiating Priest must have struck you as very antique and out of fashion. Nor is this surprising, for if you saw a lady enter church today with a head-dress such as worn in the days of Queen Elizabeth, her appearance would look to you very singular. Now, our priestly vestments are far older in style than the days of Queen Elizabeth; much older even than the British Empire. Eusebius and other writers of the fourth century speak of them as already existing in their times. It is no wonder, therefore, that these vestments look odd to the unfamiliar eye.

In the Old Law God prescribed to the Priests the vestments which they should wear while engaged in their sacred office: "And these shall be the vestments which they shall make (for the Priest): a rational and an ephod, a tunic and a straight linen garment, a mitre and a girdle. They shall make the holy vestments for thy brother Aaron and his sons, that they may do the office of priesthood unto Me." [7] Guided by Heaven, the Church also prescribes sacred garments for her ministering Priests; for it is eminently proper and becoming that the minister of God, while engaged in the sacred mysteries, should be arrayed in garments which would constantly impress upon him his sacred character and remind him, as well as the congregation, of the sublime functions he is performing.

The vestments worn by the Priest while celebrating Mass are an amice, or white cloth around the neck; an alb, or white garment reaching to his ankles, and bound around his waist by a cincture; a maniple suspended from his left arm; a stole, which is placed over his shoulders and crossed at the breast; and a chasuble, or large outer garment.

The chasuble, stole and maniple vary in color according to the

[7] Exod. xxviii. 4.

occasion. Thus, *white* vestments are used at Christmas, Easter and other festivals of joy, also on feasts of Confessors and Virgins; *red* are used at Pentecost and on festivals of Apostles and Martyrs; *green* from Trinity Sunday to Advent, on days having no special feast; *purple* during Lent and Advent, and *black* in Masses for the dead.

One more word on this subject. Only a few years ago the whole Protestant world was united in denouncing the use of floral decorations on our altars, incense, sacred vestments, and even the altar itself, as abominations of Popery. But of late a better spirit has taken possession of a respectable portion of the Protestant Episcopal church. After having exhausted their wrath against our vestments, and vilified them as the rags of the wicked woman of Babylon, the members of the Ritualistic church have, with remarkable dexterity, passed from one extreme to the other. They don our vestments, they swing our censer, erect altars in their churches and adorn them with flowers and candle-sticks.

These Ritualists are, however, easily discerned from the true Priest. Should one of them ever appear before the Father of the faithful in these ill-fitting robes the venerable Pontiff would exclaim, with the Patriarch of old: "The voice indeed is the voice of Jacob, but the hands are the hands of Esau." I feel the garment of the Priest, but I hear the voice of the parson.

God grant that, as our misguided brothers have assumed our sacerdotal garments, they may adopt our faith, that their speech may conform to their dress. Then, having laid aside their earthly stoles, may they deserve, like all faithful Priests, to be seen "standing before the throne, and in sight of the Lamb, with white stoles and palms in their hands, . . . saying: "Salvation to our God, who sitteth upon the throne, and to the Lamb." [8]

[8] Apoc. vii. 9. 10.

CHAPTER XXVI

THE SACRAMENT OF PENANCE

I

THE whole history of Jesus Christ is marked by mercy and compassion for suffering humanity. From the moment of His incarnation till the hour of His death every thought and word and act of His Divine life was directed toward the alleviation of the ills and miseries of fallen man.

As soon as He enters on His public career He goes about doing good to all men. He gives sight to the blind, hearing to the deaf, vigor to paralyzed limbs; He applies the salve of comfort to the bleeding heart and raises the dead to life.

But, while Jesus occupied Himself in bringing relief to corporal infirmities, *the principal object of His mission was to release the soul from the bonds of sin.* The very name of Jesus indicates this important truth: "Thou shalt call His name Jesus," says the angel, "for He shall save His people from their sins." [1]

For, if Jesus had contented Himself with healing the maladies of our body without attending to those of our soul, He would deserve, indeed, to be called our Physician, but would not merit the more endearing titles of Savior and Redeemer. But as sin was

[1] Matt. i. 21.

277

the greatest evil of man, and as Jesus came to remove from us our greatest evils, He came into the world chiefly as the great Absolver from sin.

Magdalen seems to have a consciousness of this. She casts herself at His feet, which she washes with her tears and wipes with her hair, while Jesus pronounces over her the saving words of absolution. The very demons recognized Jesus as the enemy of sin, for they dreaded His approach, knowing that He would drive them out of the bodies of men.

Our Lord makes the healing of the body secondary to that of the soul. When He delivers the body from its distempers His object is to win the confidence of the spectators by compelling them to recognize Him as the soul's Physician. He says, for instance, to the palsied man, "Thy sins are forgiven." [2] The scribes are offended at our Savior for presuming to forgive sins. He replies, in substance: If you do not believe My words, believe My acts; and He at once heals the man of his disease. After he had cured the man that had been languishing for thirty-eight years He whispered to him this gentle admonition, "Sin no more, lest some worst thing may happen to thee." [3]

As much as our spiritual substance excels the flesh that surrounds it, so much more did our Savior value the resurrection of a soul from the grave of sin than the resurrection of the body from that of death. Hence St. Augustine pointedly remarks that, while the Gospel relates only three resurrections of the body, our Lord, during His mortal life, raised thousands of souls to the life of grace.

As the Church was established by Jesus Christ to perpetuate the work which he had begun, it follows that the reconciliation of sinners to God was to be the principal office of sacred ministers.

But the important question here presents itself: How was man to obtain forgiveness in the Church after our Lord's ascension?

Was Jesus Christ to appear in person to every sinful soul and say to each penitent, as He said to Magdalen, "Thy sins are for-

[2] Matt. ix. 2.　　　　[3] John. v. 14.

given thee," or did He intend to delegate this power of forgiving sins to ministers appointed for that purpose?

We know well that our Savior never promised to present Himself visibly to each sinner, nor has He done so.

His plan, therefore, must have been to appoint ministers of reconciliation to act in His name. It has always, indeed, been the practice of Almighty God, both in the Old and the New Law, to empower human agents to execute His merciful designs.

When Jehovah resolved to deliver the children of Israel from the captivity of Egypt He appointed Moses their deliverer. When God wished them to escape from the pursuit of Pharoah across the Red Sea, did He intervene directly? No; but, by His instructions, Moses raised his hand over the waters and they were instantly divided.

When the people were dying from thirst in the desert, did God come visibly to their rescue? No; but Moses struck the rock, from which the water instantly issued. When Paul, breathing vengeance against the Christians, was going to Damascus, did our Savior personally restore his sight, convert and baptize him? No; He sent Paul to His servant Ananias, who restored his sight and baptized him.

The same Apostle beautifully describes to us in one sentence of his Epistle to the Corinthians the arrangement of Divine Providence in the reconciliation of sinners: "God," he says, "hath reconciled us to Himself through Christ, *and hath given to us the ministry of reconciliation.* . . . For Christ, therefore, we are ambassadors; God, as it were, exhorting through us." [4] That is to say, God sends Christ to reconcile sinners; Christ sends us. We are His ambassadors, reconciling sinners in His name.

When I think of this tremendous power that we possess I congratulate the members of the Church, for whose benefit it is conferred; I tremble for myself and my fellow-ministers, for terrible is our responsibility, while we have nothing to glory in. Christ is the living Fountain of grace: we are but the channels

[4] II. Cor. v. 18-20.

through which it is conveyed to your souls. Christ is the treasure; we are but the pack-horses that carry it. "We bear this treasure in earthen vessels." Christ is the shepherd; we are the pipe He uses to call His sheep. Our words sounding in the confessional are but the feeble echo of the voice of the Spirit of God that purified the Apostles in the cenacle of Jerusalem.

But have we Gospel authority to show that our Savior did confer on the Apostles and their successors the power to forgive sins?

We have the most positive testimony, and our Savior's words conferring this power are expressed in the plainest language which admits of no misconception. In the Gospel of St. Matthew our Savior thus addresses Peter: "Thou art Peter, and on this rock I will build My Church. . . . And I will give to thee the keys of the Kingdom of Heaven, and whatsoever thou shalt bind on earth shall be bound also in heaven, and whatsoever thou shalt loose on earth shall be loosed also in heaven." [5]

And to all the Apostles assembled together on another occasion He uses the same forcible language: "Whatsoever you shall bind on earth shall be bound also in heaven, and whatsoever you shall loose on earth shall be loosed also in heaven." [6] The soul is enchained by sin. I give you power, says our Lord, to release the penitent soul from its galling fetters, and to restore it to the liberty of a child of God.

In the Gospel of St. John we have a still more striking declaration of the absolving power given by our Savior to His Apostles.

Jesus, after His resurrection, thus addresses His disciples: "Peace be to you. As the Father hath sent Me, I also send you. . . . Receive ye the Holy Ghost; whose sins ye shall forgive, they are forgiven them, and whose sins ye shall retain, they are retained." [7]

That peace which I give to you you will impart to repentant souls as a pledge of their reconciliation with God. The absolving power I have from My Father, the same I communicate to you. Receive the Holy Ghost, that you may impart this Holy Spirit

[5] Matt. xvi. 18, 19.   [6] Matt. xviii. 18.   [7] John xx. 21-23.

to souls possessed by the spirit of evil. "If their sins are as scarlet, they shall be made as white as snow; and if they be red as crimson, they shall be white as wool." [8] If they are as numerous as the sands on the seashore, they shall be blotted out, provided they come to you with contrite hearts. The sentence of mercy which you shall pronounce on earth I will ratify in heaven. From these words of St. John I draw three important conclusions:

It follows, first, that the forgiving power was not restricted to the Apostles, but extended to their successors in the ministry unto all times and places. The forgiveness of sin was to continue while sin lasted in the world; and as sin, alas! will always be in the world, so will the remedy for sin be always in the Church. The medicine will co-exist with the disease. The power which our Lord gave the Apostles to preach, to baptize, to confirm, to ordain, etc., was transmitted by them to their successors. Why not also the power which they had received to forgive sins, since man's greatest need is his reconciliation with God by the forgiveness of his offences?

It follows, secondly, that forgiveness of sin was ordinarily to be obtained only through the ministry of the Apostles and their successors, just as it was from them that the people were to receive the word of God and the grace of Baptism. The pardoning power was a great prerogative conferred on the Apostles. But what kind of prerogative would it be if people could always obtain forgiveness by confessing to God secretly in their rooms? How few would have recourse to the Apostles if they could obtain forgiveness on easier terms! God says to His chosen ministers: I give you the keys of My kingdom, that you may dispense the treasures of mercy to repenting sinners. But of what use would it be to give the Apostles the keys of God's treasures for the ransom of sinners, if every sinner could obtain his ransom without applying to the Apostles? If I gave you, dear reader, the keys of my house, authorizing you to admit whom you please, that they might partake of the good things contained in it, you would conclude that I had done you a small favor if you discovered that every one

[8] Isaiah i. 18.

was possessed of a private key, and could enter when he pleased without consulting you.

I have said that forgiveness of sins is *ordinarily* to be obtained through the ministry of the Apostles and of their successors, because it may sometimes happen that the services of God's minister cannot be obtained. A merciful Lord will not require in this conjuncture more than a hearty sorrow for sin joined with a desire of having recourse as soon as practicable, to the tribunal of Penance; for God's ordinances bind only such as are able to fulfil them.

It follows, in the third place, that the power of forgiving sins, on the part of God's minister, involves the obligation of confessing them on the part of the sinner. The Priest is not empowered to give absolutioin to every one indiscriminately. He must exercise the power with judgment and discretion. He must reject the impenitent and absolve the penitent. But how will he judge of the disposition of the sinner unless he knows his sins, and how will the Priest know his sins unless they are confessed? Hence, we are not surprised when we read in the Acts that "Many of them who believed came confessing and declaring their deeds" [9] to the Apostles. Why did they confess their sins unless they were bound to do so? Hence, also, we understand why St. John says: "If we confess our sins, He is faithful and just to forgive us our sins and to cleanse us from all iniquity." [10]

The strength of these texts of Scripture will appear to you much more forcible when you are told that all the Fathers of the Church, from the first to the last, insist upon the necessity of Sacramental Confession as a Divine institution. We are not unfrequently told by those who are little acquainted with the doctrine and history of the Church, that Sacramental Confession was not introduced into the Church until 1,200 years after the time of our Savior. In vindication of their bold assertion they even introduce quotations from SS. Basil, Ambrose, Augustine, Jerome and Chrysostom. These quotations are utterly irrelevant; but, if seen in the context, they will tend to prove, instead of dis-

[9] Acts xix. 18.   [10] I. John i. 9.

proving, the Catholic doctrine of Confession. For the sake of brevity I shall cite only a few passages from the Fathers referred to. These citations I take, almost at random, from the copious writings of these Fathers on Confession. From these extracts you can judge of the sentiments of all the Fathers on the subject of Confession. *"Ab uno disce omnes."*

St. Basil writes: "In the confession of sins the same method must be observed as in laying open the infirmities of the body; for as these are not rashly communicated to every one, but to those only who understand by what method they may be cured, so the confession of sins must be made to such persons as have the power to apply a remedy." [11] Later on he tells us who those persons are. "Necessarily, our sins must be confessed to those to whom has been committed the dispensation of the mysteries of God. Thus, also, are they found to have acted who did penance of old in regard of the saints. It is written in the Acts, they confessed to the Apostles, by whom also they were baptized." [12] Two conclusions obviously follow from these passages of St. Basil: First, the necessity of confession. Second, the obligation of declaring our sins to a Priest to whom in the New Law is committed "the dispensation of the mysteries of God."

St. Ambrose, of Milan, writes: "The poison is sin; the remedy, the accusation of one's crime: the poison is iniquity; confession is the remedy of the relapse. And, therefore, it is truly a remedy against poison, if thou declare thine iniquities, that thou mayest be justified. Art thou ashamed? This shame will avail thee little at the judgment seat of God." [13]

The following passage clearly shows that the great Light of the Church of Milan is speaking of confession to Priests: "There are some," continues St. Ambrose, "who ask for penance that they may at once be restored to Communion. These do not so much desire to be loosed as to bind the Priest; for they do not unburden their conscience, but they burden his, who is commanded

[11] In Reg. Brev., quæst, ccxxix., T. II., p. 492.
[12] Ibid., cclxxxviii., p. 516.
[13] See Faith of Catholics, Vol. III., p. 74 and seq.

not to give holy things unto dogs—that is, not easily to admit impure souls to the Holy Communion." [14]

Paulinus, the secretary of St. Ambrose, in his life of that great Bishop relates that he used to weep over the penitents whose confessions he heard.

St. Augustine writes: "Our merciful God wills us to confess in this world that we may not be confounded in the other." [15] And again: "Let no one say to himself, I do penance to God in private, I do it before God. Is it then in vain that Christ hath said, 'Whatsoever thou shalt loose on earth shall be loosed in heaven?' Is it in vain that the keys have been given to the Church? Do we make void the Gospel, void the words of Christ?" [16]

In this extract how well doth the great Doctor meet the sophistry of those who, in our times, say that it is sufficient to confess to God!

St. Chrysostom, in his thirtieth Homily, says: "Lo! we have now, at length, reached the close of Holy Lent; now especially we must press forward in the career of fasting, . . . and exhibit a *full* and *accurate confession of our sins*, . . . that with these good works, having come to the day of Easter, we may enjoy the bounty of the Lord. . . . For, as the enemy knows that having confessed our sins and *shown* our wounds to the *physician* we attain to an abundant cure, he in an especial manner opposes us."

Again he says: "Do not *confess to me* only of fornication, nor of those things that are manifest among all men, but bring together also thy secret calumnies and evil speakings, . . . and all such things." [17]

The great Doctor plainly enjoins here a detailed and specific confession of our sins not to God, but to His minister, as the whole context evidently shows.

The same Father, in an eloquent treatise on the power of the sacred ministry, uses the following words: "To the Priests is given a power which God would not grant either to angels or

---

[14] Apud Wiseman's Doctrines of the Church.   [15] Hom. xx.
[16] Sermo cccxcii.   [17] Tom. vii Comm. in Matt.

archangels; inasmuch that what the Priests do below God ratifies above, and the Master confirms the sentence of His servants. For, He says, 'Whose sins you shall retain, they are retained.'

"What power, I ask, can be greater than this? The Father hath given all power to the Son; and I see all this same power delivered to them by God the Son.

"To cleanse the leprosy of the body, or rather to pronounce it cleansed, was given to the Jewish Priests alone. But to our Priests is granted the power not of declaring healed the leprosy of the body, but of absolutely cleansing the defilements of the soul." [18]

And again: "If a sinner, as becomes him, would use the aid of his conscience, and hasten to confess his crimes and disclose his ulcer to his physician, who may heal and not reproach, and receive remedies from him; if he would speak to him alone, without the knowledge of any one, and with care lay all before him, easily would he amend his failings; *for the confession of sins is the absolution of crimes.*" [19]

St. Jerome writes: "If the serpent, the devil, secretly bite a man and thus infect him with the poison of sin, and this man shall remain silent, and do not penance, nor be willing to make known his wound to his brother and master; the master, who has a tongue that can heal, cannot easily serve him. For if the ailing man be ashamed to open his case to the physician no cure can be expected; for medicine does not cure that of which it knows nothing." [20]

Elsewhere he says: "With us the Bishop or Priest binds or looses—not them who are merely innocent or guilty—but *having heard, as his duty requires, the various qualities of sin* he understands who should be bound and who loosed." [21]

Could the Catholic doctrine regarding the power of the Priests and the obligation of confession be expressed in stronger language than this?

And yet these are the very Fathers who are represented to be opposed to Sacramental Confession! With a reckless disregard of

[18] Lib. iii., De Sacerdotio.
[20] Comment in Eccles.
[19] Ibid., Hom. xx.
[21] Comm. in Matt.

the unanimous voice of antiquity our adversaries have the hardihood to assert that private or Sacramental Confession was introduced at a period subsequent to the twelfth century. They do
not, however, vouchsafe to inform us by what Pope or Bishop or
Father of the Church, or by what Council, or in what country,
this monstrous innovation was foisted on the Christian Republic.
Surely, an institution which, in their estimation, has been fraught
with such dire calamity to Christendom, ought to have its origin
marked with more precision. It is sometimes prudent, however,
not to be too particular in fixing dates.

I shall now, I trust, show to the satisfaction of the reader: First
—That Sacramental Confession was not introduced. Second—
That it could not have been introduced into the Church since the
days of the Apostles, and consequently that it is Apostolic in its
origin.

That Confession was not invented since the days of the Apostles
is manifest as soon as we attempt to fix the period of its first
establishment. Let us go back, step by step, from the nineteenth
to the first century.

It had not its origin in the present century, as everybody will
admit.

Nor did it arise in the sixteenth century, since the General
Council of Trent, held in that age, speaks of it as an established
and venerable institution and Luther says that "auricular Confession, as now in vogue, is useful, nay, necessary; nor would I,"
he adds, "have it abolished, since it is the remedy of afflicted con-
sciences." [22] Even Henry VIII., before he founded a new sect,
wrote a treatise in defence of the Sacraments, including Penance
and Confession.

It was not introduced in the thirteenth century, for the Fourth
Council of Lateran passed a decree in 1215 obliging the faithful
to confess their sins at least once a year. This decree, of course,
supposes Confession to be already an established fact.

Some Protestant writers fall into a common error in interpreting the decree of the Lateran Council by saying "Sacramental

[22] Lib. de Capt. Babyl. cap de Pœnit.

Confession was never required in the Church of Rome until the thirteenth century." The Council simply prescribed a limit beyond which the faithful should not defer their confession.

These writers seem incapable of distinguishing between a law obliging us to a certain duty and a statute fixing the time for fulfilling it. They might as well suppose that the revenue officer creates the law regarding the payment of taxes when he issues a notice requiring the revenue to be paid within a given time.

Going back to the ninth century we find that Confession could not have had its rise then. It was at that period that the Greek schism took its rise, under the leadership of Photius. The Greek schismatic church has remained since then a communion separate from the Catholic Church, having no spiritual relations with us. Now, the Greek church is as tenaciously attached to private Confession as we are.

For the same reasons Confession could not date its origin from the fifth or fourth century. The Arians revolted from the Church in the fourth century, and the Nestorians and Eutychians in the fifth. The two last-named sects still exist in large numbers in Persia, Abyssinia and along the coast of Malabar, and retain Confession as one of their most sacred and cherished practices.

In fine, no human agency could succeed in instituting Confession between the first and fourth century, for the teachings of our Divine Redeemer and of His disciples had made too vivid an impression on the Christian community to be easily effaced; and the worst enemies of the Church admit that no spot or wrinkle had yet deformed her fair visage in this, the golden age of her existence.

These remarks suffice to convince us that Sacramental Confession *was not instituted since the time of the Apostles.* I shall now endeavor to prove to your satisfaction *that its introduction into the Church, since the Apostolic age, was absolutely impossible.*

There are two ways in which we may suppose that error might insinuate itself into the Church, viz.: suddenly, or by slow process. Now, the introduction of Confession in either of those ways was simply impossible.

First, nothing can be more absurd than to suppose that Confession was immediately forced upon the Christian world. For experience demonstrates with what slowness and difficulty men are divested of their religious impressions, whether true or false. If such is the case with individuals, how ridiculous would it seem for whole nations to adopt in a single day some article of belief which they had never admitted before. Hence, we cannot imagine, without doing violence to our good sense, that all the good people of Christendom went to rest one night ignorant of the Sacrament of Penance, and rose next morning firm believers in the Catholic doctrine of auricular Confession. As well might we suppose that the citizens of the United States would retire to rest believing they were living under a Republic, and awake impressed with the conviction that they were under the rule of Queen Victoria.

Nor is it less absurd to suppose that the practice of Confession was introduced by degrees. How can we imagine that the Fathers of the Church—the Clements, the Leos, the Gregories, the Chrysostoms, the Jeromes, the Basils and Augustines, those intrepid High Priests of the Lord, who, in every age, at the risk of persecution, exile and death have stood like faithful sentinels on the watch-towers of Israel, defending with sleepless eyes the outskirts of the city of God from the slightest attack—how can we imagine, I say, that they would suffer the enemy of truth to invade the very sanctuary of God's temple? If they were so vigilant in cutting off the least withered branch of error, how would they tamely submit to see so monstrous an exotic engrafted on the fruitful tree of the Church?

What gives additional weight to these remarks is the reflection that Confession is not a speculative doctrine, but a doctrine of the most practical kind, influencing our daily actions, words and thoughts—a Sacrament to which thousands of Christians have constant recourse in every part of the world. It is a doctrine, moreover, hard to flesh and blood, and which no human power, even if it had the will, could impose on the human race. It is only a God that, in such a case, could exact the homage of our assent.

THE SACRAMENT OF PENANCE 289

In whatever light, therefore, we view the present question—
whether we consider the circumstances of time, place, manner
of its introduction—the same inevitable conclusion stares us in the
face: that Sacramental confession is not the invention of man, but
the institution of Jesus Christ.

But the doctrine of priestly absolution and the private confession of sins is not confined to the Roman Catholic and Oriental
schismatic churches. The same doctrine is also taught by a large
and influential portion of the Protestant Episcopal Church of
England.

The Rev. C. S. Grueber, a clergyman of the Church of England,
has recently published a catechism in which the absolving power
of the minister of God, and the necessity and advantage of confession, are plainly set forth. I will quote from the Rev. gentleman's book his identical words:

Question. What do you mean by absolution?

Answer. The pardon or forgiveness of sin.

Q. By what special ordinance of Christ are sins committed
after Baptism to be pardoned?

A. By the sacrament of absolution.

Q. Who is the minister of absolution?

A. A Priest.

Q. Do you mean that a Priest can really absolve?

A. Yes.

Q. In what place of the Holy Scripture is it recorded that
Christ gave this power to the priesthood?

A. In John xx. 23; see also Matt. xviii. 18.

Q. What does the prayer-book (or Book of Common Prayer)
say?

A. In the office for the ordaining of Priests the Bishop is directed to say, "Receive the Holy Ghost for the office and work of
a Priest in the Church of God. Whose sins thou dost forgive,
they are forgiven." In the office for the visitation of the sick it is
said, "Our Lord Jesus Christ hath left in His Church power to
absolve all sinners that truly repent and believe in Him." In
the order for morning and evening prayer we say again, "Al-

mighty God hath given power and commandment to his ministers to declare and pronounce to His people, being penitent, the
absolution and remission of their sins."

Q. For what purpose hath Christ given this power to Priests
to pronounce absolution in His name?

*A. For the consolation of the penitent; the quieting of his
conscience.*

Q. What must precede the absolution of the penitent?

A. Confession. . . . Before absolution privately given, confession must be made to a Priest privately.

Q. In what case does the Church of England order her ministers to move people to private, or, as it is called, to auricular confession?

A. When they feel their conscience troubled with any weighty
matter.

Q. What is weighty matter?

A. Mortal sin certainly is weighty; sins of omission or commission of any kind that press upon the mind are so, too. Anything may be weighty that causes scruple or doubtfulness.

Q. At what times in particular does the Church so order?

A. In the time of sickness, *and before coming to the Holy
Communion.*

Q. Is there any other class of persons to whom confession is
profitable?

A. Yes; to those *who desire to lead a saintly life. These, indeed, are the persons who most frequently resort to it.*

Q. Is there any other object in confession, besides the seeking
absolution for past sin and the quieting of the penitent's conscience?

A. Yes; the practice of confessing each single sin is a great
check upon the commission of sin and a preservative of purity
of life.[23]

Here we have the Divine institution of priestly absolution and
the necessity and advantage of Sacramental confession plainly

[23] See "A Catechism on the Church." By the Rev. C. S. Grueber, Hambridge,
Diocese of Bath and Wells. London: Palmer. 1870.

taught, not in a speculative treatise, but in a practical catechism, by a distinguished minister of the Church of England; taught by a minister who draws his salary from the funds of the Protestant Episcopal church; who preaches and administers in a church edifice recognized as a Protestant Episcopal church, and who is in strict communion with a Bishop of the Protestant Episcopal Church of England.

And these doctrines are upheld, not by one eminent Divine only, but by hundreds of clergymen, as well as by thousands of the Protestant Episcopalians of England.

What a strange spectacle to behold the same church teaching diametrically opposite doctrines! What is orthodox in the diocese of Bath and Wells is decidedly heterodox in the diocese of North Carolina. An ordinance which Rev. Mr. Grueber proclaims to be of Divine faith is characterized by Rt. Rev. Bishop Atkinson[24] as the invention of men. What Dr. Grueber inculcates as a most salutary practice Dr. Atkinson anathematizes as pernicious to religion. Confession, which, in the judgment of the former, is a great "check upon the commission of sin," is stigmatized by the latter as an incentive to sin. "Behold how good and pleasant it is for brethren to dwell together in unity." [25]

Suppose that the venerable Protestant Episcopal Bishop of North Carolina, in passing through England, were invited by the Rev. Mr. Grueber to preach in his church in the morning, and that the Rt. Rev. Prelate chose for his subject a sermon on confession; and suppose that the Rev. Mr. Grueber selected in the evening, as the subject of his discourse, the doctrine advanced by him in his catechism.

Let us imagine some benighted dissenter attending Mr. Grueber's church at the morning and evening service, with the view to being enlightened in the teachings of the Protestant church. Would not our dissenter be sorely perplexed, on returning home at night, as to what the Protestant Episcopal church really *did teach*?

[24] The Protestant Episcopal Bishop of North Carolina.
[25] Ps. cxxxii.

Some Episcopalians are pleased to admit that confession may be resorted to with spiritual profit in certain abnormal cases— for instance, in time of sickness. So that, in their judgment, a religious observance which is salutary to a sick man is pernicious to him in good health. For the life of me, I cannot see how the circumstances of bodily health can affect the moral character of a religious act.

That a minister of the Baptist or the Methodist church should deny the power of priestly absolution I readily understand, since these churches disclaim, in their confessions of faith, any such prerogative for their clergy. But I cannot well conceive why a Protestant Episcopalian should repudiate the pardoning power, which is plainly asserted in his standard prayer-book.

Whenever an Episcopalian Bishop imposes hands on candidates for the ministry he employs the following words, which are found in the Book of Common Prayer: "Receive the Holy Ghost for the office and work of a Priest in the Church of God, now committed unto thee by the imposition of our hands. Whose sins thou dost forgive, they are forgiven; and whose sins thou dost retain, they are retained." [26] If these words do not mean that the minister receives by the imposition of the Bishop's hands the power of forgiving sin, they mean nothing at all. When the Bishop pronounces this sentence, either he intends to convey this power of absolution, or he does not. If he intended to confer this power, he could not employ more clear and precise language to express his idea; if he did not intend to confer this power, then his language is calculated to mislead.

Just imagine that prelate addressing a candidate for Holy Orders, in the morning, with the words: "Whose sins thou dost forgive they are forgiven;" and after Divine service saying to the young minister: "Remember, sir, you have no power to forgive sins. The words of ordination are a mere figure of speech."

When a Catholic Bishop ordains Priests he uses the precise words which I have quoted, because the Book of Common Prayer borrows them from our Pontifical. But he means exactly what he

[26] The Ordering of Priests.

says, viz: That the Priest receives through the ministration of the Bishop the power of forgiving sins.

To sum up: We have seen that the Sacrament of Penance and absolution by the Priest is taught in Scripture, proclaimed by the Fathers, upheld not only by Roman Catholics throughout the world, but also by all the schismatic Christians of the East. It is inculcated in those old and genuine editions of the *Book of Common Prayer,* which have not been enervated by being subjected to the pruning-knife in this country, and the same practice is encouraged by an influential portion of the Protestant Episcopal church in England, and I will add, also, in the United States.

Again, some object to priestly absolution on the assumption that the exercise of such a function would be a usurpation of an incommunicable prerogative of God, who alone can forgive sins. This was precisely the language addressed by the Scribes to our Savior. They exclaimed: "He blasphemeth! who can forgive sins but God only?" [27] My answer, therefore, will be equally applicable to old and modern objectors. It is not blasphemy for a Priest to claim the power of forgiving sins, since he acts as the delegate of the Most High. It would, indeed, be blasphemous if a Priest pretended to absolve in his own name and by virtue of his own authority. But when the Priest absolves the penitent sinner he acts in the name, and by the express authority, of Jesus Christ; for he says: "I absolve thee in the name of the Father, and of the Son, and of the Holy Ghost." Let it be understood once for all that the Priest arrogates to himself no Divine powers. He is but a feeble voice. It is the Holy Spirit that operates sanctity in the soul of the penitent.

Not a few Protestant Episcopalians, I believe, still admit that original sin is washed away in the Sacrament of Baptism. If the minister is not guilty of blasphemy in being the instrument of God's mercy, in forgiving sins by Baptism, how can a Priest blaspheme in being the instrument of Divine mercy, in absolving sinners in the Sacrament of Penance? The same Lord who instituted Baptism for the remission of original sin established

[27] Mark ii. 7.

Penance for the forgiveness of sins committed after Baptism. Did not the Apostles exercise Divine power in raising dead bodies to life, and in raising souls that were dead to the life of grace? And yet no one but Scribes and Pharisees accused them of usurping God's powers. Cannot the Almighty, without derogating from His own glory, give to men in the nineteenth century privileges which He accorded to them in the first age of the Church?

Far, then, from dishonoring, we honor God by having recourse to the earthly physician whom He has appointed for us, and, like the multitude in the Gospel, we "glorify God, who hath given such power to men." [28]

Others object thus: Why confess to a Priest, when you may confess to God in secret. I will retort by asking, why do you build fine temples when you can worship God in the great temple of nature? Why pray in church when you can pray in your chamber? Why listen to a minister expounding the Word of God when you can read the Gospel at your leisure at home. You answer that the Lord authorizes these things. So does He authorize priestly absolution. This objection is not new. It is very old.

St. Augustine, who lived fourteen hundred years ago, will answer the objection for me: "Let no one," remarks this illustrious Doctor, "say to himself, I do penance to God in private; I do it before God. Is it, then, in vain that Christ has said: 'Whatsoever ye shall loose on earth shall be loosed in heaven'? Is it in vain that the keys have been given to the Church?" The question for us is not what God is able to do, but what *He has willed to do*. God *might* have adopted other means for the justification of the sinner, as He might have created a world different from the present one. But it is our business to take our Father at His word, and to have recourse with gratitude to the system He has actually established for our justification. Now, we are assured by His infallible word that it is by having recourse to His consecrated ministers that our sins will be forgiven us.[29]

[28] Matt. ix. 8.
[29] John xx.

It is related in the Book of Kings that Naaman, the Syrian, was afflicted with a grievous leprosy, which baffled the skill of the physicians of his country. He had in his household a Jewish maid-servant. She spoke to her master of the great prophet Eliseus, who lived in her native country, to whom the Lord had given the power of performing miracles. She besought her master to consult the prophet. Naaman, accordingly, set out for the country of Israel and begged Eliseus to heal him. The prophet told him to go and wash seven times in the Jordan; but Naaman, instead of doing as he was directed, became very angry, and said: "I thought he would have come out to me, . . . and touched with his hand the place of the leprosy, and healed me. Are not the Abana and the Pharfar rivers of Damascus, better than all the waters of Israel, that I may wash in them, and be made clean?" [30] But the servants of Naaman remonstrated with him, and besought him to comply with the prophet's injunction, telling him that the conditions were easy and the Jordan was at hand. Naaman went and washed and was cleansed. Our opponents, like Naaman, cry out: "Why should you go to a Priest, a sinner like yourself, when secretly, in your own room, you can approach God, the pure fountain of grace, to be washed from your sins?" I answer, because Jesus Christ, a prophet, and more than a prophet, has commanded you to do so.

The last charge that I will notice is the most serious and the most offensive. We are told that private confession is lawless; that the conscience soon becomes "enfeebled and chained and starved" by it, and, worse and worse, that sins are more readily committed, if followed by an absolution conveying pardon—in other words, that the more attached Catholics are to the practice of their holy religion the more depraved and corrupt they become. Or, if they remain faithful to God, this is not by reason of, but in spite of, their religious exercises.

Surely, this was not the sentiment of the late Dr. Ives, once Protestant Bishop of North Carolina, and of many other illustrious converts, who, from the day of their conversion to the hour

[30] IV. Kings v.

of their death never failed to receive consolation and strength from the sacred tribunal.

Nor is it the sentiment of Rev. Father Lyman, a Catholic Priest, of Baltimore, and brother of the assistant Protestant Bishop of North Carolina, nor of the present Archbishops of Baltimore and Philadelphia, of the Bishops of Wilmington, Cleveland, Columbus and Ogdensburg, and a host of others, both of the Protestant clergy and laity, who within the last fifty years have entered the Catholic Church.

If we compare the Protestant and Catholic systems for the forgiveness of sins, the Catholic system will not suffer by the comparison. According to the Protestant system, repentance is necessary and sufficient for justification. The Catholic system also requires repentance on the part of the sinner as an indispensable prerequisite for the forgiveness of sin. But it requires much more than this. Before the penitent receives absolution he must carefully examine his conscience and confess his sins, according to their number and kind. He is obliged to have a firm purpose of amendment, to promise restitution, if he has defrauded his neighbor, to repair any injury done his neighbor's character, to be reconciled with his enemies and to avoid the occasions of sin. Do not these obligations afford a better safeguard against a relapse into sin than a simple internal act of contrition?

Many most eminent Protestant, and even infidel, writers, who were conversant with the practical workings of the confessional in the countries in which they lived, bear testimony to the moral reformation produced by it. The famous German philosopher, Leibnitz, admits that it is a great benefit conferred on men by God that He left in His Church the power of forgiving sins.[31]

Voltaire, certainly no friend of Christianity, avows "that there is not perhaps a more useful institution than confession." [32]

Rousseau, not less hostile to the Church, exclaims: "How many restitutions and reparations does not confession cause among Catholics!" [33]

The Protestant authorities of Nuremberg, in Germany, shortly

[31] Systema Theol.   [32] Remarques sur l'Olympe.   [33] Emile.

after the establishment of the reformed doctrines in that city, were so much alarmed at the laxity of morals which succeeded after the abolition of confession that they petitioned their Emperor, Charles V., to have it restored.

It is a favorite custom for the adversaries of the Catholic Church to refer to the alleged loose morals prevailing in France and in other Catholic countries as a proof of the inferior standard of Catholic morality. This is a safe, and at the same time not the most honorable, mode of attack, as the people of those nations are too far off to defend themselves. For my part, I have spent a considerable time in various portions of France, and more edifying Christians I have never witnessed than those I met in that country. For six years I had for my professors French Priests, whose exemplary lives were a daily sermon to all around them.

I submit that the cosmopolitan city of Paris (waiving, for the present, the enormities of which it is accused), is not to be adduced as a fair criterion of French morality. Let us stay at home and judge of Catholic morals by the examples furnished under our eyes.

The influence of the confessional has been fairly tested in this country since the foundation of our Republic. Are practical Catholics enfeebled in conscience? Is their conscience chained and starved? Has the absolution they received whetted their appetites for more sin? Are they monsters of immorality? I think that an enlightened Protestant public will pronounce a contrary verdict.

I feel that I can say, with truth, that Catholics who frequent the confessional are generally virtuous in their private lives, just and honorable in their dealings with others, and that they cultivate charity and good-will toward their fellow-citizens.

It will not do to reply that it is the system, not the individual, that is attacked. How can we judge of a system unless by its practical working in the individual? "By their fruits ye shall know them," says our Redeemer.

Vices, indeed, we have to deplore among certain classes of our people, which are often superinduced by their migratory habits and irregular mode of life. But they are commonly sins of frailty, and these are not the persons that are accustomed to approach the confessional. If they did their lives would be very different from what they are.

The best of us, alas! are not what we ought to be, considering the graces we receive. But if you seek for canting hypocrites, or colossal defaulters, or perpetrators of well-laid schemes of forgery, or of systematic licentiousness, or of premeditated violence, you will seek for such in vain among those who frequent the confessional.

There is another objection which it is difficult to kill. It dies hard and, like Banquo's ghost, it will not down. If you drive it from the city, it will fly to the town. If you expel it from the town, it will take refuge in the village. If you eject it from the village, it will hide itself like some noxious animal, in some desert place until it makes its rounds again.

I allude to the charge that a price has to be paid for remitting sins. "You have only (say these slanderers) to pay a certain toll at the confessional gate, and you can pass the biggest load of sin."

It is hard to treat these objections seriously. I have been hearing confessions for fifty years, and of all who have come to me, not one has had the sense of duty to offer me any compensation for absolving them, and this is true of every Priest with whom I have been acquainted. The truth is, the Priest who would solicit a fee for absolution knows that he would be guilty of simony, and would be liable to suspension.

But we are told that confession is an intolerable yoke, that it makes its votaries the slaves of the Priests.

Before answering this objection, let me call your attention to the inconsistency of our adversaries, who blow hot and cold in the same breath. They denounce confession as being too hard a remedy for sin and condemn it, at the same time, as being a smooth road to heaven. In one sentence they style it a bed of roses; in the next a bed of thorns.

In a preceding objection it was charged that the votaries of confession had no moral constraint at all. Now it is said that their conscience is bound in chains of slavery. Surely, confession cannot be hard and easy at the same time.

I have already refuted, I trust, the former charge. I shall now answer the second. I am not aware in what sense our people are less independent than those of any other class of the community. The only restraint, as far as I know, imposed on Catholics by their Priests is the yoke of the Gospel, and to this restraint no Christian ought to object. In my estimation, no body of Christians enjoys more Apostolic freedom than those of the Catholic communion, because they are guided in their conduct, not by the ever-changing *ipse dixit* of any minister, but by the unchangeable teachings of the Church of Jesus Christ.

But if to love their Priest, to reverence his sacred character, to obey his voice as the voice of God; if to be willing to make any sacrifice for their spiritual father; if, I say, you call this slavery, then our Catholic people are slaves, indeed, and, what is more, they are content with their chains.

Even our Manuals of Devotion have not escaped the lash of wanton criticism. They have excited the pious horror of some modern Pharisees because they contain a table of sins for the use of those preparing for confession. The same flower that furnishes honey to the bee supplies poison to the wasp; and, in like manner, the same book that gives only the honey of consolation to the devout reader has nothing but moral poison for those that search its pages for nothing else.

How can anyone object to the table of sins in our prayer-books and consistently advocate the circulation of the Bible, which contains incomparably plainer and more palpable allusions to gross crimes than are found in our books of devotion? Let us not forget the adage, *"Honi soit qui mal y pense."*

I may be permitted, in concluding this subject, to add the testimony of my own experience on the beneficent influence of the confessional; for, like my brethren in the ministry, I am, in the language of Dryden,

> "One bred apart from worldly noise,
> To study souls, their cures, and their diseases."

Since the time of my ordination up to the present hour I have been accustomed to hear confessions almost every day. I have therefore, had a fair opportunity of ascertaining the value of the "system." The impressions forced upon my mind, far from being peculiar to myself, are shared by every Catholic Priest throughout the world charged with the care of souls. The testimony of ten experienced confessors ought, in my estimation, to have more weight in enabling men to judge of the moral tendencies of the confessional than the gratuitous assertions of a thousand individuals who have no personal experience of it, but who draw on their heated imaginations or on the pages of sensational novels for the statements they offer.

My experience is that the confessional is the most powerful lever ever erected by a merciful God for raising men from the mire of sin. It has more weight in withdrawing people from vice than even the pulpit. In public sermons we scatter the seed of the Word of God; in the confessional we reap the harvest. In sermons, to use a military phrase, the fire is at random, but in confession it is a dead shot. The words of the Priest go home to the heart of the penitent. In a public discourse the Priest addresses all in general, and his words of admonition may be applicable to very few of his hearers. But his words spoken in the confessional are directed exclusively to the penitent, whose heart is open to receive the Word of God. The confessor exhorts the penitent according to his spiritual wants. He cautions him against the frequentation of dangerous company and other occasions of sin, or he recommends special practices of piety suited to the penitent's wants.

Hence missionaries are accustomed to estimate the fruit of a mission more by the number of penitents who have approached the sacred tribunal than by the number of persons who have listened to their sermons.

Of all the labors that our sacred ministry imposes on us, there is none more arduous or more irksome than that of hearing confessions. If I may make a revelation of my own life, I deferred receiving Holy Orders for two years, from a sense of the dread responsibility connected with the confessional. It is no trifling task to sit for six or eight consecutive hours on a hot summer day, listening to stories of sin and sorrow and misery. It is only the consciousness of the immense good he is doing that sustains the confessor in the sacred tribunal. He is one "who can have compassion on the ignorant and erring, because he himself is also encompassed with infirmity." [34]

I have seen the man whose conscience was weighed down by the accumulated sins of twenty winters. Upon his face were branded guilt and shame, remorse and confusion. There he stood by the confessional, with downcast countenance, ashamed, like the Publican, to look up to heaven. He glided into the little mercy-seat. No human ear will ever learn what there transpired. The revelations of the confessional are a sealed book.

But during the brief time spent in the confessional a resurrection occurred more miraculous than the raising of Lazarus from the tomb—it was the resurrection from the grave of sin of a soul that had long lain worm-eaten. During those precious moments a ray from heaven dispelled the darkness and gloom from that self-accuser's mind. The genial warmth of the Holy Spirit melted his frozen heart, and the purifying influence of the same Spirit that came on the Apostles, "like a mighty wind from heaven," scattered the poisonous atmosphere in which he lived and filled his soul with Divine grace. When he came out there was quickness in his step, joy on his countenance, a new light in his eye. Had you asked him why, he would have answered: "Because I was lost, and am found. Having been dead, I am come to life again." [35]

[34] Heb. v. 2.
[35] Luke xv. 32.

II

ON THE RELATIVE MORALITY OF CATHOLIC AND PROTESTANT COUNTRIES

It has been gravely asserted that the confession of sin and the doctrine of absolution tend to the spread of crime and immorality. Statistics are produced to show that murder and illegitimate births are largely in excess in countries under Catholic influence, and that this prevalence of wickedness is the *result of confession and easy absolution.*

If our system of absolving those only who both repent and *confess* leads to laxity of morals, how much more must the Protestant system, which omits that which is most humiliating and admits the sinner to reconciliation on condition of mere interior dispositions? As all our catechisms teach, and as every Catholic knows, there is no pardon of sin without sorrow of heart and purpose of amendment. It is a great mistake to suppose that the most ignorant Catholic believes he can procure the pardon of his sins by simply confessing them without being truly sorry for them. The estimate which so many Protestants set on the virtue of even the lower classes of Roman Catholics is clearly enough evinced in the preference which they constantly manifest in their employment of Catholics—practical Catholics—Catholics who go to confession. I maintain, therefore, that confession, far from being an incentive to sin, as our adversaries have the hardihood to affirm, is a most powerful check on the depravity of men and a most effectual preventive of their criminal excesses.

But is it true that crimes, especially murder and illegitimacy, are more prevalent in Catholic than in Protestant countries? I utterly deny the assertion, and also appeal to statistics in support of the denial. Whence do our opponents derive their information? Forsooth, from Rev. M. Hobart Seymour's "Nights Among Romanists" and similar absolutely unreliable compilations, the false statements of which have been again and again refuted.

Rev. Mr. Seymour gives the following list of the number of murders in England, France and Ireland:

Ireland...................... 19 homicides to the million of inhabitants
France...................... 31   "   "   "
England.................... 4   "   "   "

The reader of the above might well draw back in astonishment and exclaim, "Truly moral atmosphere of England!" But how do these statements compare with the official records which I submit to the unprejudiced reader? Recent returns from the "Hand-Book" for France, and "Thom's Official Directory for England and Ireland, 1869," are as follows:

	Convictions (and sentences to death)	Executions
1864.—France......................	9	5
1867.—England and Wales...........	27	10
Ireland......................	3	0

These figures, which are from authenticated sources, do not bear out our accusers in their assertion that murders are more prevalent in Catholic than in Protestant countries. The statistics of this crime are limited, or they are not in very general circulation. But we have more extensive information in reference to the other great crime which, it is charged, prevails to a much more alarming extent in countries under Catholic influence, viz., illegitimacy. Here again we shall meet statistics with counter-statistics to refute unjust declarations. We do not wish to be understood as advocating the immaculateness of Catholic communities. We frankly admit and heartily deplore the disorders which Catholics commit, but we deny that they are worse than their Protestant neighbors; and still more emphatically do we deny that the Church is responsible for their disorders.

The Journal of the Statistical Society of London, of the years 1860, '62, '65, '67, gives the number of illegitimate births in England and Wales as 6½ in every hundred, whilst in the Catholic kingdom of Sardinia the number is slightly over two in the hundred, and in Ireland three in every hundred. If the test of illegitimacy is a correct index of the morality of a country, how refreshing to pass from Protestant England across to Catholic

Ireland or to the Continent and visit Sardinia! The moral atmosphere of these countries, compared with England, must be as a healthful breeze to a pestilential marsh.

That we may see at a glance the real condition of European countries in reference to this species of crime, I will here insert as correct a table as can be made from the latest reports. (Vid. *Catholic World*, Vol. XI., p. 112.)

PERCENTAGE OF ILLEGITIMACY IN PROTESTANT AND CATHOLIC COUNTRIES OF EUROPE

Protestant	Per cent
Holland	4.6
Switzerland	5.5
Prussia (Protestant)	10.0
England and Wales	6.5
Sweden and Norway	9.6
Scotland	10.1
Denmark	11.0
German States	14.8
Wurtemburg	16.4

Catholic	
Italy	5.1
Spain	5.5
France	7.2
Prussia (Catholic)	6.5
Belgium	7.2
Austria	11.1
Ireland	3.0

We have divided Prussia into Protestant and Catholic because statistics are kept according to the religious creed of the people; and we discover that, whilst among the Catholic portion of the empire there is but a percentage of six and a half of illegitimate births, among the Protestants it runs up to ten per cent. And the same remark is applicable to Ireland.

The *Scotman,* whose statements are based on the report of the British Registrar-General, publishes the following statistics:

"The proportion of illegitimate births to the total number of births is in Ireland 3.8 per cent.; in England the proportion is 6.4; in Scotland 9.9; in other words, England is nearly twice, and

Scotland nearly thrice worse, than Ireland. Something worse has to be added, from which no consolation can be derived. The proportion of illegitimacy is very unequally distributed over Ireland, and the inequality rather humbling to us as Protestants, and still more as Presbyterians and Scotchmen. Taking Ireland according to the registration divisions, the proportion of illegitimate births varies from 6.2 to 1.3. The division showing this lowest figure is the western, being substantially the Province of Connaught, where about nineteen-twentieths of the population are Celtic and Roman Catholic. The division showing the highest proportion of illegitimacy is the northeastern, which comprises, or almost consists of, the Province of Ulster, where the population is almost equally divided between Protestants and Roman Catholics, and where the great majority of Protestants are of Scotch blood and of the Presbyterian church. The sum of the whole matter is, that semi-Presbyterian and semi-Scotch Ulster is fully three times more immoral than wholly Popish and wholly Irish Connaught—which corresponds with wonderful accuracy to the more general fact that Scotland, as a whole, is three times more immoral than Ireland as a whole."

It is worthy, too, of notice, that in the tabular statement above presented the percentage of illegitimacy in Holland and Switzerland, where there are large Catholic minorities, is lower than in any other Protestant country.

We have at hand evidences, furnished by Protestant writers, of the hideous immoralities of certain European nations that are more thoroughly Protestantized than England itself. Thus, Mr. Laing writes: "Of the 2,714 children born in Stockholm, 1,577 were legitimate, 1,137 illegitimate; making only a balance of 440 chaste mothers out of 2,714; and the proportion of illegitimate to legitimate children not as one to two and three-tenths, but as one to one and a half."—*A Tour in Sweden in* 1838.

But we are not disposed to parade these monstrous vices, no matter by whom committed. We allude to them with feelings of shame, not of pleasure; and give them a passing notice merely in self-defence against the gratuitous assertions of our adversaries.

We certainly do not wish to excuse or palliate the evil deeds of Catholics, who, with all the blessed aids which their religion affords, ought to be much better than they are. Yet we will add, quoting the words of the *Catholic World*: "If we are not very much better than our neighbors, we are not any worse; and are not to be hounded down with the cry of vice and immorality by a set of Pharisees who are constantly lauding their own superiority and thanking God they are so much better than we poor Catholics."

CHAPTER XXVII

INDULGENCES

THERE are few tenets of the Catholic Church so little understood, or so grossly misrepresented by her adversaries, as her doctrine regarding Indulgences.

One of the reasons of the popular misapprehension of an Indulgence may be ascribed to the change which the meaning of that term has gradually undergone. The word Indulgence originally signified *favor, remission or forgiveness.* Now, it is commonly used in the sense of unlawful gratification, and of free scope to the passions. Hence, when some ignorant or prejudiced persons hear of the Church granting an Indulgence the idea of license to sin is at once presented to their minds.

An Indulgence is simply a remission in whole or in part, through the superabundant merits of Jesus Christ and His saints, of the temporal punishment due to God on account of sin after the guilt and eternal punishment have been remitted.

It should be borne in mind that, even after our guilt is removed, there often remains some temporal punishment to be undergone, either in this life or the next, as an expiation to Divine sanctity and justice. The Holy Scripture furnishes us with many examples of this truth. Mary, the sister of Moses, was pardoned the sin which she had committed by murmuring against her brother. Nevertheless, God inflicted on her the penalty of leprosy and of seven days' separation from the people.[1]

Nathan, the prophet, announced to David that his crimes were

[1] Num. xii.

forgiven, but that he should suffer many chastisements from the hand of God.[2]

That our Lord has given to the Church the power of granting Indulgences is clearly deduced from the Sacred Text. To the Prince of the Apostles He said: "Whatsoever thou shalt bind on earth shall be bound also in heaven; and whatsoever thou shalt loose on earth shall be loosed also in heaven."[3] And to all the Apostles assembled together He made the same solemn declaration.[4] By these words our Savior empowered His Church to deliver her children (if properly disposed) from every obstacle that might retard them from the Kingdom of Heaven. Now there are two impediments that withhold a man from the heavenly kingdom—sin and the temporal punishment incurred by it. And the Church having power to remit the greater obstacle, which is sin, has power also to remove the smaller obstacle, which is the temporal punishment due on account of it.

The prerogative of granting Indulgence has been exercised by the teachers of the Church from the beginning of her existence.

St. Paul exercised it in behalf of the incestuous Corinthian whom he had condemned to a severe penance proportioned to his guilt, "that his spirit might be saved in the day of the Lord."[5] And having learned afterwards of the Corinthian's fervent contrition the Apostle absolves him from the penance which he had imposed: "To him, that is such a one, this rebuke is sufficient, which is given by many. So that contrariwise you should rather pardon and comfort him, lest, perhaps, such a one be swallowed up with over-much sorrow. . . . And to whom you have pardoned anything, I also. For, what I have pardoned, if I have pardoned anything, for your sakes I have done it in the person of Christ."[6]

Here we have all the elements that constitute an Indulgence. First—A penance, or temporal punishment proportioned to the gravity of the offence, is imposed on the transgressor. Second—

[2] II. Kings xii.   [3] Matt. xvi. 19.   [4] Ibid., xviii. 18.
[5] I. Cor. v. 5.   [6] II. Cor. ii. 6-10.

The penitent is truly contrite for his crime. Third—This determines the Apostle to remit the penalty. Fourth—The Apostle considers the relaxation of the penance ratified by Jesus Christ, in whose name it is imparted.

We find the Bishops of the Church, after the Apostle, wielding this same power. No one disputes the right, which they claimed from the very first ages, of inflicting canonical penances on grievous criminals, who were subjected to long fasts, severe abstinences and other mortifications for a period extending from a few days to five or ten years and even to a lifetime, according to the gravity of the offence. These penalties were, in several instances, mitigated or cancelled by the Church, according to her discretion; for a society that can inflict a punishment can also remit it. Our Lord gave His Church power not only to bind, but also to loose. This discretionary prerogative was often exercised by the Church at the intercession of those who were condemned to martyrdom, when the penitents themselves gave strong marks of fervent sorrow, as we learn from the writings of Tertullian and Cyprian.

The General Council of Nice and other Synods authorize Bishops to mitigate, or even to remit altogether, public penances, whenever, in their judgment, the penitent manifested special marks of repentance. Now, in relaxing the canonical penances, or in substituting for them a milder satisfaction, the Bishops granted what we call an Indulgence. This sentence of remission on the part of the Bishops was valid not only in the sight of the Church, but also in the sight of God. Although the Church imposes canonical penances no longer, God has never ceased to inflict temporal punishment for sin. Hence Indulgences continue to be necessary now, if not a substitute for canonical penances, at least as a mild and merciful payment of the temporal debt due to God.

An Indulgence is called plenary or partial, according as it remits the whole or a part of the temporal punishment due to sin. An Indulgence, for instance, of forty days remits, before God,

so much of the temporal punishment as would have been ex-
piated in the primitive Church by a canonical penance of forty
days.

Although the very name of Indulgence is now so repugnant
to our dissenting brethren, there was a time when the Protestant
Church professed to grant them. In the canons of the Church of
England reference is made to Indulgences, and to the disposition
to be made of the money paid for them.[7]

From what I have said you may judge for yourself what to
think of those who say that an Indulgence is the remission of past
sins, or a license to commit sin granted by the Pope as a spiritual
compensation to the faithful for pecuniary offerings made him.
I need not inform you that an Indulgence is neither the one nor
the other. It is not a remission of sin, since no one can gain an
Indulgence until he is already free from sin. It is still less a license
to commit sin; for every Catholic child knows that neither Priest
nor Bishop nor Pope nor even God Himself—with all reverence
be it said—can give license to commit the smallest fault.

But are not Indulgences at variance with the spirit of the Gospel, since they appear to be a mild and feeble substitute for alms-
giving, fasts, abstinences and other penitential austerities, which
Jesus Christ inculcated and practised, and which the primitive
Church enforced?

The Church, as every one must know who is acquainted with
her history, never exempts her children from the obligation of
doing works of penance.

No one can deny that the practices of mortification are more
frequent among Catholics than among Protestants. Where will
you find the evangelical duty of fasting enforced, if not from
the Catholic pulpit? It is well known that, among the members
of the Catholic Church, those who avail themselves of the boon

---

[7] Articuli pro Clero, A. D. 1584. Sparrow, 194. I admit, indeed, that Protestant
canons have but a fleeting and ephemeral authority even among themselves, and
that the canons must yield to the spirit of the times, not the times to the canons.
I dare say that even few Protestant theologians are familiar with the canons to
which I have referred. Some people have a convenient faculty of forgetting
unpleasant traditions.

of Indulgences are usually her most practical, edifying and fervent children. Their spiritual growth far from being retarded, is quickened by the aid of Indulgences, which are usually accompanied by acts of contrition, devotion, self-denial and the reception of the Sacraments.

But, do what we will, we cannot please our opponents. If we fast and give alms; if we crucify our flesh, and make pilgrimages and perform other works of penance, we are accused of clinging to the rags of dead works, instead of "holding on to Jesus" by faith. If, on the other hand, we enrich our souls with the treasures of Indulgences we are charged with relying on the vicarious merits of others and of lightening too much the salutary burden of the cross. But how can Protestants consistently find fault with the Church for *mitigating* the austerities of penance, since their own fundamental principle rests on *faith alone without good works?*

But have not Indulgences been the occasion of many abuses at various times, particularly in the sixteenth century?

I will not deny that Indulgences have been abused; but are not the most sacred things liable to be perverted? This is a proper place to refer briefly to the Bull of Pope Leo X. proclaiming the Indulgence which afforded Luther a pretext for his apostasy. Leo determined to bring to completion the magnificent Church of St. Peter, commenced by his predecessor, Julius II. With that view he issued a Bull promulgating an Indulgence to such as would contribute some voluntary offering toward the erection of the grand cathedral. Those, however, who contributed nothing shared equally in the treasury of the Church, provided they complied with the essential conditions for gaining the Indulgence. The only indispensable conditions enjoined by the Papal Bull were sincere repentance and confession of sins. D'Aubigne admits this truth, though in a faltering manner, when he observes that "in the Pope's Bull something was said of the repentance of the heart and the confession of the lips." [8] The applicants for the Indulgence knew well that, no matter how munificent were

[8] Vol. I. p. 214.

their offerings, these would avail them nothing without true contrition of heart.

No traffic or sale of Indulgences was, consequently, authorized or countenanced by the Head of the Church, since the contributions were understood to be voluntary. In order to check any sordid love of gain in those charged with preaching the Indulgence, "the hand that delivered the Indulgence," as D'Aubigne testifies, "could not receive the money: that was forbidden under the severest penalties." [9]

Wherein, then, was the conduct of the Pope reprehensible? Certainly not in soliciting the donations of the faithful for the purpose of erecting a temple of worship, a temple which today stands unrivalled in majesty and beauty!

> "But thou of temples old, or altars new,
> Standest alone, with nothing like to thee;
> Worthiest of God, the holy and the true,
> Since Sion's desolation, when that He
> Forsook His former city, what could be
> Of earthly structures, in His honor piled,
> Of a sublimer aspect? Majesty,
> Power, Glory, Strength, and Beauty, all are aisled
> In this eternal ark of worship undefiled." [10]

If Moses was justified in appealing to the Hebrew people, in the Old Law, for offerings to adorn the tabernacle, why should not the Pope be equally justified in appealing for similar offerings to the Christian people, among whom he exercises supreme authority, as Moses did among the Israelites?

Nor did the Pope exceed his legitimate powers in promising to the pious donors spiritual favors in exchange for their donations. For if our sins can be redeemed by alms to the poor,[11] as the Scripture tells us, why not as well by offerings in the cause of religion? When Protestant ministers appeal to their congregations in behalf of themselves and their children, or in support of a church, they do not fail to hold out to their hearers spiritual blessings in reward for their gifts. It is not long since a Methodist parson of New York addressed these sacred words to Cornelius

[9] Ibid.   [10] Bryon.   [11] Daniel iv. 24.

Vanderbilt, the millionaire, who had endowed a Methodist college: "Cornelius, thy prayer is heard, and thy alms are had in remembrance in the sight of God." [12] The minister is more *indulgent* than even the Pope, to whom were given the keys of the Kingdom of Heaven; for the minister declares Cornelius absolved without the preliminary of confession or contrition, while even, according to D'Aubigne, the inflexible Pope insisted on the necessity of "repentance of the heart and confession of the lips" before the donor's offering could avail him to salvation.

John Tetzel, a Dominican monk, who had been appointed the chief preacher to announce the Indulgence in Germany, was accused by Luther of exceeding his powers by making them subservient to his own private ends. Tetzel's conduct was disavowed and condemned by the representative of the Holy See. The Council of Trent, held some time after, took effectual measures to put a stop to all irregularities regarding Indulgences and issued the following decree: "Wishing to correct and amend the abuses which have crept into them, and on occasion of which this signal name of Indulgences is blasphemed by heretics, the Holy Synod enjoins in general, by the present decree, that all wicked traffic for obtaining them, which has been the fruitful source of many abuses among the Christian people, should be wholly abolished." [13]

[12] Acts x. 31.
[13] Sess. xxv. Dec. de Indulgentia.

CHAPTER XXVIII

EXTREME UNCTION

EXTREME Unction is a Sacrament in which the sick, by the anointing with holy oil and the prayers of the Priests, receive spiritual succor and even corporal strength when such is conducive to their salvation. This unction is called *Extreme,* because it is usually the last of the holy unctions administered by the Church.

The Apostle St. James clearly refers to this Sacrament and points out its efficacy in the following words: "Is any man sick among you; let him bring in the Priests of the Church, and let them pray over him, anointing him with oil in the name of the Lord, and the prayer of faith shall save the sick man; and the Lord shall raise him up; and if he be in sins, they shall be forgiven him." [1]

Several of the ancient Fathers allude to this Sacrament. Origen (third century) writes: "There is also a remission of sins through penitence, when the sinner . . . is not ashamed to declare his sin to the Priest of the Lord, and to seek a remedy . . . wherein that also is fulfilled which the Apostle James saith: *'But if any be sick among you, let him call in the Priests of the Church, and let them impose hands on him, anointing him with oil in the name of the Lord.'* [2]

St. Chrysostom (fourth century) says: "Not only when they (the Priests) regenerate us, but they have also power to forgive sins committed afterward; for he says: 'Is any man sick among

[1] James v. 14, 15. [2] Homil. ii. in Levit.

314

you; let him call in the Priests of the Church, and let them pray over him, anointing him with oil in the name of the Lord.' " [3]

Pope Innocent I. (fifth century), in a letter to a Bishop named Decentius, after quoting the words of St. James, proceeds: "These words, there is no doubt, ought to be understood of the faithful who are sick, who can be anointed with the holy oil, which, having been prepared by a Bishop, may be used not only for Priests, but for all Christians." [4]

The Sacramentary, or ancient Roman Ritual, revised by Pope St. Gregory in the sixth century, prescribes the blessing of oil by the Bishop, and the prayers to be recited in the anointing of the sick.

The venerable Bede of England, who lived in the eighth century, referring to the words of St. James, writes: "The custom of the Church requires that the sick be anointed by the Priests with consecrated oil and be sanctified by the prayer which accompanies it." [5]

The Greek Church, which separated from the Roman Catholic Church in the ninth century, says in its profession of faith: "The seventh Sacrament is Extreme Unction, prescribed by Christ; for, after He had begun to send His disciples two and two (Mark vi. 7-13), they anointed and healed many, which unction the Church has since maintained by pious usage, as we learn from the Epistle of St. James: 'Is any man sick among you,' etc. The fruits proper to this Sacrament, as St. James declares, are the remission of sins, health of soul, strength—in fine, of body. But though it does not always produce this last result, it always, at least, restores the soul to a better state by the forgiveness of sins." This is precisely the Catholic teaching on this subject. All the other Oriental churches, some of which separated from Rome in the fifth century, likewise enumerate Extreme Unction among their Sacraments.

Such identity of doctrine proclaimed during so many ages by

[3] Lib. iii. de Sacred.
[4] Epist. xxv. ad Decentum.
[5] Comment in locum.

churches so wide apart can have no other than an Apostolic origin.

The eminent Protestant Leibnitz makes this candid admission: "There is no room for much discussion regarding the unction of the sick. It is supported by the words of Scripture, the interpretation of the Church, in which pious and Catholic men safely confide. Nor do I see what any one can find reprehensible in that practice which the Church accepts." [6]

Protestants, though professing to be guided by the Holy Scripture, entirely disregard the admonition of St. James. Luther acted with more consistency. Finding that the injunction of the Apostle was too plain to be explained away by subtlety of words, he boldly rejected the entire Epistle, which he contemptuously styled "a letter of straw." [7]

It is sad to think that our separated brethren discard this consoling instrument of grace, though pressed upon them by an Apostle of Jesus Christ; for, surely, a spiritual medicine which diminishes the terrors of death, comforts the dying Christian, fortifies the soul in its final struggle, and purifies it for its passage from time to eternity, should be gratefully and eagerly made use of, especially when prescribed by an inspired Physician.

[6] Systema Theol., p. 280.
[7] Lib. de Captiv. Babyl.

CHAPTER XXIX

THE PRIESTHOOD

THE Apostles were clothed with the powers of Jesus Christ. The Priest, as the successor of the Apostles, is clothed with their power. This fact reveals to us the eminent dignity of the priestly character.

The exalted dignity of the Priest is derived not from the personal merits for which he may be conspicuous, but from the sublime functions which he is charged to perform. To the carnal eye the Priest looks like other men, but to the eye of faith he is exalted above the angels, because he exercises powers not given even to angels.

The Priest is the *ambassador of God,* appointed to vindicate His honor and to proclaim His glory. "We are ambassadors for Christ," says the Apostle; "God, as it were, exhorting by us." [1] If it is esteemed a great privilege for a citizen of the United States to represent our country in any of the courts of Europe, how much greater is the prerogative to represent the court of heaven among the nations of the earth! "As the Father hath sent Me," says our Lord to His Apostles, "I also send you." [2] "Going, therefore, teach ye all nations, . . . teaching them to observe all things, whatsoever I have commanded you. And, behold, I am with you all days, even to the consummation of the world." [3] The jurisdiction of earthly representatives is limited, but the authority of the ministers of God extends over the whole earth. "Go ye into the

[1] II. Cor. v. 20.
[2] John xx. 21.
[3] Matt. xxviii. 19, 20.

whole world and preach the Gospel," says Christ, "to every creature." [4]

Not only does Jesus empower His ministers to preach in His name, but he commands their hearers to listen and obey. "Whosoever will not receive you, nor hear your words, going forth from that house or city, shake off the dust from your feet. Amen, I say to you, it shall be more tolerable for the land of Sodom and Gomorrha in the day of judgment than for that city." [5] "He that heareth you heareth Me; and he that despiseth you despiseth Me; and he that despiseth Me despiseth Him that sent Me." [6]

God requires not only that His Gospel should be heard with reverence, but that the persons of His Apostles should be honored. As no greater insult can be offered to a nation than to insult its representative at a foreign court, so no greater injury can be offered to our Lord than to do violence to His representatives, the Priests of His Church. "Touch not My anointed, and do no evil to My prophets." [7] God avenged the crime of two and forty boys who mocked the prophet Eliseus by sending wild beasts to tear them in pieces. The frightful death of Maria Monk, the calumniator of consecrated Priests and Virgins, who ended her life a drunken maniac on Blackwell's Island, proves that our religious institutions are not to be mocked with impunity.

When an ambassador is accredited from this country to a foreign court, he is honored with the confidence of the President, from whom he receives private instructions. So does Jesus honor His ambassadors with His friendship and communicate to them the secrets of heaven: "I will not now call you servants; for, the servant knoweth not what his Lord doeth. But I have called you friends, because all things whatsoever I have heard of My Father I have made known to you." [8]

What a privilege to be the herald of God's law to the nations of the earth! "How beautiful on the mountains are the feet of him that bringeth good tidings and that preacheth peace: of him that showeth forth good, that preacheth salvation, that saith

---

[4] Mark xvi. 15. [5] Matt. x. 14, 15. [6] Luke x. 16.
[7] Paralip, xvi. 22. [8] John xv. 15.

to Sion: Thy God shall reign." [9] How cherished a favor to be the bearer of the olive branch of peace to a world deluged by sin; to be appointed by Heaven to proclaim a Gospel which brings glory to God, and peace to men; that Gospel which strengthens the weak, converts the sinner, reconciles enemies, consoles the afflicted heart and holds out to all the hope of eternal salvation!

I have often reflected on a remark made to me by Senator Bayard of Delaware: "You of the clergy," he said, "have a great advantage as public speakers over us political men. You enjoy the confidence of your hearers. You can speak as long as you please, you can admonish and rebuke as much as you please, without any fear of contradiction; while we are constantly liable to interruption."

O! what a tremendous power is wielded by the Catholic preacher! Hundreds of souls are hanging on his words; hundreds are sustained by him in spiritual life, and leave the Church depending on him whether they go forth fortified with the Bread of life, or famished and disappointed. I can say of every Priest what Simeon said of our Lord, "This man is set for the fall and the resurrection of many in Israel."

Not only are Priests the ambassadors of God, but they are also the *dispensers of His graces* and the almoners of His mercy. "Let a man so regard us," says the Apostle, "as ministers of Christ and dispensers of the mysteries of God." [10]

How can he be called a dispenser of God's mysteries whose labors are confined to preaching? But he is truly a dispenser of Divine mysteries who distributes to the faithful the Sacraments, the mysterious symbols and efficient causes of grace.

As St. John Chrysostom observes, it was not to angels or archangels, but to the Priests of the New Law that Christ said: "Whatsoever you shall bind on earth shall be bound also in heaven; and whatsoever you shall loose on earth shall be loosed also in heaven." To them alone He gave the power to forgive sins, saying: "Whose sins you shall forgive, they are forgiven." To them alone He gave the power of consecrating His Body and

[9] Isaiah lii. 7.   [10] I. Cor. iv. 1.

Blood and dispensing the same to the faithful. He has empowered the Priests of the New Law to impart the grace of regeneration in Baptism. He has assigned to them the solemn duty of
preparing the dying Christian for his final journey to eternity:
"Is any man sick among you? Let him bring in the priests of the
Church, and let them pray over him, anointing him with oil, in
the name of the Lord." [11]

As far as heaven is above earth, as eternity is above time, and
the soul is above the body, so far are the prerogatives vested in
God's ministers higher than those of any earthly potentate. An
earthly prince can cast into prison or release therefrom. But his
power is over the body. He cannot penetrate into the sanctuary
of the soul; whereas the minister of God can release the soul
from the prison of sin, and restore it to the liberty of a child of
God.

To sum up in a few brief sentences the titles of a Catholic
Priest:

He is a *king,* reigning not over unwilling subjects, but over the
hearts and affections of his people.

His spiritual children pay him not only the tribute of their
money, but also the tribute of their love which royalty can neither
purchase nor exact.

He is a *shepherd,* because he leads his flock into the delicious
pastures of the Sacraments and shelters them from the wolves that
lie in wait for their souls.

He is a *father,* because he breaks the bread of life to his spiritual children, whom he has begotten in Christ Jesus through the
Gospel. [12]

He is a *judge,* whose office it is to pass sentence of pardon on
self-accusing criminals.

He is a *physician,* because he heals their souls from the loath-
some distempers of sin.

St. John, in his Apocalypse, represents the Church under the
figure of a city. "I saw the holy city, the new Jerusalem, coming
down from heaven, from God, prepared as a bride adorned for

[11] James v. 14.   [12] I. Cor. iv. 15.

her husband." [13] Our Savior is the Architect and Founder of this celestial city. The Apostles are its foundation. The faithful are the living stones of the edifice. The anointed ministers of the Lord are the workmen chosen to adjust and polish these stones, that they may reflect the beauty and glory of the sun of justice that perpetually illumines this city. The Priests are engaged in adorning the interior of the heavenly Jerusalem by enriching, with virtue, the precious souls entrusted to their charge. "God gave some, indeed, Apostles, and some Prophets, and others Evangelists, and others Pastors and Doctors, for the perfecting of the saints, for the work of the ministry, for the building up of the body of Christ," [14] which is His Church. What an honor is this to the Priest of the New Law! Surely God "hath not done alike to every nation, and His judgments He hath not made manifest to them." [15]

With how much more force may we apply to the successors of the Apostles the words which God spoke to the Priests of the Old Law: "Hear, ye sons of Levi. Is it a small thing unto you, that the God of Israel hath separated you from all the people and joined you to Himself, that ye should serve Him in the service of the tabernacle, and should stand before the congregation of the people and minister unto Him?"

Our Savior affectionately puts this question three times to Peter: "Simon, lovest thou Me?" And three times Peter answers Him, "Lord, Thou knowest that I love Thee." What proof of love, then, does Jesus exact of Peter? Does He say: If thou lovest Me, chastise thy body by fasting and stripes, prophesy, work miracles, lay down thy life for Me? No, but "feed My lambs," "feed My sheep." This was to be the closest bond of Peter's devotion to his Master, and of the Master's affection for His disciple.

And our Lord declares that the reward of His disciples would be commensurate with the dignity of their ministry: "Behold," says Peter, "we have left all things and have followed Thee. What, therefore, shall we have? And Jesus said to them, Amen, I say to you that you who have followed Me, in the regeneration,

[13] Apoc. xxi. 2.   [14] Eph. iv. 11, 12.   [15] Ps. cxlvii. 20.

when the Son of man shall sit on the seat of His majesty, you shall also sit on twelve seats, judging the twelve tribes of Israel." And immediately after He adds that the worthy successors of the Apostles shall share in their felicity: "And every one that hath left house, or brethren, or sisters, or father, or mother, or wife, or children, or lands for my name's sake shall receive a hundredfold and shall possess life everlasting." [16]

I know that there are many in our days who deny that Priests possess any spiritual power—as if God could not communicate such power to men. I understand why atheists and rationalists, who reject all revelation, should deny all supernatural authority to the ministers of God. But that professing Christians who accept the testimony of Scripture should share in this unbelief passes my comprehension.

Has not the Almighty, in numberless instances recorded in Holy Writ, made man the instrument of His power? Did not Moses convert the rivers of Egypt into blood? Did he not cause water to issue from the barren rock? Did not the prophets predict future events? Did not the sun stand still in the heavens at the command of Josue? Did not Eliseus, the prophet, raise the dead to life? Why do we believe all these prodigies? Because the Scriptures record them. Does not the same Word of God declare that the Apostles received power to confer the Holy Ghost by the imposition of hands, to forgive sins, to consecrate the Body and Blood of Christ, etc.? Is not the New Testament as worthy of belief as the Old? Has not Jesus Christ solemnly promised to be always with the ministers of His Church, "even to the consummation of the world," strengthening them to repeat those miracles of mercy that were wrought by His first disciples? Can the God of truth be unfaithful to His promises? Is He not as strong and merciful now as He was in days of the Prophets and Apostles, and are not we as much in need of the Holy Ghost as the primitive Christians were? If God could make feeble men the ministers of His mercy then, why not now?

But should a Priest consider himself greater than other men be-

[16] Matt. xix. 27-29.

cause he exercises such authority? Far from it. He ought to humble himself beneath others when he reflects to what weak hands God assigns power so tremendous. He should remember what our Savior said to the seventy-two disciples, who, returning with joy from their first mission, cried out to Him: "Lord, even the devils are subject to us in Thy name." But Jesus checked their vain-glory, saying: "I saw Satan like lightning fall from heaven. Behold, I have given you power . . . but rejoice not in this, that spirits are subject to you; but rejoice in this, that your names are written in heaven." [17] The Priest does not forget that "the most severe judgment shall be for them that bear rule," [18] and that "judgment should begin at the house of God." [19] The words of the Apostle are present to his mind: "What hast thou that thou hast not received? And if thou hast received, why dost thou glory as if thou hadst not received it?" [20] As well might the vessel that is filled with precious liquor boast of being superior to the vessel that is filled with water. The Priest knows full well that the powers he has received from God are given to him not to feed his own vanity, but to enrich the hearts of the faithful; and that, though instrumental in pointing out to others the way to heaven, he himself, unless adorned with personal virtues, will become a reprobate, like those unhappy Priests of Jerusalem who directed the Magi to Jesus in Bethlehem, but did not go thither themselves.

"I have planted," says the Apostle, "Apollo watered, but God gave the increase. Therefore, neither he that planteth is anything, nor he that watereth, but God that giveth the increase." [21] We perform the outward ceremony; God alone supplies the grace.

The obligations of the minister of God are, therefore, commensurate with his exalted dignity.

The Priest is required to be a man of profound learnings and of solid piety. "The lips of the Priest shall keep knowledge, and they (the people) shall seek the law at his mouth." [22] The Lord

---

[17] Luke x. 18, 20.
[19] I. Pet. iv. 17.
[21] Cor. iii. 6, 7.

[18] Wisd. vi. 6.
[20] I. Cor. iv. 7.
[22] Malach. ii. 7.

denounces the Priests of the Old Law because they neglected to study the Sacred Sciences: "Because thou hast rejected knowledge, I will reject thee, that thou shalt not do the office of priesthood for Me, and thou hast forgotten the law of thy God, I will also forget thy children." [23]

"To you," says our Lord to His Apostles, "it is given to know the mystery of the Kingdom of God, to the rest, in parables." The Priests of the New Law, like the Apostles, are the custodians of the mysteries of religion.

Now we know that the knowledge of God's Kingdom is not imparted to us by inspiration or revelation. Christ does not personally teach us as He taught His Apostles. It is by hard study that the knowledge of His law is acquired by us. He does not lift us up on Angels' wings to the spiritual Parnassus. It is only by the royal road of earnest labor that we can attain those heights which will enable us to contemplate the Kingdom of heaven and describe it to others.

As physician of the soul, he must be conversant with its various distempers and must know what remedy is to be applied in each particular case. If society justly holds the unskilful physician responsible for the fatal consequences of his malpractice, surely God will call to a strict account the spiritual physician who, through criminal ignorance, prescribes injudicious remedies to the souls of the patients committed to his charge.

As judge of souls, he must know when to bind and when to loose, when to defer and when to pronounce sentence of absolution. If nothing is so disastrous to the Republic as an incompetent judge, whose decisions, though involving life and death, are rendered at haphazard and not in accordance with the merits of the case, so nothing is more detrimental to the Christian commonwealth than an ignorant priesthood, whose decisions injuriously affect the salvation of souls.

The advocate in our courts of justice feels bound in conscience and in honor to study the case of his client with the utmost diligence, and to defend him before the jury with all the elo-

[23] Osee. iv. 6.

quence he can master. And yet the suit may not involve more than a brief imprisonment or even a limited fine.

But the Priest, like Moses, stands before God to intercede for His people, and before the people to advocate the cause of God. He not only ascends daily the altar to plead for the people and to cry out with the prophet, "Spare, O Lord, spare Thy people, and give not Thy inheritance to reproach;" but every Sunday he mounts the pulpit to vindicate the claims which God has on His subjects. Certainly, if an attorney is bound to study his client's cause before he defends it, no matter how trifling the issue, how much more imperative is the obligation of the Priest to study well his case, when he reflects that an immortal soul is on trial, and before men who are often the worst enemies of their own soul. He has to convince the people that the narrow road, which their inclinations abhor, is to be followed; and that the broad road, which their self-love and their passions tend to pursue, is to be abandoned. Conviction in this case requires rare tact as well as eloquence and learning.

But the minister of religion has to defend the soul not only against the corruptions of the heart, but also against those doctrinal errors that are daily springing up in every direction, and which are plausibly preached by false teachers, who bring to their support the most specious arguments, couched in the most attractive language. To refute these errors often requires the most consummate skill and a profound knowledge of history and the Holy Scripture.

It is no wonder, then, that the Church insists that her clergy be educated men. Hence our ecclesiastical students are usually obliged to devote from ten to fourteen years to the diligent study of the modern and ancient languages, of history and philosophy, of the great science of theology and Holy Scripture, before they are elevated to the sacred ministry.

It is true, indeed, that, owing to the rapidly-increasing demand for clergy in the United States, our Bishops have hitherto been sometimes compelled to abridge the course of studies of the candidates for the ministry; but now that the Church is more thoroughly organized, and that seminaries are multiplied among us, they are happily enabled to extend to their young levites the advantages of a full term of literary and theological training.

If the Priest should be eminent for his learning, he should be still more conspicuous for his virtues, for he is expected to preach more by example than by precept. If in the Old Law God charged His Priests with the admonition: "Be sanctified, ye that carry the vessels of the Lord," [24] how much more strictly is holiness of life enjoined on the Priests of the New Dispensation, who not only touch the sacred vessels, but drink from them the Precious Blood of the Lord?

"Purer," says St. Chrysostom, "than any solar ray should that hand be which divides that flesh, that mouth which is filled with spiritual fire, that tongue which is purpled with that most awful blood."

In order to foster in us the spirit of personal piety, we are constantly admonished by the Church to be men of prayer. The Priest should be like those angels whom Jacob saw in a vision, ascending to heaven and descending therefrom on the mystical ladder. He is expected to ascend by prayer and to descend by preaching. He ascends to heaven to receive light from God; he descends to communicate that light to his hearers. He ascends to draw at the Fountain of Divine grace, he descends to diffuse those living waters among the faithful, that their hearts may be refreshed. He ascends to light his torch at the ever-burning furnace of Divine love; he descends to communicate the flame to the souls of his people.

The Church, indeed, considers prayer so indispensable to her clergy that, besides the voluntary exercises of piety which their private devotion may suggest, she requires them to devote at least an hour each day to the recitation of the Divine Office, which chiefly consists of the Psalms and other portions of Holy Scripture, the Homilies of the early Fathers and prayers of marvelous force and unction.

[24] Isaiah lii. 11.

CHAPTER XXX

CELIBACY OF THE CLERGY

THE CHURCH requires her Priests to be pure in body as well as in soul, and to "present their bodies a living victim, holy, well-pleasing unto God."[1]

Our Savior and His Apostles, though recognizing matrimony as a holy state, have proclaimed the superior merits of voluntary continency, particularly for those who consecrate their lives to the sacred mininstry. "There are eunuchs who have made themselves such for the Kingdom of Heaven's sake. He who can take it, let him take it."[2] Our Lord evidently recommends here the state of celibacy to such as feel themselves called to embrace it, in order to attain greater perfection.

St. Paul gives the reason why our Savior declares continency to be a more suitable state for His ministers than that of matrimony: "He who is unmarried careth for the things of the Lord— how he may please God. But he who is married is solicitous about the things of the world—how he may please his wife—and he is divided."[3]

Jesus Christ manifestly showed His predilection for virginity, not only by always remaining a virgin, but by selecting a Virgin-Mother and a virgin-precursor in the person of St. John the Baptist, and by exhibiting a special affection for John the Evangelist, because, as St. Augustine testifies, that Apostle was chosen a virgin and such he always remained.

Not only did our Lord thus manifest while on earth a marked predilection for virgins, but He exhibits the same preference for

[1] Rom. xii. 1.   [2] Matt. xix. 12.   [3] I. Cor. vii. 32, 33.

them in heaven; for the hundred and forty-four thousand who are chosen to sing the New Canticle and who follow the Lamb whithersoever He goeth are all virgins, as St. John testifies. (Apoc. xiv.)

The Apostle of the Gentiles assures us that he led a single life, and he commends that state to others: "I say to the unmarried, and to the widows it is good for them if they so continue, even as I." [4]

There is no evidence from Scripture that any of the Apostles were married except St. Peter. St. Jerome says that if any were married they certainly separated from their wives after they were called to the Apostolate. Even St. Peter, after his vocation, did not continue with his wife, as may be inferred from his own words: "Behold, we have left all things, and followed Thee." [5] Among "all things" must be reckoned the fellowship of his wife, for he could hardly say with truth that he had left all things if he had not left his wife. Our Savior immediately after enumerates the wife among those cherished objects, the renunciation of which, for His sake, will have its reward. [6]

St. Paul declares that "a Bishop must be sober, just, holy, contintent." [7] And writing to Timothy, whom he had consecrated Bishop, he says: "Be thou an example to the faithful . . . in charity, in faith, in *chastity*." [8] In another place, he enumerates chastity among the virtues that should adorn the Christian minister: "In all things let us exhibit ourselves as the ministers of God in much patience, . . . in chastity." [9]

Although celibacy is not expressly enforced by our Savior, it is, however, commended so strongly by Himself and His Apostles, both by word and example, that the Church felt it her duty to lay it down as a law.

The discipline of the Church has been exerted from the beginning in prohibiting Priests to marry *after* their ordination. St. Jerome observes that "Bishops, Priests and Deacons are chosen from virgins or widowers, or, at least, they remain perpetually

[4] I. Cor. vii. 8.   [5] Matt. xix. 27.   [6] Ibid., xix. 29.
[7] Tit. i. 8.   [8] I. Tim. iv. 12.   [9] II. Cor. vi. 46.

chaste after being elevated to the priesthood." [10] To Jovinian he writes: "You certainly admit that he cannot remain a Bishop who begets children in the episcopacy; for, if convicted, he will not be esteemed as a husband, but condemned as an adulterer." [11] Again he says: "What will the churches of the East, of Egypt and of the Apostolic See do, which adopt their clergy from among virgins, or if they have wives, they cease to live as married men." [12]

St. Epiphanius declares that "he who leads a married life is not admitted by the Church to the order of Deacon, Priest, Bishop or sub-Deacon." [13]

In the primitive days of the Church, owing to the scarcity of vocations among the unmarried, married men were admitted to sacred orders, but they were enjoined, as we learn from various canons, to live separated from their wives after their ordination.

This discipline, it is true, was relaxed to some extent in favor of a portion of the clergy of the Oriental Church, who were permitted to live with their wives if they happened to espouse them before ordination; but, like the Priests of the Western Church, the Eastern clergy were forbidden to contract marriage after their ordination. It is important also to observe that the unmarried clergy of the East are held in much higher esteem by the people than the married Priests.

It cannot, indeed, be denied that at certain epochs of the Church's history, especially in periods of disordered society, there were too many instances of the violation of clerical celibacy. But the repeated violations of a law are no evidence of its non-existence. Whenever the voice of the Church could be heard it always spoke in vindication of the law of priestly chastity.

Let me now call your attention to the propriety and advantages of clerical celibacy.

First—The Priest is the representative of Jesus Christ. He continues the work begun by his Divine Master. It is his duty to preach the word, to administer the Sacraments, and, above all, to

---

[10] Ep. ad Pammach.
[11] Adv. Jovin., lib. 1.
[12] Adv. Vigilantium.
[13] Hæres. 59, c. 4.

consecrate the Body and Blood of Christ and to distribute the same to the faithful. Is it not becoming that a chaste Lord should be served by chaste ministers?

If the Jewish Priests, while engaged in their turn in offering the sacrifice of animals in the Temple, were obliged to keep apart from their wives, should not the Priests of the New Law, who offer daily the sacrifice of the Immaculate Lamb, practise continual chastity?

If David and his friends were not permitted to eat the bread of Proposition till he had avowed that for the three preceding days they had refrained from women,[14] how pure in body and soul should be the Priest who daily partakes of that living Bread of which the bread of Proposition was but the type; and if the people at Mount Sinai were forbidden to come near their wives for three days before receiving the Law,[15] should not they whose office it is to preach the Law at all times abstain altogether?

Thorndyke, an eminent Protestant Divine, in his work entitled, *Just Weights and Measures,* makes the following observation: "The reason for single life for the clergy is firmly grounded, by the Fathers and canons of the Church, upon the precept of St. Paul, forbidding man and wife to depart unless for a time, to attend unto prayer (1 Cor. vii. 5). For, Priests and Deacons being continually to attend upon occasions of celebrating the Eucharist, which ought continually to be frequented; if others be to abstain from the use of marriage for a time, then they always."[16]

Second—Writers frequently discuss the secret cause of the marvelous success which marks the growth of the Catholic Church everywhere in spite of the most formidable opposition. Some ascribe this progress to her thorough organization; others to the far-seeing wisdom of her chief pastors. Without undervaluing these and other auxiliaries, I incline to the belief that, under God, the Church has no tower of strength more potent than the celibacy of her clergy. The unmarried Priest, as St. Paul observes (1 Cor. vii.), is free to give his whole time undivided to

---

[14] I. Kings xxi.   [15] Exod. xix.   [16] Page 239.

the Lord, and can devote his attention not to one or two children, but to the entire flock whom he has begotten in Christ Jesus, through the Gospel; while the married minister is divided between the cares of his family and his duties to the congregation. "A single life," says Bacon, "doth well with churchmen; for, charity will hardly water the ground where it must first fill a pool." [17]

Third—The world has hitherto been converted by unmarried clergymen, and only by them will it continue to be converted. St. Francis Xavier and St. Francis de Sales could not have planted the faith in so many thousands of souls if they were accompanied on their journeys by their wives and children. Of all the gems that adorn the priestly diadem, none is so precious and indispensable in the eyes of the people as the peerless jewel of chastity. Without this pearl the voice of a Hyacinthe "becomes as sounding brass and a tinkling cymbal;" with it, the humblest missioner gains the hearts of multitudes.

Everybody is aware of the numerous conversions to Christianity effected by St. Francis Xavier in Japan in the sixteenth century. After the lapse of many years from the death of St. Francis, when a French squadron was permitted to enter the Japanese ports, a native Christian, named Peter, having learned that French Priests were on board, put their faith to the test by proposing to them these three questions: "Are you followers of the great Father in Rome? Do you honor Mary, the Blessed Virgin? Have you wives?" The French priests having satisfied their interrogator on these points, and especially on the last, Peter and his companions fell at the missioners' feet, exclaiming with delight: "Thanks, thanks! they are virgins and true disciples of our Apostle Francis." [18]

A contemporary writer has wittily remarked that "perhaps the most ardent admirer of hymeneal rites would cheerfully admit that he could not conceive St. Paul or St. John starting on a nuptial tour, accompanied by the latest fashions from Athens or

[17] Essays, p. 17.
[18] Annals of the Propagation of the Faith, March, 1868.

Ephesus, and the graceful brides whom they were destined to adorn. They would feel that Christianity itself could not survive such a vision as that. Nor could the imagination, in its wildest moods, picture the majestic adversary of the Arian Emperor attended in his flight up the Nile by Mistress Athanasius, nor St. John Chrysostom escorted in his wanderings through Phrygia by the wife of his bosom arrayed in a wreath of orange-blossoms. Would Ethelbert have become a Christian if St. Augustine had introduced to him his lady and her bridesmaids?" [19]

We frequently hear of unmarried Bishops and Priests laying down their lives for the faith in China and Corea and imprisoned in Germany. Heroic sacrifices such as these are, however, too much to be expected from men enjoying the domestic luxury and engrossed by the responsibility of a wife and children.

But does not St. Paul authorize the marriage of the clergy when he says: "Have we not power to carry about a woman, a sister, as well as the rest of the Apostles?" [20] The Protestant text mistranslates this passage by substituting the word *wife* for *woman.* It is evident that St. Paul does not speak here of his wife, since he had none; but he alludes to those pious women who voluntarily waited on the Apostles, and ministered to them in their missionary journeys.

It is also objected that the Apostle seems to require that a Bishop be "the husband of one wife." [21] The context certainly cannot mean that a Bishop must be a married man, for the reason already given, that St. Paul himself was never married. The sense of the text, as all tradition testifies, is that no candidate should be elected to the office of Bishop who had been married more than once. It was not possible in those days always to select single men for the Episcopal office. Hence the Church was often compelled to choose married persons, but always with this restriction, that they had never contracted nuptials a second time. They were obliged, moreover, if not widowers, to live separated from their wives.

Others adduce against clerical celibacy these words of St.

[19] Marshall, Comedy of Convocation.
[20] I. Cor. ix. 5.
[21] I. Tim. iii. 2.

Paul: "In the last times some shall depart from the faith, giving heed to spirits of error, . . forbidding to marry." (I. Tim. iv. 1-3) This passage, however, alludes to the Ebionites, Gnostics and Manicheans, who positively taught that marriage is sinful. The Catholic Church, on the contrary, holds that matrimony is not only a lawful state, but that it is also a Sacrament, and that the highest degree of holiness is attainable in conjugal life.

Some go so far as to declare continency impracticable. Our dissenting brethren in the ministry are so uxoriously inclined that, perhaps, for this reason they dispute the possibility, as well as the privilege of priests to remain single. But in making this assertion they impugn the wisdom of Jesus Christ and His Apostle, who lived in this state and recommended it to others; they slander consecrated Priests and nuns, and they unwittingly question the purity of their own unmarried sisters, daughters and sons. How many men and women are there in the world who spend years, nay, their whole lives, in the single state? And who shall dare to accuse such a multitude of incontinency?

Nor should any one complain of the severity of the law of clerical celibacy, since the candidate voluntarily accepts the obligations after mature consideration.

Finally, it cannot be urged against celibacy that it violates the Divine precept to "increase and multiply;" for this command surely cannot require all marriageable persons to be united in wedlock. Otherwise, bachelors and spinsters would also be guilty of violating the law. The number of men and women consecrated to God by vows of chastity forms but an imperceptible fraction of the human family, their proportion in the United States, for instance, being only one individual to about every four thousand. Moreover, it is an incontrovertible fact that the population increases most in those countries in which the Catholic clergy exercise the strongest influence; for there married people are impressed with the idea that marriage was instituted not for the gratification of the flesh, but for the procreation and Christian education of children.

CHAPTER XXXI

MATRIMONY

MATRIMONY is not only a natural contract between husband and wife, but it has been elevated for Christians, by Jesus Christ, to the dignity of a Sacrament: "Husbands," says the Apostle, "love your wives, as Christ also loved the Church and delivered Himself up for it, . . . so also ought men to love their wives as their own bodies. . . . For this cause shall a man leave his father and mother, and shall adhere to his wife and they shall be one flesh. This is a great sacrament: but I speak in Christ and in the Church." [1]

In these words the Apostle declares that the union of Christ with His Church is the type or model of the bond subsisting between man and wife. Now the union between Christ and His Church is supernatural and sealed by Divine grace. Hence, also, is the fellowship of a Christian husband and wife cemented by the grace of God. The wedded couple are bound to love one another during their whole lives, as Christ has loved His Church, and to discharge the virtues proper to the married state. In order to fulfil these duties special graces of our Savior are required.

The Fathers, Councils and Liturgies of the Western and the Oriental Churches, including the Coptic, Jacobite, Syriac, Nestorian and other schismatic bodies, which for upwards of fourteen centuries have been separated from the Catholic communion, all agree in recognizing Christian marriage as a Sacrament.

Hence the Council of Trent, speaking of Matrimony, says:

[1] Ephes. v. 25-32.

"Christ Himself, the Institutor and Perfector of the venerable sacraments, merited for us by His passion the grace which might perfect that natural love, and confirm that indissoluble union, and sanctify the married; as the Apostle Paul intimates, saying: 'Husbands, love your wives, as Christ also loved the Church, and delivered Himself for it;' adding shortly after: 'This is a great sacrament, but I speak in Christ and in the Church.' (Ephes. v.) Whereas, therefore matrimony, in the evangelical law, excels in grace, through Christ, the ancient marriages; with reason have our holy Fathers and Councils and the tradition of the universal Church always taught that it is to be numbered among the sacraments of the new law." [2]

The Gospel forbids a man to have more than one wife, and a wife to have more than one husband. "Have you not read," says our Savior, "that He who made man in the beginning made them male and female? And He said, for this cause shall a man leave father and mother, and shall cleave unto *his wife, and they two shall be in one flesh*. Wherefore they are no more two, but one flesh." [3] Our Lord recalls marriage to its primitive institution as it was ordained by Almighty God. (Gen. ii.) Now, marriage in its primitive ordinance was the union of one man with one woman, for Jehovah created but one helpmate to Adam. He would have created more, if His design had been to establish polygamy. The Scripture says that "man shall adhere to his *wife*"—not *his wives*. It does not declare that they shall be three or more, but that "they shall be two in one flesh."

Hence Mormonism, unhappily so prevalent in the United States, is at variance with the plain teachings of the Gospel, and is consequently condemned by the Catholic Church. Polygamy, wherever it exists, cannot fail to be a perpetual source of family discord and feuds. It fosters deadly jealousy and hate among the wives of the same household; it deranges the laws of succession and primogeniture and breeds rivalry among the children, each endeavoring to supplant the other in the affections and the inheritance of their common father.

[2] Sess. xxiv.   [3] Matt. xix. 4-6.

Marriage is the most inviolable and irrevocable of all contracts that were ever formed. Every human compact may be lawfully dissolved but this. Nations may be justified in abrogating treaties with each other; merchants may dissolve partnerships; brothers will eventually leave the paternal roof, and, like Jacob and Esau, separate from one another. Friends, like Abraham and Lot, may be obliged to part company. But by the law of God the bond uniting husband and wife can be dissolved only by death. No earthly sword can sever the nuptial knot which the Lord has tied; for, "what God hath joined together, let no man put asunder."

It is worthy of remark that three of the Evangelists, as well as the Apostle of the Gentiles, proclaim the indissolubility of marriage and forbid a wedded person to engage in second wedlock during the life of his spouse. There is, indeed, scarcely a moral precept more strongly enforced in the Gospel than the indissoluble character of marriage validly contracted.

"The Pharisees came to Jesus, tempting Him and saying: Is it lawful for a man to put away his wife for every cause? Who, answering, said to them: Have ye not read that He who made man from the beginning made them male and female? And He said: For this cause shall a man leave father and mother, and shall cleave to his wife, and they two shall be one flesh. Therefore now they are not two, but one flesh. What, therefore, God hath joined together let no man put asunder. They say to Him: Why, then, did Moses command to give a bill of divorce and to put away? He said to them: Because Moses, by reason of the hardness of your heart, permitted you to put away your wives; but from the beginning it was not so. And I say to you, that whosoever shall put away his wife, except it be for fornication, and shall marry another committeth adultery: and he that shall marry her that is put away committeth adultery." [4] Our Savior here emphatically declares that the nuptial bond is ratified by God Himself, and hence that no man, nor any legislation framed by men, can validly dissolve the contract.

[4] Matt. xix. 3-9.

To the Pharisees interposing this objection, if marriage is not to be dissolved, why then did Moses command to give a divorce, our Lord replies that Moses did not command, but simply *permitted* the separation, and that in tolerating this indulgence the great lawgiver had regard to the violent passion of the Jewish people, who would fall into a greater excess if their desire to be divorced and to form a new alliance were refused. But our Savior reminded them that in the primitive times no such license was granted.

He then plainly affirms that such a privilege would not be conceded in the New Dispensation, for He adds: "I say to you: whosoever shall put away his wife and shall marry another committeth adultery." Protestant commentators erroneously assert that the text justifies an injured husband in separating from his adulterous wife and in marrying again. But the Catholic Church explains the Gospel in the sense that, while the offended consort may obtain a divorce from bed and board from his unfaithful wife, he is not allowed a divorce *a vinculo matrimonii,* so as to have the privilege of marrying another.

This interpretation is confirmed by the concurrent testimony of the Evangelists Mark and Luke and by St. Paul, all of whom prohibit divorce *a vinculo* without any qualification whatever.

In St. Mark we read: "Whosoever shall put away his wife and marry another committeth adultery against her. And if the wife shall put away her husband and be married to another she committeth adultery." [5]

The same unqualified declaration is made by St. Luke: "Every one that putteth away his wife and marrieth another committeth adultery; and he that marrieth her that is put away from her husband committeth adultery." [6] Both of these Evangelists forbid either husband or wife to enter into second wedlock, how aggravating soever may be the cause of their separation. And surely, if the case of adultery authorized the aggrieved husband to marry another wife, those inspired penmen would not have failed to mention that qualifying circumstance.

[5] Mark x. 11, 12.   [6] Luke xvi. 18.

Passing from the Gospels to the Epistle of St. Paul to the Corinthians, we find there also an absolute prohibition of divorce. The Apostle is writing to a city newly converted to the Christian religion. Among other topics he inculcates the doctrine of the Church respecting Matrimony. We must suppose that as an inspired writer and a faithful minister of the Word he discharges his duty conscientiously, without suppressing or extenuating one iota of the law. He addresses the Corinthians as follows: "To them that are married not I, but the Lord, commandeth that the wife depart not from her husband. And if she depart that she remain unmarried, or be reconciled to her husband. And let not the husband put away his wife." [7] Here we find the Apostle, in his Master's name, commanding the separated couple to remain unmarried, without any reference to the case of adultery. If so important an exception existed, St. Paul would not have omitted to mention it; otherwise he would have rendered the Gospel yoke more grievous than its Founder intended.

We must, therefore, admit that, according to the religion of Jesus Christ, conjugal infidelity does not warrant either party to marry again, or we are forced to the conclusion that the vast number of Christians whose knowledge of Christianity was derived solely from the teachings of Saints Mark, Luke and Paul were imperfectly instructed in their faith.

Nor can we suppose that St. Matthew gave to the married Christians of Palestine a privilege which St. Paul withheld from the Corinthians; for then the early Christian Church might have witnessed the disedifying spectacle of aggrieved husbands seeking in Judea for a divorce from their adulterous wives which they could not obtain in Corinth, just as discontented spouses, in our times, sue in a neighboring State for a legal separation which is denied them in their own. Christ is not divided, nor do the Apostles contradict one another.

The Catholic Church, following the light of the Gospel, forbids a divorced man to enter into second espousals during the life of his former partner. This is the inflexible law she first pro-

[7] I. Cor. vii. 10, 11.

claimed in the face of Pagan Emperors and people and which she
has ever upheld, in spite of the passions and voluptuousness of
her own rebellious children.

Henry VIII., once an obedient son and defender of the Church,
conceived in an evil hour, a criminal attachment for Anne Boleyn,
a lady of the queen's household, whom he desired to marry after
being divorced from his lawful consort, Catherine of Aragon.
But Pope Clement VII., whose sanction he solicited, sternly refused to ratify the separation, though the Pontiff could have easily
forseen that his determined action would involve the Church in
persecution, and a whole nation in the unhappy schism of its
ruler. Had the Pope acquiesced in the repudiation of Catherine,
and in the marriage of Anne Boleyn, England would, indeed,
have been spared to the Church, but the Church herself would
have surrendered her peerless title of Mistress of Truth.

When Napoleon I. repudiated his devoted wife, Josephine, and
married Marie Louise, of Austria, so well assured was he of the
fruitlessness of his attempt to obtain from the Holy See the sanction of his divorce and subsequent marriage that he did not even
consult the Holy Father on the subject.

A few years previously Napoleon appealed to Pius VII. to
annul the marriage which his brother Jerome had contracted with
Miss Patterson of Baltimore. The Pope sent the following reply
to the Emperor: "Your majesty will understand that upon the
information thus far received by us it is not in our power to pronounce a sentence of nullity. We cannot utter a judgment in
opposition to the rules of the Church, and we could not, without
laying aside those rules, decree the invalidity of a union which,
according to the Word of God, no human power can sunder."

Christian wives and mothers, what gratitude you owe to the
Catholic Church for the honorable position you now hold in
society! If you are no longer regarded as the slave, but the equal
of your husband; if you are no longer the toy of his caprice and
liable to be discarded at any moment, like the women of Turkey
and the Mormon wives of Utah; but if you are recognized as the
mistress and queen of your household, you owe your emancipa-

tion to the Church. You are especially indebted for your liberty to the Popes who rose up in all the majesty of their spiritual power to vindicate the rights of injured wives against the lustful tyranny of their husbands.

How opposite is the conduct of the fathers of the so-called Reformation, who, with the cry of religious reform on their lips, deformed religion and society by sanctioning divorce.

Henry VIII. was divorced from his wife, Catherine, by Cranmer, the first Reformed Primate of England.

Luther and his colleagues, Melanchthon and Bucer, permitted Philip, Landgrave of Hesse, to have two wives at the same time.[8] Karlstadt, another German Reformer, justified polygamy.[9]

Modern Prussia is now reaping the bitter fruits of the seeds that were then sown within its borders. Seventy-five per cent. of the marriages now contracted outside of the Catholic Church in Berlin are performed without any religious ceremony whatever. A union not bound by the strong ties of religion is easily dissolved.

This subject excites a painful interest in our own country, in consequence of the facility with which divorce from the marriage bond is obtained in many of our States. We have here another exemplification of the dangerous consequences attending a private interpretation of the sacred text. When Luther and Calvin proclaimed to the world that "it was not wise to prohibit the divorced adulterer from marrying again," [10] they little dreamed of the fruitful progeny which was destined before long to spring from this isolated monster of their creation. There are already about thirty causes which allow the conjugal tie to be broken, some of which are of so trifling a nature as to provoke merriment were it not for the gravity of the subject, which is well calculated to excite alarm for the moral and social welfare of our country.

---

[8] Bossuet, Variations, Vol. 1.   [9] Audin, p. 339.

[10] American Cyclop., art Divorce. Our Savior declares that he who marrieth an adulteress committeth adultery. Yet Luther and Calvin declare that it is unwise to oppose such a marriage. But "the foolishness of God is wiser than men." And Wisdom has said: "I will destroy the wisdom of the wise." (I. Cor. i.)

Persons are divorced by the courts not only for infidelity, but also without even the shadow of Scripture authority—for alleged cruelty, intemperance, desertion, prolonged absence, mental incapacity, sentence to the penitentiary, incompatibility of temper and *such other causes as the court, in its discretion, may deem sufficient.*

For the year ending June, 1874, seventeen hundred and forty-two applications for divorce were presented in the State of Ohio. If such is Ohio's record, what must be the matrimonial condition of Indiana, which is called the paradise of discontented spouses.

In Connecticut there were, in 1875, four thousand three hundred and eighty-five marriages, and four hundred and sixty-six divorces from the marriage bond. The number of divorces obtained in the same State during the last fifteen years has reached five thousand three hundred and ninety-one. This is the record of a State whose public school system is considered the most thorough and perfect in the country. The statistics given of Ohio and Connecticut will enable us to form some idea of the fearful catalogue of divorces annually obtained in the United States.

There are some who regard the Catholic Church as too severe in proclaiming the absolute indissolubility of marriage. But it should be borne in mind that it is not the Church, but the Divine Founder of the Christian religion, that has given us the law. She merely enforces its observance.

The law, how rigorous soever, is mercy itself, when compared with the cruel consequences which follow from the easy concession of divorce.

The facility with which marriage is annulled is most injurious to the morals of individuals, of the family and of society. It leads to ill-assorted and hasty marriages, because persons are less circumspect in making a compact which may be afterwards dissolved almost at will. It stimulates a discontented and unprincipled husband or wife to lawlessness, quarrels and even adultery, well knowing that the very crime will afford a pretext and legal grounds for a separation. It engenders between husband and wife fierce litigations about the custody of their offspring. It deprives the children of the protecting arm of a father, or of the gentle care of a mother, and too frequently consigns them to the cold charity of the world; for the married couple who are wanting in conjugal love for one another are too often destitute also of parental affection. In a word, it brings into the household a blight and desolation which neither wealth nor luxury can repair.

There is but one remedy to this social distemper, and that is an absolute prohibition of divorce *a vinculo,* in accordance with the inflexible rule of the Gospel and of the ancient Church. In Catholic countries divorces are exceedingly rare, and are obtained only by such as have thrown off the yoke of the Church. If the sacred laws of Matrimony are still happily observed by so large a portion of the Protestant community, the purity of morals is in no small measure due to the presence among them of the Catholic religion, which exercises a beneficial influence even over those who are outside the pale of her communion, like the sun, whose benignant light and heat are felt even in those secluded spots which his rays can but obliquely and dimly penetrate.

INDEX

343

means of sanctification, 16; encourages communion with God, 17; a watchful mother—supplies us at each step, 17; fruitful in saints, 18; still produces saints and apostles, 18; has her martyrs in our day, 18; still numbers confessors in her ranks, 18; saves sinners, 19; refuge of the poor, 20; her inheritance—the afflicted, 20; possesses means of reform, 22; cosmopolitan, 25; Catholic in name and reality, 28; gaining numerically at present, 29; apostolical, 32; built upon foundation of the Apostles, 32; derives her origin from the Apostles, 40; indestructible, 44; and the barbarous hordes, 45; and Mohammedanism, 45; and the Arian heresy, 46; et seq.; and the Irish people, 46; and state, 49; her relation to other religious bodies, 49; does not need temporal power for preservation, 50; and modern progress, 50; benefited by scientific appliances and inventions, 50; fosters intellectual progress, 51; encourages scientific investigation, 50; science indebted to her— has no fear from human liberty, 52; outlasts all other governments, 52, et seq.; authority comes from God, 54; her teaching directed by the Holy Ghost, 54; her infallibility proved from Scripture, 55, et seq.; Christ's promise in favor of the, 58; her doctrines incapable of reform, 60; her doctrinal decrees irrevocable, 62; divinely appointed teacher of revelation, 63; guardian and depository of the Bible, 73; requires a head, 80; unity maintained by supreme head, 63; only one founded by Christ, 82; built on Peter, 82; revealed Word of God her Magna Charta, 102; exhorts all to honor Mary, 154; her practice proves existence of purgatory, 176; et seq.; Fathers of the—unanimous in praying for the dead, 178; has always promoted civil liberty, 186; defends civil rights and liberties, 190; conflict with state, 190; and American Independence, 197; desires no governmental aid, 202; does not sanction persecution or bloodshed, 204; disavows the excesses of the Spanish

Inquisition, 212; her practice and the procedure of the Supreme Court compared, 106; organization—American system of, 202; her doctrine on unbaptized infants, 223; perpetuates Christ's work, 278; grants indulgences, 308.

Churches—earliest Christian were Catacombs, 112; fallible—consequences, 58.

Clement of Alexandria bears witness to spread of Christianity, 26.

Clerical celibacy—necessity, 327; propriety and advantages of, 329.

Clement VII, Pope, refused to sanction divorce of Henry VIII, 339.

Communion with God encouraged by Church, 17.

Communion under both forms given by Christ, 245.

Communion under form of bread, 248, et seq.

Communion of Saints—a comforting thought, 131.

Confession of sins obligatory, 282; various views, 298; sacramental, of divine institution, 282, et seq.

Confirmation—graces of, 17; defined, 230; signs that follow, 231; described by St. Augustine, 232; abolished by the Protestants, 234.

Constantine gives peace to the Church, 112.

Continence—voluntary, superior to matrimony, 327.

Cross—held in reverence, 2; instrument of the crucifixion, 2; adorns our sanctuaries, 2; surmounts our Churches, 2; emblem of salvation, 2.

Cross—sign of the, ancient and pious practice, 2; how made, 2; taught by tradition, 2; profession of faith, 3; salutary act of religion, 3.

D

D'AUBIGNE on Protestant Reformation, 217—comments on divorce of Henry VIII.

David and Nathan, 307.

Deacons, priests and bishops in Protestant sects, 8.

Death does not dissever love among friends, 131.

H

HABEAS CORPUS, 191.

Hail Mary explained, 143, et seq.

Hamlet, Shakespeare's, advised by the dead, 181.

Hebrews believed in intercessory prayer, 130.

Henry VIII excommunicated, 8; divorce refused, 38.

Henry VIII and Elizabeth persecuted Catholics, 206.

Heresy and schism opposed to unity, 4; likened to murder and idolatry, 4; heresy defined, 4; and the Church, 46; a crime against church and state, 210.

Holy Eucharist—St. Paul's testimony on, 241.

Holiness a mark of the Church, 14.

Holmes, Oliver Wendell, praises Mary, 147.

Holy Ghost sent by Christ, 3; on Pentecost, 3; guides the Church's teaching, 54.

Holy Scripture—depository of God's Word, 63.

Holy Orders and Matrimony—graces of, 17.

I

IMAGE — MAKING COMMANDED BY GOD, 166.

Images, Sacred—advantages of, 168, et seq.; and the Reformers, 163; and the Council of Trent, 164, et seq.; and the Book of Exodus, 165; veneration of, 162; Catacombs abound in, 162.

Immaculate Conception implied in Scripture, 141; in our earliest history, 142; dogma formulated in 1854, 141.

Indestructibility of the Church due to finger of God, 48.

Infallible Bible not sufficient, 96, et seq.

Infallibility a special guidance of the Holy Ghost, 54; implied in the attributes of the Church, 54; of Apostolic teaching, 54; proved from Scripture, 55, et seq.; transmitted by Apostles to successors, 54; blessings attendant on—for the faithful, 60; Catholic idea of, reasonable and satisfactory, 110; misapprehended, 99; what it does not mean, 99, et seq.;

what it is, 101; founded on Bible, 102, et seq.; not a new doctrine, 106.

Incense, its use, 273.

Indians, American — worshiped the Great Spirit, 252.

Indulgence defined, 307; granted by the Church, 308; elements required, 308; classes, 309; does not exempt from doing penance, 310; abused, 311.

Infant Baptism proved from early Doctors, 222; and the Council of Carthage, 222; not to be delayed, 225.

Inquisition, Spanish—cruelties, 204; its true character, 209; explained, 209; excesses disavowed by the Church, 208.

Inventions and scientific appliances beneficial to Church, 50.

Invocation of the Saints defined, 124.

Ireland and the Ancient Church, 46.

Irish clergy persecuted by Cromwell, 206.

J

JEREMIAH, after death, prays for Jewish people, 130.

Jesus Christ, second person of Blessed Trinity, 1; perfect God and perfect man, 1; assumes human nature, 1; born on Christmas Day, 1; led a life of obscurity at Nazareth, 1; commences public career, 1; associates with his Apostles, 1; doing good, 1; preaches new gospel, 1; crucified on Mount Calvary, 2; purchases our redemption, 2; is our Saviour and Redeemer, 2; example to be imitated, 2; manifested Divine power on Easter Sunday, 3; raised Himself to life, 3; ascended into heaven, 3; spends forty days on earth, 3; sends Holy Ghost, 3; requires unity of faith, 4; prays for unity, 4; mission evidenced in unity of Church, 4; speaks of His Church, not churches, 5; our model, 14; wrote no line of Scripture, 66; established supreme head of the Church, 80, et seq.; founded but one Church, 82; the one Mediator, 132; came on earth to wash away sins, 220; our Victim in the Mass, 259; a Physician and Saviour, 278.

Jesus' prayer is always heard, 103; name

Christ's lessons tend to sanctification, 13; inculcated by the Church, 15; moral law standard of perfection, 15.

More, Sir Thomas, quoted on Bible in English, 75.

Mormons claim Biblical authorization for polygamy, 72.

Mormonism at variance with Gospel, 335.

Mysteries, principal, incentive to holiness, 14; proposed by the Church, 14; surround us everywhere, 240.

N

NAAMAN THE SYRIAN cured, 295.

Napoleon's demands on Pope Pius VII, 199, et seq.

Nathan and David, 307.

Nuptial bond ratified by God, 336.

O

ONIAS, after death, prays for the people of God, 130.

Oracles, rashness of following discordant, 59.

Origen bears witness to the spread of Christianity, 26.

Original sin, all men born in, 220; Blessed Virgin alone exempted, 220; universal, 223.

P

PAGANS RETAINED primitive traditions about sacrifices, 252.

Papal jurisdiction—examples, 90, et. seq.

Papal states a convenience for the Holy Father, 118.

Paul, St. on heresy and schism, 4, et seq.; asks intercession, 129.

Penance—effects of Sacrament, 17.

Pentecost—Christ sends Holy Ghost, 3.

Perpetuity of the Church, 43; defined, 43; foretold in the Scriptures, 43.

Persecutions lasted 280 years, 44.

Persecution and bloodshed not sanctioned by the Church, 204.

Persecutions by Queen Mary of England, 215; compared with those under Elizabeth, 215, et seq.

Pepin, King of the Franks, defeats Lombards, 115.

Peter, St., primacy of, 78; foundation of the Church, 82; first Bishop of

Rome, 87; supremacy handed down, 89; and Washington compared, 89; oracle of the Apostles, 103, et seq.

Photius appeals to Pope Nicholas I to confirm his election to the Patriarchate of Constantinople, 92.

Plebescitum, Roman, explained, 119.

Plutarch declares: "No nations without priests and altars," 252.

Poe, Edgard Allan, invokes Mary, 157.

Pontiff, Supreme, is commander-in-chief of the Church, 96.

Pope is Vicar of Christ, 104; father and doctor of Christians, chief pastor of the Church, 106; confirms or rejects decrees of councils, 107; a prisoner in his own house, 118.

Popes succeed to Peter's supremacy, 89; send Apostolic missionaries, 94; go to confession regularly, 100; oracles of the early Church, 104, et seq.; recognized in all ages as infallible teachers, 107.

Prayer for unity, 4; and Sacraments—means of sanctification, 16; a duty binding in conscience, 16; of Jesus Christ, always heard, 103; for the dead, consoling, 184.

Priest, Catholic obliged to read word of God, 76; ambassador of God, 317; dispenser of God's graces, 319; titles, 320; physician of souls, 324; must be man of prayer, 326.

Priestly obligations, 323; stands before God, intercessor for his people, 325; experience in sacred ministry, 299 et seq.

Primacy of St. Peter, 78; promised, 80 et seq.; and supremacy similarly demonstrated, 90.

Progress, Modern, and the Church, 50; intellectual fostered by the Church, 51; cannot destroy the Church, 50.

Prophecies of Christ fulfilled by spread of Christianity, 25.

Protestant sects make no claim to Catholicity, 27; Episcopalians sometimes usurp the title of Catholic, 27; inconsistency between teaching and practice, 67 et seq.

Protestantism not traceable to Apostolic times, 40; and Arianism paralleled, 47, et seq.

Protestants differ in belief among them-

OTHER TITLES AVAILABLE

Imitation of the Sacred Heart of Jesus. Arnoudt.
Catholic Prophecy—The Coming Chastisement. Dupont.
The Church Teaches—Documents of the Church.
The Life of the Blessed Virgin. Emmerich.
Purgatory. Schouppe.
Treatise on the Love of God. St. Francis de Sales.
My Changeless Friend. Le Buffe.
Mary, Mother of the Church. Ripley.
St. Joan of Arc. Beevers.
The Secret of the Rosary. St. Louis De Montfort.
Evidence of Satan in the Modern World. Cristiani.
The Book of Destiny (Apocalypse). Kramer.
Who Is Teresa Neumann? Carty.
Clean Love in Courtship. Lovasik.
Padre Pio—The Stigmatist. Carty.
Beyond Space—A Book about the Angels. Parente.
Thirty Favorite Novenas.
Pere Lamy. Biver.
The Holy Shroud and Four Visions. O'Connell.
St. Anthony—The Wonder-Worker of Padua. Stoddard.
Christ's Appeal for Love. Menendez.
The Reign of Antichrist. Culleton.
The Prophets of Our Times. Culleton.
The New Regulations on Indulgences. Herbst.
Devotion to the Infant Jesus of Prague.
The Agony of Jesus. Padre Pio.
Meditation Prayer on Mary Immaculate. Padre Pio.
Fundamentals of Catholic Dogma. Ott.
Child's Bible History. Knecht.
Bible History of the Old & New Testament. Schuster.
Why Squander Illness. Prayerbook.
Who is Padre Pio?
History of Antichrist. Huchede.
The Priest, The Man of God. St. Joseph Cafasso.
Hidden Treasure—Holy Mass. St. Leonard.
Baltimore Catechism No. 3. Original Ed.
Purgatory and Heaven. Arendzen.
The Blessed Eucharist. Mueller.
The Stigmata and Modern Science. Carty.
A Brief Life of Christ. Rumble.
The Way of Divine Love. Menendez.
The Fatima Secret. Culligan.
Dialogue of St. Catherine of Siena. St. Catherine.
Soul of the Apostolate. Chautard.
The Prophecies of St. Malachy. Bander.
Begone Satan. Vogl.
Douay-Rheims Bible.

Available wherever Catholic books are sold.

OTHER TITLES AVAILABLE

Wife, Mother and Mystic. Bessiers.
The Life of Anne Catherine Emmerich. Schmöger.
The Evolution Hoax Exposed. Field.
The Cure D'Ars. Trochu.
The Glories of Mary. St. Alphonsus Liguori.
The Convert's Catechism of Catholic Doctrine. Geiermann.
The Rosary in Action. Johnson.
Dogmatic Canons and Decrees.
The Three Ways of the Spiritual Life. Garrigou-Lagrange.
Latin Grammar. Scanlon.
Second Latin. Scanlon.
Saint Therese — The Little Flower. Beevers.
Bible Quizzes. Rumble & Carty.
Purgatory Quizzes. Rumble & Carty.
Indulgence Quizzes. Rumble & Carty.
Confession Quizzes. Rumble & Carty.
Marriage Quizzes. Rumble & Carty.
Hell Quizzes. Rumble & Carty.
Birth Prevention Quizzes. Rumble & Carty.
Eucharist Quizzes. Rumble & Carty.
True Church Quizzes. Rumble & Carty.
Virgin and Statue Worship Quizzes. Rumble & Carty.
Set of 10 Quizzes Above.
Dogmatic Theology for the Laity. Premm.
Is It a Saint's Name.
What Catholics Believe. Lovasik.
The Incredible Creed of the Jehovah's Witnesses. Rumble.
Uniformity with God's Will. St. Alphonsus Liguori.
Saint Gertrude the Great.
Chats With Converts. Forrest.
Humility of Heart. Bergamo.
St. Francis of Paola. Simi/Segreti.
Incorruptibles. Cruz.
St. Pius V, His Life and Times. Anderson.
Where We Got the Bible. Graham.
Humanum Genus. (On Freemasonry). Pope Leo XIII.

Available wherever Catholic books are sold.

NOTES

NOTES

NOTES

NOTES

NOTES

NOTES

NOTES

NOTES